THE PRACTICAL STYLIST Fifth Edition

Sheridan Baker
THE UNIVERSITY OF MICHIGAN

HARPER & ROW, PUBLISHERS, New York

Cambridge, Hagerstown, Philadelphia, San Francisco,
London, Mexico City, São Paulo, Sydney

1817

Sponsoring Editor: Phillip Leininger
Developmental Editor: Walter D. Brownfield
Project Editor: Holly Detgen
Designer: Helen Iranyi
Production Manager: Marion A. Palen
Compositor: Ruttle, Shaw & Wetherill, Inc.
Printer and Binder: Halliday Lithograph Corporation
Art Studio: Danmark & Michaels Inc.
Cover Design: Chris Kristiansen

THE PRACTICAL STYLIST, Fifth Edition

Library of Congress Cataloging in Publication Data

Baker, Sheridan Warner, 1918–
  The practical stylist.

  Includes index.
  1. English language – Rhetoric.   I. Title.
PE1408.B283   1981   808'.042   80-16744
ISBN 0-06-040454-X

THE
PRACTICAL
STYLIST

Contents

9. RESEARCH 94

A WRITER'S HANDBOOK

10. A WRITER'S GRAMMAR 133

Preface

This is a rhetoric primarily for freshman English, but it has also proved useful to others – advanced or struggling – who have found themselves facing a blank page and the problems of exposition. From the freshman's first essay through the senior's last paper (and on through the doctoral dissertation and the corporate annual report), the expository problems are always the same. Indeed, they all come down to two fundamental questions: one of form, one of style. And even form is spatial styling. Since, in general, writing well is writing in style, I have found it practical to teach writing almost as a tactile art, in which students learn how to shape their material and bring out the grain to best advantage. Hence *The Practical Stylist* – again revised extensively.

In this Fifth Edition, I have strengthened the first chapter concerning the student's overwhelming problem of getting started, adding help with discovering a subject, with sharpening a thesis, with projecting one's private responses into written validity, and finding one's written voice. I have similarly strengthened the essential strategies of structure and the ways of coherent paragraphing. I have written, in Chapter 4, a new treatment of rhetorical tactics, relying on such durable organizational patterns as cause and effect, comparison and contrast, classification, and definition. I have strenghtened the chapter on "evidence" by considering the basic inductive and deductive patterns. A wholly new term paper on nuclear power and renewable energy shows the students how to assemble and present timely evidence as it stimulates further research and debate of their own. From the suggestion of many users, I have consolidated and expanded my discussion of fragments, run-ons, and comma splices, and I have renovated examples and exercises throughout. Side headings down the margins reinforce the student's reading with focal points. But in its content, its size, its approach, and its practical intent, *The Practical Stylist* remains essentially the same.

I continue to emphasize argument because I believe that argument subsumes all other expository principles and that it teaches clearly and easily the firmest organization of one's ideas. Many books on writing begin with simple units and build upward. I have found the opposite approach far more efficient—beginning with the thesis, the big idea. Once students can push their material into an argumentative thesis and grasp the large essentials of structural arrangement, they then can proceed easily to the smaller and more powerful elements—to paragraphs, to sentences, and on to the heart of the matter, to words, where the real dynamite of rhetoric is.

I have included exercises in thesis-making, in paragraphing, in writing various kinds of sentences and punctuating them, in using words and spelling them, and in handling various figures of speech. I have tried to encourage the student to play with language, to write unusual and complicated sentences for exercise, to juggle with words. The chapter on the research paper then draws these points together, bringing the student's expository skills fully to bear. The book concludes with a handbook of grammar, punctuation, spelling, capitalization, and usage—for supplementary teaching and permanent reference—with further exercises as needed. Inside the front cover is a "do's" list against which the students may check their work; inside the back cover, a set of symbols for marking the "don'ts." Especially if the teacher likes to concentrate on students' writing in weekly essays arising from the exercises, the book serves well alone, or in company with *Practice in Exposition: Supplementary Exercises for The Practical Stylist* and with the expository readings of *The Essayist*, Fourth Edition, both designed to reinforce this book.

The teacher will find plenty of room here for any convenient approach, and ample opportunity for that almost necessary bonus of academic gratification, disagreeing with the book, out of which much of our best teaching comes. A great deal will certainly be familiar. Nothing here is really new; I am simply describing the natural linguistic facts discovered again and again by the heirs of Aristotle, in which lineage I seem inescapably to belong. For I have found that one practical need in all writing is to mediate gracefully between opposite possibilities—between simplicity and complexity, clarity and shade, economy and plenitude, the particular and the general.

I wish to acknowledge my great debt to the teachers who, from the responses of more than a million students, have given me their encouragement and their suggestions. I am no less grateful to the many individual students and private citizens who have written me from as far away as Kenya and as near home as Ann Arbor.

SHERIDAN BAKER

THE
PRACTICAL
STYLIST

1

Subject and Thesis

THE STYLISTIC APPROACH

Style in writing is like style in a car, a gown, a Greek temple—the ordinary materials of this world so poised and perfected as to stand out from the landscape and compel a second look, something that hangs in the reader's mind, like a vision. It is your own voice, with the hems and haws chipped out, speaking the common language uncommonly well. It calls for a craftsman who has discovered the knots and potentials in his material, one who has learned to like words as some people like polished wood or stones, one who has learned to enjoy phrasing and syntax, and the very punctuation that keeps them straight. It is a labor of love, and like love it can bring pleasure and satisfaction.

Style is not for the gifted only. Quite the contrary. Everyone, indeed, already has a style, and a personality, and can develop both. The stylistic side of writing is, in fact, the only side that can be analyzed and learned. The stylistic approach is the practical approach: you learn some things to do and not to do, as you would learn strokes in tennis. Your ultimate game is up to you, but you can at least begin in

1

good form. Naturally, it takes practice. You have to keep at it. Like the doctor and the lawyer and the golfer and the tennis player, you just keep practicing—even to write a practically perfect letter. But if you like the game, you can probably learn to play it well. You will at least be able to write a respectable sentence, and to express your thoughts clearly, without puffing and flailing.

In the essay, as in business, trying to get started and getting off on the wrong foot account for most of our lost motion. So you will start by learning how to find a subject, then a thesis, which will virtually organize your essay for you. Next, you will study the relatively simple structure of the essay, and the structure of the paragraph—the architecture of styling. Then, for exercise, you will experiment with various styles of sentence, playing with length and complexity. And finally you will get down to words themselves. Here is where writing tells; and here, as in ancient times, you will be in touch with the mystery. But again, there are things to do and things not to do, and these can be learned. So, to begin.

WHAT SHALL I WRITE?

First you need a subject, and then you need a thesis. Yes, but *what shall I write?* That is the question, persisting from the first Christmas thank-you letter down to this very night. Here you are, an assignment due and the paper as blank as your mind. The Christmas letter may give us a clue. Your mother probably told you, as mine did, to write about what you had been doing. Almost anything would do—Cub Scouts, Brownies, the birthday party, skating—so long as you had been doing it. As you wrote, it grew interesting all over again. Finding a mature subject is no different: look for something you have experienced, or thought about. The more it matters to you, the more you can make it matter to your readers. It might be skiing. It might be clothes. It might be roommates, wives, husbands, the Peloponnesian War, running for office, a personal discovery of racial tensions, an experience on the job. But do not tackle a big philosophical abstraction, like Freedom, or a big subject, like the Supreme Court. They are too vast; your time and space and knowledge, all too small. You would probably manage no more than a collection of platitudes. Start rather with something specific, like apartment-hunting, and let the ideas of freedom and justice and responsibility arise from there. An abstract idea is a poor beginning. To be sure, as you move ahead through your course in writing, you will work more directly with ideas, with problems posed by literature, with questions in the great civilizing debate about what we are doing in this strange world and universe. But again, look for something within your concern. The best subjects lie nearest at hand, and nearest the heart.

Suppose we start with Adulthood. That is certainly something close enough to all of us in prospect or achievement. It will illustrate conveniently how to generalize from personal experience, and how to narrow a subject down to manageable size. Your first impulse will be to describe your first realization that you were grown up, say, a recent test of responsibility: drugs, theft, speeding, sex. Written as autobiography, in the first person, "I," it would doubtless be interesting, even amusing or heartrending, as are most things human. But it would remain merely personal, a kind of confession, or hymn of self-praise. It would probably lack an important ingredient of intellectual maturity. You would still be working in that bright, self-centered spotlight of consciousness in which we live before we really begin to grow up and beyond which many of us never learn to step — where the child assumes that all his experiences are unique. If you shift from "me" to "the adult," however, you will be actually stepping into the perspective of maturity: acknowledging that others have gone through exactly the same thing, that your particular experiences have illustrated once again the general dilemma of responsibility versus the group at some perilous threshold to adulthood. So you will write not "I was afraid to say anything" but:

> **The teen-ager fears going against the group more than death itself. When the speedometer hits 100, silence is the rule, though terror is screaming in every throat.**

By *generalizing* your private feelings, you change your subject into a thesis by asserting something about it, by finding publicly valid reasons for your private convictions. You simply assume you are normal and fairly representative, and you then generalize with confidence, transposing your particular experiences, your particular thoughts and reactions, into statements about the general ways of the world. You might want to sharpen your statement a little more, as you turn your subject into a thesis, asserting something like: "The teen-ager's thrilling high-speed ride, if survived, can be a sobering lesson in the dynamics of the group and adult responsibility." Put your proposition into one sentence. This will get you focused. And now you are ready to begin.

WHERE ESSAYS FAIL

You can usually blame a bad essay on a bad beginning. If your essay falls apart, it probably has no primary idea to hold it together. "What's the big idea?" we used to ask. The phrase will serve as a reminder that you must find the "big idea" behind your several smaller thoughts and musings before you start to write. In the beginning was the *logos*, says the Bible — the idea, the plan, caught in a flash as if in a single word. Find your *logos*, and you are ready to round out your essay and set it spinning.

The big idea behind our ride in the speeding car was that in adolescence, especially, the group can have a deadly influence on the individual. If you had not focused your big idea in a thesis, you might have begun by picking up thoughts at random, something like this:

> **Everyone thinks he is a good driver. There are more accidents caused by young drivers than any other group. Driver education is a good beginning, but further practice is very necessary. People who object to driver education do not realize that modern society, with its suburban pattern of growth, is built around the automobile. The car becomes a way of life and a status symbol. When teen-agers go too fast they are probably only copying their own parents, without any sense of responsibility.**

A little reconsideration, aimed at a good thesis-sentence, could turn this into a reasonably good opening paragraph, with your thesis, your big idea, asserted at the end to focus your reader's attention:

> **Modern society is built on the automobile. Children play with tiny cars; teen-agers long to take out the car alone. Soon they are testing their skills at higher and higher speeds, especially with a group of friends along. One final test at extreme speeds usually suffices. It is usually a sobering experience, if survived, and can open one's eyes to the deadly dynamics of the group and the emerging sense of an adult responsibility for oneself and others.**

Thus the central idea, or thesis, is your essay's life and spirit. If your thesis is sufficiently clear, it may tell you immediately how to organize your supporting material. But if you do not find a thesis, your essay will be a tour through the miscellaneous. Essays replete with scaffolds and catwalks — "We have just seen this; now let us turn to this" — are essays in which the inherent idea is weak or nonexistent. A purely expository and descriptive essay, one simply about "Cats," for instance, will have to rely on outer scaffolding alone (some orderly progression from Persia to Siam) since it really has no idea at all. It is all subject, all cats, instead of being based on an idea *about* cats, with a thesis *about* cats.

THE ARGUMENTATIVE EDGE
Find Your Thesis.

The *about*-ness puts an argumentative edge on the subject. When you have something to say *about* cats, you have found your underlying idea. You have something to defend, something to fight about: not just "Cats," but "The cat is really a person's best friend." Now the hackles on all dog people are rising, and you have an argument on your hands. You have something to prove. You have a thesis.

"What's the big idea, Mac?" Let the impudence in that time-honored demand remind you that the most dynamic thesis is a kind of affront to somebody. No one will be very much interested in listening to you expound the thesis "The dog is a person's best friend." Everyone knows that already. Even the dog lovers will be uninterested, convinced they know better than you. But the cat. . . .

So it is with any unpopular idea. The more unpopular the viewpoint and the stronger the push against convention, the stronger the thesis and the more energetic the essay. Compare the energy in "Democracy is good" with that in "Communism is good," for instance. The first is filled with platitudes, the second with plutonium. By the same token, if you can find the real energy in "Democracy is good," if you can get down through the sand to where the roots and water are, you will have a real essay, because the opposition against which you generate your energy is the heaviest in the world: boredom. Probably the most energetic thesis of all, the greatest inner organizer, is some tired old truth that you cause to spurt with new life, making the old ground green again.

To find a thesis and to put it into one sentence is to narrow and define your subject to a workable size. Under "Cats" you must deal with all felinity from the jungle up, carefully partitioning the eons and areas, the tigers and tabbies, the sizes and shapes. The minute you proclaim the cat the friend of humanity, you have pared away whole categories and chapters, and need only think up the arguments sufficient to overwhelm the opposition. So, put an argumentative edge on your subject—and you will have found your thesis.

Simple exposition, to be sure, has its uses. You may want to tell someone how to build a doghouse, how to can asparagus, how to follow the outlines of relativity, or even how to write an essay. Performing a few exercises in simple exposition will no doubt sharpen your insight into the problems of finding orderly sequences, of considering how best to lead your readers through the hoops of writing clearly and accurately. It will also illustrate how much finer and surer an argument is.

You will see that picking an argument immediately simplifies the problems so troublesome in straight exposition: the defining, the partitioning, the narrowing of the subject. Not that you must be constantly pugnacious or aggressive. I have overstated my point to make it stick. Actually, you can put an argumentative edge on the flattest of expository subjects. "How to build a doghouse" might become "Building a doghouse is a thorough introduction to the building trades, including architecture and mechanical engineering." "Canning asparagus" might become "An asparagus patch is a course in economics." "Relativity" might become "Relativity is not so inscrutable as many suppose." Literary subjects take an argumentative edge almost by nature. You simply assert what the essential point of a poem or play seems to be: *"Hamlet* is essentially about a world that has lost its values." You assume that your readers are in search of clarity, that you have a loyal opposition consisting of the interested but uninformed. You have given your subject its edge; you have limited and organized it at a single stroke. Pick an *argument,* then, and you will automatically be defining and narrowing your subject, and all the partitions you don't need will fold up. Instead of dealing with things, subjects, and pieces of subjects, you will be dealing with an idea and its consequences.

Sharpen Your Thesis.

Come out with your subject pointed. Take a stand, make a judgment of value, make a *thesis.* Be reasonable, but don't be timid. It is helpful to think of your thesis, your main idea, as a debating question —"Resolved: Welfare payments must go"—taking out the "Resolved" when you actually write your thesis down. But your resolution will be even stronger, your essay clearer and tighter, if you can sharpen your thesis even further—"Resolved: Welfare payments must go because ————." Fill in that blank, and your worries are practically over. The main idea is to put your whole argument into one sentence.

Try, for instance: "Welfare payments must go because they are making people irresponsible." I don't know at all if that is true, and neither will you until you write your way into it, considering probabilities and alternatives and objections, and especially the underlying assumptions. In fact, no one, no master sociologist or future historian, can tell absolutely if it is true, so multiplex are the causes in human affairs, so endless and tangled the consequences. The basic assumption —that irresponsibility is growing—might be entirely false. No one, I repeat, can tell absolutely. But by the same token, your guess may be as good as another's. At any rate, you are ready to write. You have found your *logos.*

Now put your well-pointed thesis-sentence on a scrap of paper to keep from drifting off target. But you will want to dress it for the public, to burnish it and make it comely. Suppose you try:

> **Welfare payments, perhaps more than anything else, are eroding personal initiative.**

But is this fully true? Perhaps you had better try something like:

> **Despite their immediate benefits, welfare payments may actually be eroding personal initiative and depriving society of needed workers.**

This is your full thesis; write that down on a scrap of paper too.

You might wonder if it is not astoundingly presumptuous to go around stating theses before you have studied your subject from all angles, made several house-to-house surveys, and read everything ever written. A natural uncertainty and feeling of ignorance, and a misunderstanding of what truth is, can well inhibit you from finding a thesis. But no one knows everything. No one would write anything if he waited until he did. To a great extent, the writing of a thing is the learning of it—the discovery of truth.

So, first, make a desperate thesis and get into the arena. This is probably solution enough. If it becomes increasingly clear that your thesis is untrue, no matter how hard you push it, turn it around and use the other end. If your convictions have begun to falter with:

> **Despite their immediate benefits, welfare payments undermine initiative. . . .**

try it the other way around, with something like:

> **Although welfare payments may offend the rugged individualist, they relieve much want and anxiety, and they enable many a father-less family to maintain its integrity.**

You will now have a beautiful command of the major objections to your new position. And you will have learned something about human fallibility and the nature of truth.

Persuade Your Reader.

Once you believe in your proposition, you will discover that proving it is really a venture in persuasion. *Rhetoric* is, in fact, the art of persuasion, of moving the reader to your belief. You have made a thesis, a hypothesis really—an opinion as to what the truth seems to be from where you stand, with the information you have. Belief has an unfolding energy. Write what you believe. You may be wrong, of course, but you will probably discover this as you probe for reasons, and can then reverse your thesis, pointed with your new conviction. The truth remains true, and you must at least glimpse it before you can begin to persuade others to see it. So follow your convictions, and think up reasons to convince your reader. Give him enough evidence to persuade him that what you say is probably true; find arguments that will stand up in the marketplace and survive the public haggle. You must find the public reasons for your private convictions.

THE WRITTEN VOICE
Make Your Writing Talk.

That the silent page should seem to speak with the writer's voice is remarkable. With all gestures gone, no eyes to twinkle, no notation at all for the rise and fall of utterance, and only a handful of punctuation marks, the level line of type can yet convey the writer's voice, the tone of his personality.

To achieve this tone, to find your own voice and style, simply try to write in the language of intelligent conversation, cleared of all the stumbles and weavings of talk. Indeed, our speech, like thought, is amazingly circular. We can hardly think in a straight line if we try. We think by questions and answers, repetitions and failures; and our speech, full of *you know*'s and *I mean*'s, follows the erratic ways of the mind, circling around and around as we stitch the simplest of logical sequences. Your writing will carry the stitches, not the loopings and pauses and rethreadings. It should be literate. It should be broad enough of vocabulary and rich enough of sentence to show that you have read a book. It should not be altogether unworthy to place you in the company of those who have written well in your native tongue. But it should nevertheless retain the tone of intelligent and agreeable conversation. It should be alive with a human personality—yours —which is probably the most persuasive rhetorical force on earth. Good writing should have a voice, and the voice should be unmistakably your own.

Suppose your spoken voice sounded something like this (I reconstruct an actual response in one of my classes):

> Well, I don't know. I like Shakespeare really, I guess—I mean, well, like when Lear divides up his kingdom like a fairy tale or something, I thought that was kind of silly, dividing his kingdom. Anyone could see that was silly if you wanted to keep your kingdom, why divide it? But then like, something begins to happen, like a real family, I mean. Cordelia really gets griped at her older sisters, I mean, like all older sisters, if you've ever had any. There's a kind of sibling rivalry, you know. Then she's kind of griped at her father, who she really loves, but she thinks, I mean, like saying it right out spoils it. You can't really speak right out, I mean, about love, well, except sometimes, I guess, without sounding corny.

Your written voice may then emerge with something of the same tone, but with everything straightened out, filled in, polished up:

> The play begins like a fairy tale. It even seems at first a little abstract and silly. A king has three daughters. The two elder ones are bad; the youngest is good. The king wishes to keep his kingdom in peace, and keep his title as king, by dividing his kingdom in a senseless and almost empty ceremonial way. But very soon the play seems like real life. The family seems real, complete with sibling rivalry. It is the king, not the play, who is foolish and senile. The older daughters are hypocrites. Cordelia, the youngest, is irritated at them, and at her father's foolishness. As a result, she remains silent, not only because she is irritated at the flattering words of her sisters, but because anything she could say about her real love for her father would now sound false.

You might wish to polish that some more. You might indeed have said it another way, one more truly your own. The point, however, is to write in a tidy, economical way that wipes up the lapses of talk and fills in the gaps of thought, and yet keeps the tone and movement of good conversation, in your own voice.

Consider Your Readers.

If you are to take your subject with all the seriousness it deserves and yourself with as much skeptical humor as you can bear, how are you to take your readers? Who are they, anyway? Hypothetically, your vocabulary and your tone would vary all the way from Skid Row to Oxford as you turn from social work to Rhodes scholarship; and certainly the difference of audience would reflect itself somewhat in your language. Furthermore, you must indeed sense your audience's capacity, its susceptibilities and prejudices, if you are to win even a hearing. No doubt our language skids a bit when down on the Row, and we certainly speak different tongues with our friends, and with the friends of our parents.

But the notion of adjusting your writing to a whole scale of audiences, though attractive in theory, hardly works out in practice. You are *writing,* and the written word presupposes a literate norm that immediately eliminates all the lower ranges of mere talk. Even when you speak, you do not so lose your identity as to pass for a total illiterate. You stand on your own linguistic feet, in your own linguistic personality, and the only adjustment you should assiduously practice in your writing, and in your speaking as well, is the upward one toward verbal adulthood, a slight grammatical tightening and rhetorical heightening to make your thoughts clear, emphatic, and attractive.

Consider your audience a mixed group of intelligent and reasonable adults. You want them to think of you as well informed and well educated. You wish to explain what you know and what you believe. You wish to persuade them pleasantly that what you know is important and what you believe is right. Try to imagine what they might ask you, what they might object to, what they might know already, what they might find interesting. Be simple and clear, amusing and profound, using plenty of illustration to show what you mean. *But do not talk down to them.* That is the great flaw in the slumming theory of communication. Bowing to your readers' supposed level, you insult them by assuming their inferiority. Thinking yourself humble, you are actually haughty. The best solution is simply to assume that your readers are as intelligent as you. Even if they are not, they will be flattered by the assumption. Your written language, in short, will be respectful toward your subject, considerate toward your readers, and somehow amiable toward human failings.

Don't Apologize.

"In my opinion," the beginner will write repeatedly, until he seems to be saying "It is only *my* opinion, after all, so it can't be worth much." He has failed to realize that his whole essay represents his opinion—of what the truth of the matter is. Don't make your essay into a diary, or a letter to Parent or Teacher, a confidential report of what happened to you last night as you agonized over a certain question. "*To me*, Robert Frost is a great poet"—this is really writing about yourself. You are only confessing private convictions. To find the "public reasons" often requires no more than a trick of grammar: a shift from "*To me*, Robert Frost is . . ." to "Robert Frost is . . .," from "*I thought* the poem *meant* . . ." to "The poem *means* . . .," from you and your room last night to your subject and what it *is*. The grammatical shift represents, as we have seen (p. 3), a whole change of viewpoint, from self to subject. Again you become the informed adult, showing the reader around firmly, politely, and persuasively.

Once you have effaced yourself from your thesis, once you have erased *to me* and *in my opinion* and all such signs of amateur terror, you may later let yourself back into the essay for emphasis or graciousness: "Mr. Watson errs, I think, precisely at this point." You can thus ease your most tentative or violent assertions, and show that you are polite and sensible, reasonably sure of your position but aware of the possibility of error. Again: the reasonable adult. But it is better to omit the "I" altogether than to write a junior autobiography of your discoveries and doubts (also see *Point of view*, p. 192).

Plan to Rewrite!

As you write your weekly assignments and find your voice, you will also be learning to groom your thoughts, to present them clearly and fully, to make sure you have said what you thought you said. Good writing comes only from rewriting. Even your happy thoughts will need resetting, as you join them to the frequently happier ones that a second look seems to call up. Even the letter-perfect paper will improve almost of itself if you simply sit down to type it through again. You will find, almost unbidden, sharper words, better phrases, new figures of speech, and new illustrations and ideas to replace the weedy patches not noticed before. So, *allow yourself time for revision.*

After you have settled on something to write about, plan for at least three drafts—and try to manage four. Thinking of things to say is the hardest part at first. Even a short assignment of 500 words seems to stretch ahead like a Sahara. You have asserted your central idea in a sentence, and that leaves 490 words to go. But if you step off boldly, one foot after the other, you will make progress, find an oasis or two, and perhaps end at a run in green pastures. With longer papers, you will want some kind of outline to keep you from straying, but the principle is the same: step ahead and keep moving until you've arrived. That is the first draft.

The second draft is a penciled correction of the first. Of course, if the first has been really haphazard, you will probably want to type it again, rearranging, dropping a few things, adding others, before you can do much detailed work with a pencil. But the second, or penciled, draft is where you refine and polish, checking your dubious spellings in the dictionary, sharpening your punctuation, clarifying your meaning, pruning away the deadwood, adding a thought here, extending an illustration there—running in a whole new paragraph on an inserted page. You will also be tuning your sentences, carefully adjusting your tone until it is clearly that of an intelligent, reasonable person at ease with his knowledge and his audience.

Your third draft is a smoothing of all this for public appearance. Still other illustrations and better phrases will suggest themselves as you get your penciled corrections into order. For a classroom paper, three drafts, with several rereadings of the first and the second, are usually adequate. But, if you have time, a fourth draft will do no harm. Reading aloud will frequently pick up errors, lapses in punctuation, and infelicities of phrase. You may have to retype a page of your most polished draft, as a brilliant idea hits you at last, or a terrible sentence finally rears its fuzzy head.

Here is a passage from a student's paper that has gone the full course. First you see the student's initial draft, with his own corrections on it. Next you see the passage after a second typing (and some further changes), as it was returned by the instructor with his marks on it. Then you see the final revision, handed in again, as this particular assignment required:

FIRST DRAFT

In a college education, students should be al-
lowed to ~~make~~ choose their own course. ~~Too many~~ All the requirements, they
~~are discouraging to~~ must take discourage people's creativity, and they cannot learn anything ~~which is~~ they are not motivated ~~for him~~ to
learn. ~~With~~ R requirements restrict their freedom to choose
~~what he is interested in~~ and their eagerness to learn. They are only discouraged
~~is taken away~~ by having to
study dull subjects like German, ~~which he is not in-~~ in which they can see no
~~terested in.~~ relevance to their interests.

THE PAPER, WITH INSTRUCTOR'S MARKINGS

In a college education, students <u>should be</u>
<u>allowed</u> to choose their own curricula and select
their own courses. <u>All the requirements they must take</u>
stifle their <u>creativity</u>. Moreover, they <u>cannot learn</u>
anything they are not motivated to learn. Requirements restrict their freedom to choose and their
<u>eagerness</u> to explore the subjects they are interested
in. <u>They are only discouraged by</u> having to study
dull subjects like German, in which they can see no
relevance.

can you get rid of the passive?

redundant

relevant?

true?

activate

REVISED PAPER

Students should choose their own education,
their own curricula, their own courses. Their education is really theirs alone. Every college re-
quirement threatens to stifle the very enthusiasms
upon which true education depends. Students learn
best when motivated by their own interests, but, in
the midst of a dozen complicated requirements, they
can hardly find time for the courses they long to
take. Requirements therefore not only restrict their
freedom to choose but destroy their eagerness to
explore. Dull subjects like German, in which they
can see no relevance anyway, take all their time and
discourage them completely.

EXERCISES

1. *The following sentences are all thesis statements taken from actual
students' papers. As you can see, the authors did not spot the built-in weak-
nesses. Explain what, if anything, you think wrong with each of these as
thesis-statements. Then revise them as best you can.*

1. I think we should all insist on the retention of the present abortion
   laws.

2. The campus of ——— University (College) is unique in many ways.

3. With the increasing enrollment at this university (and with the larger number of married students) steps need to be taken to increase student housing.

4. From experience, I would believe that weight-lifting can be helpful to a growing young man in more ways than one.

5. The five-mile, cross-country run is one of the most challenging of track events. It requires speed, endurance, and strategy.

6. No matter how it used to be in this country, we have an aristocracy of money now.

7. Joseph Heller's *Catch-22* is not great literature. Indeed, the book is not really a novel at all; it is just a series of little stories.

8. I believe, and will try to show, that the unequal distribution of blacks and whites in occupational groups revealed in the last Census is the result of two problems: inferior education for blacks and discriminatory hiring by white employers.

9. Could half-day sessions in elementary schools provide the same quality of education as provided by full-day sessions?

10. The tourist trade is good for people.

2. *Look over your revised thesis-statements from Exercise 1. Which is most likely to have the reader nodding in agreement even before he finishes the sentence? And which of your thesis-statements seems to be most interesting and exciting? Which seems to have the best argumentative edge? After having identified the most interesting and the least interesting of your thesis-statements, briefly explain what you think generates the greater interest in the one than in the other. The topics themselves? Your interest in the topics? The way you have stated the thesis? Try to be as specific as possible.*

3. *Pick two or three of the following subjects (or similar ones you like better) and change them into theses on the pattern of the debating resolution with a* because *("Cats make better pets than dogs because* ———*"; "Welfare must go because* ———*").*

marijuana	ecology
handguns	abortion
fraternities	the inner city

4. *Now smooth out these theses for public appearance, omitting the direct statement of* because *and adding qualifications ("Despite its many advantages, welfare may actually be eroding our heritage of personal responsibility").*

5. *Now turn your smoothed theses completely around, so that they assert the opposite ("Although welfare may offend the rugged individualist, it relieves much want and anxiety while promoting a sense of shared responsibility").*

Structure

After the thesis, the essay's basic structure is the most valuable means of putting ideas before the reader. In fact, an essay is simply a means of communicating and illustrating an idea in orderly structural steps. Writing is also your most valuable means of learning anything because you arrange for understanding its interconnections, implications, dimensions. You know a subject more thoroughly, you understand a book more clearly, after you have written about it to explain it to some-one else. Consequently, the essay's structure is the base for most of the writing you will do in the rest of your college career, and, indeed, the rest of your life: letters to the editor, proposals to the boss, direc-tives to employees, protests to authorities, minutes of the meeting. The essay is also one of your best means of discovery, seeing things you hadn't known, or hadn't known you knew, as you try to persuade someone about something you believe true. Your thesis is this belief. Your structure unfolds this belief in logical sequence, following the basic psychology of expectation and fulfillment. Arranging your thesis and its illustration along this structural line is the clearest way to both understanding and persuasion.

BEGINNING, MIDDLE, END

As Aristotle long ago pointed out, works that spin their way through time need a beginning, a middle, and an end to give them the

14

stability of spatial things like paintings and statues. You need a clear beginning to give your essay character and direction so the reader can tell where he is going and can look forward with expectation. Your beginning, of course, will set forth your thesis. You need a middle to amplify and fulfill. This will be the body of your argument, the bulk of your essay. You need an end to let readers know that they have arrived and where. This will be your final paragraph, a summation and reassertion of your theme.

Give your essay the three-part *feel* of beginning, middle, and end — the mind likes this triple order. Many a freshman's essay has no structure and leaves no impression. It is all chaotic middle. It has no beginning, it just starts; it has no end, it just stops, fagged out at two in the morning.

The beginning must feel like a beginning, not like an accident. It should be at least a full paragraph that lets your reader gently into the subject and culminates with your thesis. The end, likewise, should be a full paragraph, one that drives the point home, pushes the implications wide, and brings the reader to rest, back on the fundamental thesis to give a sense of completion. When we consider paragraphing in the next chapter, we will look more closely at beginning paragraphs and end paragraphs. The "middle," or "body," of your essay, which constitutes its bulk, needs further structural consideration now.

BASIC STRATEGIES

Arrange Your Points in Order of Increasing Interest.

Once your thesis has sounded the challenge, your reader's interest is probably at its highest pitch. He wants to see how you can prove so outrageous a thing, or to see what the arguments are for this thing he has always believed but never tested. Each step of the way into your demonstration, he is learning more of what you have to say. But, unfortunately, his interest may be relaxing as it becomes satisfied: the reader's normal line of attention is a progressive decline, arching down like a wintry graph. Against this decline you must oppose your forces, making each successive point more interesting. And save your best till last. It is as simple as that.

Here, for example, is the middle of a short, three-paragraph essay developing the thesis that "Working your way through college is valuable." The student has arranged his three points in an ascending order of interest:

> The student who works finds that the experience is worth more than the money. First, he learns to budget his time. He now supports himself by using time he would otherwise waste, and he studies harder in the time he has left because he knows it is limited. Second, he makes real and lasting friends on the job, as compared to the other casual acquaintances around the campus. He has shared rush hours,

and nighttime cleanups with the dishes piled high, and conversation and jokes when business is slow. Finally, he gains confidence in his ability to get along with all kinds of people, and to make his own way. He sees how businesses operate, and how waitresses, for instance, can work cheerfully at a really tiring job without much hope for the future. He gains an insight into the real world, which is a good contrast to the more intellectual and idealistic world of the college student.

Again, each successive item of your presentation should be more interesting than the last, or you will suddenly seem anticlimatic. Actually, minor regressions of interest make no difference so long as the whole tendency is uphill and your last item clearly the best. Suppose, for example, you were to try a thesis about cats. You decide that four points would make up the case, and that you might arrange them in the following order of increasing interest: (1) Cats are affectionate but make few demands; (2) cats actually look out for themselves; (3) cats have, in fact, proved extremely useful to society throughout history in controlling mice and other plaguy rodents; (4) cats satisfy some human need for a touch of the jungle, savagery in repose, ferocity in silk, and have been worshipped for the exotic power they still seem to represent. As you write, you might find Number 1 developing attractive or amusing instances, and perhaps even virtually usurping the whole essay. Numbers 2, 3, and 4 should then be moved ahead as interesting but brief preliminaries. Your middle structure, thus, should range from least important to most important, from simple to complex, from narrow to broad, from pleasant to hilarious, from mundane to metaphysical — whatever "leasts" and "mosts" your subject suggests.

Acknowledge and Dispose of the Opposition, Point by Point.

Your cat essay, because it is moderately playful, can proceed rather directly, throwing only an occasional bone of concession to the dogs, and perhaps most of your essays, as you discuss the Constitutional Convention or explain a poem, will have little opposition to worry about. But a serious controversial argument demands one organizational consideration beyond the simple structure of ascending interest. Although you have taken your stand firmly as a *pro*, you will have to allow scope to the *con*'s, or you will seem not to have thought much about your subject. The more opposition you can manage as you carry your point, the more triumphant you will seem, like a high-wire artist daring the impossible.

This balancing of *pro*'s against *con*'s is one of the most fundamental orders of thought: the dialectic order, which is the order of argument, one side pitted against the other. Our minds naturally swing from side to side as we think. In dialectics, we simply give one side an argumentative edge, producing a thesis that cuts a clear line through any subject: "This is better than that." The basic organizing principle here is to get rid of the opposition first, and to end on your own side. Probably you will have already organized your thesis sentence in a perfect pattern for your *con-pro* argument:

> **Despite their many advantages, welfare payments. . . .**
> **Although dogs are fine pets, cats. . . .**

The subordinate clause (see p. 59) states the subordinate part of your argument, which is your concession to the *con* viewpoint; your main clause states your main argument. As the subordinate clause comes first in your thesis sentence, so with the subordinate argument in your essay. Sentence and essay both reflect a natural psychological principle. You want, and the reader wants, to get the opposition out of the way. And you want to end on your best foot. (You might try putting the opposition last, just to see how peculiarly the last word insists on seeming best, and how, when stated last by you, the opposition's case seems to be your own.)

Get rid of the opposition first. This is the essential tactic of argumentation. You have introduced and stated your thesis in your beginning paragraph. Now start the middle with a paragraph of concession to the *con's*:

> **Dog-lovers, of course, have tradition on their side. Dogs are indeed affectionate and faithful. . . .**

And with that paragraph out of the way, go to bat for the cats, showing their superiority to dogs in every point. In a very brief essay, you can use the opposition itself to introduce your thesis in the first paragraph, and dispose of your opponents at the same time:

> **Shakespeare begins *Romeo and Juliet* with ominous warnings about fate. His lovers are "star-crossed," he says: they are doomed from the first by their contrary stars, by the universe itself. They have sprung from "fatal loins." Fate has already determined their tragic end. The play then unfolds a succession of unlucky and presumably fated accidents. Nevertheless, we soon discover that Shakespeare really blames the tragedy not on fate but on human stupidity and error.**

But usually your beginning paragraph will lead up to your thesis more or less neutrally, and you will attack your opposition head-on in paragraph two, as you launch into the middle.

If the opposing arguments seem relatively slight and brief, you can get rid of them neatly all together in one paragraph before you get down to your case. Immediately after your beginning, which has stated your thesis, you write a paragraph of concession: "Of course, security is a good thing. No one wants people begging." And so on to the end of the paragraph, deflating every conceivable objection. Then back to the main line: "But the price in moral decay is too great." The structure of the argument might be diagrammed something like the scheme shown in Diagram I.

If the opposition is more considerable, demolish it point by point, using a series of *con*'s and *pro*'s, in two or three paragraphs, before you steady down to your own side. Each paragraph can be a small argument that presents the opposition, then knocks it flat—a kind of Punch-and-Judy show: "We must admit that. . . . But. . . ." And down goes the poor old opposition again. Or you could swing your argument through a number of alternating paragraphs: first your beginning, the thesis, then a paragraph to the opposition *(con)*, then one for your side *(pro)*, then another paragraph of *con*, and so on. The main point, again, is this: get rid of the opposition first. One paragraph of concession right after your thesis will probably handle most of your adversaries, and the more complicated argumentative swingers, like the one outlined in Diagram II (p. 19), will develop naturally as you need them.

You will notice that *but* and *however* are always guides for the *pro*'s, serving as switches back to the main line. *But, however,* and *nevertheless* are the basic *pro*'s. *But* always heads its turning sentence (not followed by a comma); *nevertheless* usually does (followed by a comma). I am sure, however, that *however* is always better buried in the sentence between commas. "However, . . ." is the habit of heavy prose. *But* is for the quick turn; the inlaid *however* for the more elegant sweep.

Comparing and contrasting two poems, two stories, two ball players, are further instances of this essential process of thought, of this important way to understanding. You may wish simply to set two similars, or dissimilars, side by side to illustrate some larger point—

Diagram I

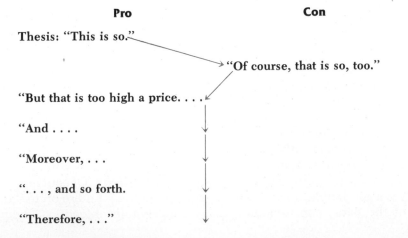

Diagram II

BANNING NUCLEAR POWER—PRO AND CON

| **Pro** | **Con** |

Thesis: "Nuclear power should
  be banned."

To be sure, fossil
  fuels are failing. . . .

But the risks of nuclear
  power are too high. . . .

Of course, no one has
  yet been harmed. . . .

Even foolproof power
  plants, however, produce
  indisposable toxic wastes. . . .

I concede that burial, or
  storage has worked so
  far. . . .

Nevertheless, proliferating
  nuclear power plants will soon
  outproduce all known means of
  storing and disposing wastes. . . .

Indeed, the more plants, the
  more the risk of subversion and
  bombs. . . .

Limiting nuclear power has already
  spurred research into alternate
  energy. . . .

Therefore, the sooner we ban
  all nuclear power, the sooner we
  will have safe and adequate
  energy. . . .

that excellence may come in very different packages, for instance. Comparing and contrasting can illuminate the unfamiliar with the familiar, or it can help you discover and convey to your readers new perspectives on things well known—two popular singers, two of Shakespeare's sonnets, two nursery rhymes. But, whether or not you are presenting one side as superior to the other, the structural tactic is the same: compare point for point, so long as the comparison illuminates.

EXERCISES

1. *In the following exercises, you will find groups of information and ideas haphazardly arranged. Rewrite the statements with the information arranged in an ascending order of interest and importance. Then, in a sentence or two, explain your reasons for using that order.*

1. We are now being made to realize the negative aspects of the technological "progress" of the twentieth century: 50,000 highway deaths per year, air and water pollution, the population explosion, nuclear warfare, loss of privacy.
2. Four different levels of government are investigating the effectiveness of the methadone treatment for heroin addiction. State, national, county, and city governments have all instituted research programs within the past few years.
3. The psychological effects of the Depression are observable in an increase in the frequency of mental breakdown, an increase in the suicide rate, and a decrease in the birth rate.
4. Although most classrooms have tile floors, carpeting is actually better in several ways. First, if you figure maintenance into the total cost of floor covering, carpeting is cheaper than tile; second, carpeting is more aesthetically pleasing than tile; and third, carpeting serves a useful acoustical function, absorbing the noise of scuffing feet and scooting chairs.
5. This car not only looks sporty, but is also equipped for sporty performance. It has a turbo charger, five-speed gear box, heavy-duty springs and shocks, high-back bucket seats, vinyl roof, a 3000cc engine, heavy-duty cooling system, power disc brakes, corduroy upholstery trim, rally accent stripes.
6. An all-volunteer army may be undesirable because it tends to draw from a limited segment of the population, to create an elitist military caste such as those in Hitler's Germany and in tsarist Russia, and to cost more. But it does away with the draft.
7. Marijuana should be legalized because people are going to use it whether it is legalized or not. Legalizing it would make a sensible distinction between hard and soft drugs, would allow authorities to control the quality of the drugs available for sale, would eliminate criminal profiteering, and would prevent numbers of people from becoming cynical violators of the law.
8. If you have gotten along without a credit card until now, applying for one is really a mistake. If you have one, you might lose it or have it stolen, and then you might be liable for a sizable part of the expenses run up by someone else using your card. Then there are the interest charges. Few people realize that the interest on most credit cards is at least 18 percent a year. And obviously, if you have a credit card, you are going to spend more than if you were using cash.

9. Talking about scientific knowledge today, she identified three of its characteristics. First, this knowledge is not within the reach of most of us. Second, this knowledge is mostly knew. And, finally, this knowledge has become almost the exclusive property of a very small group of scientists and engineers.

2. *In the exercise that follows, you will find a series of general assertions. Supply one argument* against *and one argument* for *each proposition. Then combine the statements into one thesis-sentence that includes not only the assertion, but also the reasons against and for it.*

EXAMPLE *Assertion: Movies should not be censored.*

Con: Children should not be exposed to obscene and explicitly sexual images on the screen.

Pro: Obscenity is far too subjective a thing for any person to define for anyone else.

Thesis-Statement: Although it is probably undesirable for young people to be exposed to scenes of explicit sex in films, movies still should not be censored because obscenity is so subjective a thing that no one can legitimately serve as censor for the rest of us.

1. Assertion: Discussion classes are superior to lectures.
2. Assertion: Rapid and convenient transit systems must be built in our cities.
3. Assertion: The federal government should subsidize large companies forced near bankruptcy.
4. Assertion: Medical schools should reduce the time required for a degree in general medicine from four years to two.
5. Assertion: States should prohibit the sale of beverages in nonreturnable containers.
6. Assertion: A guaranteed annual income would not wipe out poverty for all Americans.
7. Assertion: As exercise, golf is a waste of time.
8. Assertion: The law should require that all drivers and passengers in cars use seat belts.
9. Assertion: College students should study a foreign language.

3. *Choose a thesis to cover the following points (for or against public transportation, for instance). Then, underneath your thesis, list these points in an order of ascending interest, and in a* pro-con *structure, adding necessary* but's *and* of course's *and so forth, and other intermediate points of your own:*

The automobile pollutes the atmosphere.
Public transportation is going bankrupt.
The economy requires obsolescence.
Cars were once built to last.
A car is a necessity.

3

Paragraphs

THE STANDARD PARAGRAPH

A paragraph is a structural convenience — a building block to get firmly in mind. I mean the standard, central paragraph, setting aside for the moment the peculiarly shaped beginning paragraph and ending paragraph. You build the bulk of your essay with standard paragraphs, with blocks of concrete ideas, and they should fit smoothly. But they should also remain as perceptible parts, to rest your reader's eye and mind. Indeed, the paragraph originated, among the Greeks, as a resting place and place-finder, being first a mere mark (*graphos*) in the margin alongside (*para*) an unbroken sheet of handwriting — the proofreader's familiar ¶. You have heard that a paragraph is a single idea, and this is true. But so is a word, usually; and so is a sentence, sometimes. It seems best, after all, to think of a paragraph as something you use for your reader's convenience, rather than as some granitic form laid down by molten logic.

The writing medium determines the size of the paragraph. Your average longhand paragraph may look the same size to you as a typewritten one, and both may seem the same size as a paragraph in a book. But the printed page might show your handwritten paragraph so short as to be embarrassing, and your typewritten paragraph barely long enough for decency. Handwriting plus typewriting plus insecurity equals inadequate paragraphs. Your first impulse may be to write little paragraphs, often only a sentence to each. If so, you are not yet writing in any medium at all.

Journalists, of course, are habitually one-sentence paragraphers. The narrowness of the newspaper column makes a sentence look like a paragraph, and narrow columns and short paragraphs serve the rapid transit for which newspapers are designed. A paragraph from a book might fill a whole newspaper column with solid lead. It would have to be broken—paragraphed—for the reader's convenience. On the other hand, a news story on the page of a book would look like a gap-toothed comb, and would have to be consolidated for the reader's comfort.

Plan for the Big Paragraph.

Imagine yourself writing for print, but in a book, not a newspaper. Force yourself to four or five sentences at least, visualizing your paragraphs as about all of a size. Think of them as identical rectangular frames to be filled. This will allow you to build with orderly blocks, to strengthen your feel for structure. Since the beginner's problem is usually one of thinking of things to say rather than of trimming the overgrowth, you can do your filling out a unit at a time, always thinking up one or two sentences more to fill the customary space. You will probably be repetitive and wordly at first—this is our universal failing—but you will soon learn to fill your paragraph with clean and interesting details. You will get to feel a kind of constructional rhythm as you find yourself coming to a resting place at the end of your customary paragraphic frame.

Once accustomed to a five-sentence frame, say, you can then begin to vary the length for emphasis, letting a good idea swell out beyond the norm, or bringing a particular point home in a paragraph short and sharp—even in one sentence, like this.

The paragraph's structure, then, has its own rhetorical message. It tells the reader visually whether or not you are in charge of your subject and are leading him confidently to see what you already know. Tiny, ragged paragraphs display your hidden uncertainty, unless clearly placed among big ones for emphasis. Brief opening and closing paragraphs sometimes can emphasize your thesis effectively, but usually they make your beginning seem hasty and your ending perfunctory. So aim for the big paragraph all the way, and vary it only occasionally and knowingly, for rhetorical emphasis.

Find a Topic Sentence.

Looked at as a convenient structural frame, the paragraph reveals a further advantage. Like the essay itself, it has a beginning, a middle, and an end. The beginning and the end are usually each one sentence long, and the middle gets you smoothly from one to the other. Since, like the essay, the paragraph flows through time, its last sentence is the most emphatic. This is your home punch. The first sentence holds the next most emphatic place. It will normally be your *topic sentence* stating the small thesis of a miniature essay, something like this:

> *Jefferson believed in democracy because of his fearless belief in reason.* He knew that reason was far from perfect, but he also knew that it was the best faculty we have. He knew that it was better than all the frightened and angry intolerances with which we fence off our own back yards at the cost of injustice. Thought must be free. Discussion must be free. Reason must be free to range among the widest possibilities. Even the opinion we hate, and have reasons for believing wrong, we must leave free so that reason can operate on it, so that we advertise our belief in reason and demonstrate a faith unafraid of the consequences — because we know that the consequences will be right. Freedom is really not the aim and end of Jeffersonian democracy: freedom is the means by which democracy can rationally choose justice for all.

If your topic sentence covers everything within your paragraph, your paragraph is coherent, and you are using your paragraphs with maximum effect, leading your reader into your community block by block. If your end sentence brings him briefly to rest, he will know where he is and appreciate it.

BEGINNING PARAGRAPHS: THE FUNNEL
State Your Thesis at the END of Your Beginning Paragraph.

Your beginning paragraph should contain your main idea, and present it to best advantage. Its topic sentence is also the *thesis sentence* of your entire essay. The clearest and most emphatic place for your thesis sentence is at the *end* — not at the beginning — of the beginning paragraph. If you put it first, you will have to repeat some version of it as you bring your beginning paragraph to a close. If you put it in the middle, the reader will very likely take something else as your main point, probably whatever the last sentence contains. The inevitable psychology of interest, as you move your reader through your first paragraph and into your essay, urges you to put your thesis last — in the last sentence of your beginning paragraph.

Think of your beginning paragraph, then, not as a frame to be filled, but as a funnel. Start wide and end narrow:

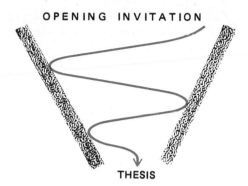

OPENING INVITATION

THESIS

If for instance, you wished to show that learning to play the guitar pays off in friendship, you would start somewhere back from your specific thesis with something more general — about music, about learning, about the pleasures of achievement, about guitars: "Playing the guitar looks easy," "Music can speak more directly than words," "Learning anything is a course in frustration." You can even open with something quite specific, even a descriptive vignette, *as long as the idea is more general than your thesis:* "Pick up a guitar, and you bump into people"; "She leaned over her guitar as if in a trance, playing only for herself." As you can see from these examples, a handy way to find an opener is to take one word from your thesis — *learning, play,* or *guitar,* for instance — and make a sentence out of it. Say something about it, and you are well on your way to your thesis, three or four sentences later.[*] This will keep you from starting too far back, and losing your reader in puddles of platitudes: "Everyone likes to be popular. Most people like music. . . ." Your opening line, in other words, should clearly look forward to your thesis, should be something to engage interest easily, something to which most readers would assent without a rise in blood pressure. (Antagonize and startle if you wish, but beware of having the door slammed before you have a chance, and of making your thesis an anticlimax.) Therefore: broad and genial. From your opening geniality, you move progressively down to smaller particulars. You narrow down: from learning the guitar, to its musical and social complications, to its rewards in friendship (your thesis). Your paragraph might run, from broad to narrow, thus:

> Learning anything has unexpected rocks in its path, but the guitar seems particularly rocky. It looks so simple. A few chords, you think, and you are on your way. Then you discover not only the musical and technical difficulties, but a whole unexpected crowd of human com-

[*]I am grateful to James C. Raymond, of the University of Alabama, for this helpful idea.

plications. Your friends think you are showing off; the people you meet think you are a fake. Then the frustrations drive you to achievement. You learn to face the music and the people honestly. You finally learn to play a little, but you also discover something better. You have learned to make and keep some real friends, because you have discovered a kind of ultimate frienship with yourself.

Now, that paragraph turned out a little different from what I anticipated. I overshot my original thesis, discovering, as I wrote, a thesis one step farther—an underlying cause—about coming to friendly terms with oneself. But it illustrated the funnel, from the broad and general to the one particular point that will be your essay's main idea, your thesis. Here is another example:

> The environment is the world around us, and everyone agrees it needs a cleaning. Big corporations gobble up the countryside and disgorge what's left into the breeze and streams. Big trucks rumble by, trailing their fumes. A jet roars into the air, and its soot drifts over the trees. Everyone calls for massive action, and then tosses away his cigarette butt or gum wrapper. The world around us is also a sidewalk, a lawn, a lounge, a hallway, a room right here. Cleaning the environment can begin by reaching for the scrap of paper at your feet.

MIDDLE PARAGRAPHS

Make Your Middle Paragraphs Full, and Use Transitions.

The middle paragraph is the standard paragraph, the little essay in itself, with its own little beginning and little end. But it must also declare its allegiance to the paragraphs immediately before and after it. Each topic sentence must somehow hook onto the paragraph above it, must include some word or phrase to ease the reader's path: a transition. You may simply repeat a word from the sentence that ended the paragraph just above. You may bring down a thought left slightly hanging in air: "Smith's idea is different" might be a tremendously economical topic sentence with automatic transition—or an even bolder "Not at all" or "Nonsense." Or you may get from one paragraph to the next by the usual stepping-stones, like *but, however, nevertheless, therefore, indeed, of course.* One brief transitional touch in your topic sentence is usually sufficient.

The topic sentences in each of the following three paragraphs by James Baldwin contain neat transitions, here shown in italics. I have just used an old standby myself: repeating the words *topic sentence* from the close of my preceding paragraph. Baldwin has just described the young people of Harlem who have given up, escaping into day-long TV, or the local bar, or drugs. He now begins his next paragraph with *And the others,* a strong and natural transition, referring back, reinforced with the further transitional reference *all of these deaths.* In the next paragraph, *them* does the trick; in the last, *other* again makes the transition and sets the contrast. The paragraphs are nearly the same length, all cogent, clear, and full. Notice how Baldwin repeats *They* in the first paragraph, *remembers* in the second, and *console* in the third to carry the thought in smooth transitions from sentence to sentence. No one-sentence paragraphing here, no gaps, but all a vivid, orderly progression:

> *And the others,* who have avoided *all of these deaths,* get up in the morning and go downtown to meet "the man." *They* work in the white man's world all day and come home in the evening to this fetid block. *They* struggle to instill in their children some private *sense* of honor or dignity which will help the child to survive. This means, of course, that *they* must struggle, stolidly, incessantly, to keep *this sense* alive in themselves, in spite of the insults, the indifference, and the cruelty *they* are certain to encounter in their working day. *They* patiently browbeat the landlord into fixing the heat, the plaster, the plumbing; this demands prodigious patience; nor is patience usually enough. In trying to make their hovels habitable, *they* are perpetually throwing good money after bad. Such frustration, so long endured, is driving many strong, admirable men and women whose only crime is color to the very gates of paranoia.
>
> *One remembers them* from another time—playing handball in the playground, going to church, wondering if they were going to be promoted at school. *One remembers* them going off to war—gladly, to escape this block. *One remembers* their return. Perhaps one remembers their wedding day. And one sees where the girl is now—vainly looking for salvation from some other embittered, trussed, and struggling boy—and sees the all-but-abandoned children in the streets.
>
> Now I am perfectly aware *that* there are *other* slums in which white men are fighting for their lives, and mainly losing. I know *that* blood is also flowing through those streets and *that* the human damage there is incalculable. People are continually pointing out to me the wretchedness of white people in order to *console* me for the wretchedness of blacks. But an itemized account of the American failure does not *console* me and it should not *console* anyone else. *That* hundreds of thousands of white people are living, in effect, no better than the "niggers" is not a fact to be regarded with complacency. The social and moral bankruptcy suggested by this fact is of the bitterest, most terrifying kind.*

*From "Fifth Avenue Uptown: A Letter from Harlem" in *Nobody Knows My Name* (New York: Dial Press, 1961), pp. 59–61. Copyright © 1960 by James Baldwin. Reprinted by permission of Dial Press. Originally published in *Esquire.*

Check Your Paragraphs
for Clarity and Coherence.

Baldwin's paragraphs run smoothly from first sentence to last. They are coherent. The *topic sentence* is the key. It assures that your subsequent sentences will fall into line, and it is the first point to check when you look back to see if they really do. Many a jumbled and misty paragraph can be unified and cleared by writing a broader topic sentence. Consider this disjointed specimen:

> **Swimming is healthful. The first dive into the pool is always cold. Tennis takes a great deal of energy, especially under a hot sun. Team sports, like basketball, baseball, and volleyball, always make the awkward player miserable. Character and health go hand in hand.**

What is all that about? From the last sentence, we can surmise something of what the writer intended. But the first sentence about swimming in no way covers the paragraph, which treats several sports not in the least like swimming, and seems to be driving at something other than health. The primary remedy, as always, is to find the paragraph's thesis and to devise a topic sentence that will state it, thus covering everything in the paragraph. Think of your topic sentence as a roof—covering your paragraph and pulling its lines and contents together.

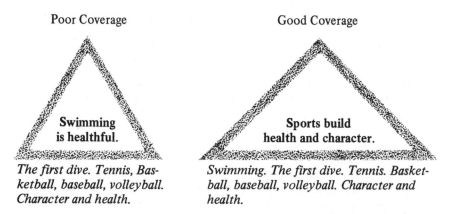

Poor Coverage   Good Coverage

**Swimming
is healthful.**

**Sports build
health and character.**

*The first dive. Tennis, Bas-   Swimming. The first dive. Tennis. Basket-
ketball, baseball, volleyball.   ball, baseball, volleyball. Character and
Character and health.*   health.

Suppose we leave the paragraph unchanged for the moment, adding only a topic sentence suggested by our right-hand diagram. It will indeed pull things together:

Topic   *Sports demand an effort of will and muscle that is healthful for the*
sentence   *soul as well as the body.* **Swimming is healthful. The first dive into
                 the pool is always cold. Tennis takes a great deal of energy, espe-
                 cially under a hot sun. Team sports, like basketball, baseball, and
                 volleyball, always make the awkward player miserable. Character
                 and health go hand in hand.**

But the paragraph is still far from an agreeable coherence. The islands of thought still need some bridges. Gaining coherence is primarily a filling in, or a spelling out, of submerged connections. You may fill in with (1) thought and (2) specific illustrative detail; you may spell out by tying your sentences together with (3) transitional tags and (4) repeated words or syntactical patterns (see the passage from James Baldwin, p. 27.) Let us see what we can do with our sample paragraph.

From the first, you probably noticed that the writer was thinking in pairs: the pleasure of sports is balanced off against their difficulty; the difficulty is physical as well as moral; character and health go hand in hand. We have already indicated this doubleness of idea in our topic sentence. Now to fill out the thought, we need merely expand each sentence so as to give each half of the double idea its due expression. We need also to qualify the thought here and there with *perhaps, often, some, sometimes, frequently, all in all*, and the like. As we work through the possibilities, more specific detail will come to mind. We have already made the general ideas of *character* and *health* more specific with *will, muscle, soul*, and *body* in our topic sentence, and we shall add a touch or two more of illustration, almost automatically, as our imagination becomes more stimulated by the subject. We shall add a number of transitional ties like *but, and, of course, nevertheless*, and *similarly*. We shall look for chances to repeat key words, like *will*, if we can do so gracefully; and to repeat syntactical patterns, if we can emphasize similar thoughts by doing so, as with *no matter how patient his teammates . . . no matter how heavy his heart*, toward the end of our revision below (the original phrases are in italics):

Topic sentence	**Sports demand an effort of will and muscle that is healthful for the soul as well as the body.** *Swimming* is physically *healthful*, of course, although it may seem undemanding and highly conducive to lying for hours inert on a deck chair in the sun. But *the first dive into the pool*
Illustrative sentences with transitions	*is always cold:* taking the plunge always requires some effort of will. And the swimmer soon summons his will to compete, against himself or others, for greater distances and greater speed, doing twenty laps where he used to do one. Similarly, *tennis takes* quantities *of energy*, physical and moral, *especially* when the competition stiffens *under a hot sun. Team sports, like basketball, baseball, and volleyball,* perhaps demand even more of the amateur. *The awkward player* is miserable when he strikes out, or misses an easy fly, or an easy basket, no matter how patient his teammates. He must drive himself to keep on trying, no matter how heavy his heart. Whatever the sport, a little determination can eventually conquer one's awkwardness and timid-
End sentence: the point	ity, and the reward will be more than physical. *Character and health* frequently *go hand in hand.*

Remember these four points about middle paragraphs. First, think of the middle paragraph as a miniature essay, with a beginning, a middle, and an end. Its beginning will normally be its topic sentence, the thesis of this miniature essay. Its middle will develop, explain, and illustrate your topic sentence. Its last sentence will drive home the idea. Second, see that your paragraph is coherent, not only flowing smoothly but with nothing in it not covered by the topic sentence. Third, make your paragraphs full and well developed, with plenty of details, examples, and full explanations, or you will end up with a skeletal paper with very little meat on its bones. Fourth, remember transitions. Though each paragraph is a kind of miniature essay, it is also part of a larger essay. Therefore, hook each paragraph smoothly to the paragraph preceding it, with some transitional touch in each topic sentence.

END PARAGRAPHS:
THE INVERTED FUNNEL

Reassert Your Thesis.

If the beginning paragraph is a funnel, the end paragraph is a funnel upside down: the thought starts moderately narrow—it is more or less the thesis you have had all the time—and then pours out broader and broader implications and finer emphases. The end paragraph reiterates, summarizes, and emphasizes with decorous fervor. This is your last chance. This is what your readers will carry away—and if you can carry *them* away, so much the better. All within decent intellectual bounds, of course. You are the person of reason still, but the person of reason supercharged with conviction, sure of your idea and sure of its importance.

The final paragraph conveys a sense of assurance and repose, of business completed. Its topic sentence should be some version of your original thesis sentence, since the end paragraph is the exact structural opposite and complement of the beginning one. Its transitional word or phrase is often one of finality or summary—*then, finally, thus*, and *so:*

> **So, the guitar is a means to a finer end.**
> **The environment, then, is in our lungs and at our fingertips.**

The paragraph would then proceed to expand and elaborate this revived thesis. We would get a confident assertion that both the music and the friendships are really by-products of an inner alliance; we would get an urgent plea to clean up our personal environs and strengthen our convictions. One rule of thumb: the longer the paper, the more specific the summary of the points you have made. A short paper will need no specific summary of your points at all; the renewed thesis and its widening of implications are sufficient.

Here is an end paragraph by Sir James Jeans. His transitional phrase is *for a similar reason.* His thesis was that previous concepts of physical reality had mistaken surfaces for depths:

> The purely mechanical picture of visible nature fails for a similar reason. It proclaims that the ripples themselves direct the workings of the universe instead of being mere symptoms of occurrences below; in brief, it makes the mistake of thinking that the weathervane determines the direction from which the wind shall blow, or that the thermometer keeps the room hot.*

In the following end paragraph of Richard Hofstadter's, his transitional word is *intellectuals,* carried over from the preceding paragraphs. His thesis was that intellectuals should not abandon their defense of intellectual and spiritual freedom, as they have tended to do, under pressure to conform:

> This world will never be governed by intellectuals — it may rest assured. But *we* must be assured, too, that intellectuals will not be altogether governed by this world, that they maintain their piety, their longstanding allegiance to the world of spiritual values to which they should belong. Otherwise there will be no intellectuals, at least not above ground. And societies in which the intellectuals have been driven underground, as we have had occasion to see in our own time, are societies in which even the anti-intellectuals are unhappy.†

THE WHOLE ESSAY

You have now discovered the main ingredients of a good essay. You have learned to find and to sharpen your thesis in one sentence, to give your essay that all-important argumentative edge. You have learned to arrange your points in order of increasing interest, and you have practiced disposing of the opposition in a *pro-con* structure. You have seen that your beginning paragraph should seem like a funnel, working from broad generalization to thesis. You have tried your hand at middle paragraphs, which are almost like little essays with their own beginnings and ends. And finally, you have learned that your last paragraph should work like an inverted funnel, broadening and embellishing your thesis.

Some students have pictured the essay as a Greek column, with a narrowing beginning paragraph as its top, or capital, and a broadening end paragraph as its base. Others have seen it as a keyhole (see the diagram).‡ But either way, you should see a structure, with solid begin-

---

The New Background of Science (Cambridge: Cambridge University Press, 1933), p. 261.

†"Democracy and Anti-Intellectualism in America," *Michigan Quarterly Review*, 59 (1953), 295.

‡Mrs. Fran Measley of Santa Barbara, California, has devised for her students a mimeographed sheet to accompany my discussion of structure and paragraphing — to help them to visualize my points, through a keyhole, as it were. I am grateful to Mrs. Measley to be able to include it here (p. 32).

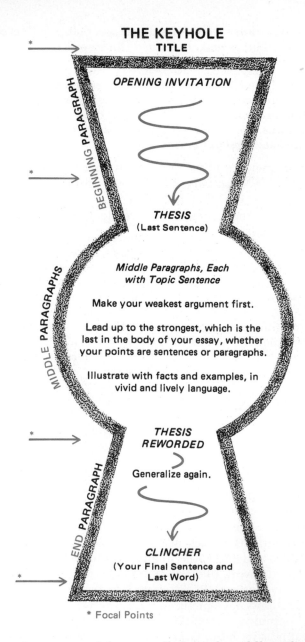

THE KEYHOLE
TITLE

OPENING INVITATION

BEGINNING PARAGRAPH

THESIS
(Last Sentence)

MIDDLE PARAGRAPHS

*Middle Paragraphs, Each
with Topic Sentence*

Make your weakest argument first.

Lead up to the strongest, which is the
last in the body of your essay, whether
your points are sentences or paragraphs.

Illustrate with facts and examples, in
vivid and lively language.

*THESIS
REWORDED*

Generalize again.

END PARAGRAPH

CLINCHER
(Your Final Sentence and
Last Word)

* Focal Points

ning and end, supported by a well-shaped middle. The student's essay that follows illustrates this structure. The assignment, early in the semester, had been to find something in a newspaper or magazine from which to develop a thesis, and then to illustrate that thesis with (1) the newspaper or magazine item and (2) a personal experience. Again, the writer's language has not fully ripened. He probably overuses *I*, and he could cut some excess wordage. But he has grasped the basic ideas of structure: a thesis well set, and a good sense of beginning, middle, and end.

THE VALUE OF WORK

America is materialistic. Newspapers and magazines are full of articles about the way greedy American materialism is burning up the world's supply of fuel, eating great quantities of food while others starve, and polluting the rivers and the atmosphere. The "Protestant Work Ethic," inherited from our Pilgrim forefathers, is supposed to be driving us to materialistic ruin. Nevertheless, the Pilgrims had a point. Work is not only essential to modern society but beneficial to the individual in nonmaterialistic ways.

An article in the *Milhaven Daily* last summer outlined the difficulty teenagers and college students were having in finding work, and it showed pictures of teenagers painting a mural on the side of a large brick building, under the supervision of an artist. The project was funded by the government, and it was frankly intended to give the teenagers something constructive to do, improving property instead of destroying it through vandalism because they had nothing else to do. Money and materialistic gain were not the purpose of the project, although the workers were paid and probably enjoyed getting their paychecks.

Work can in this way satisfy a person's need to feel useful, to do something constructive, which other people will respect. I discovered this last year during my final year in high school. Like many others, I had completed most of my college requirements and was feeling restless and discontented. I answered an ad for a dishwasher in one of our town's popular steak houses. I did not need the money. I had an allowance, and there was no problem about sending me to college. For some reason, I wanted to work for the sake of work. Like the teenagers painting the brick wall, I had almost no materialistic motivation.

My first clear motivation was just not to give up. My parents thought that working on school nights, sometimes until midnight, was a poor idea, both because of grades and health. The dishwashing, even with a monster garbage disposal and dishwashing machine, was hard and almost revolting, like stirring around for hours in hot liquid garbage. But I kept up with the load, and I satisfied myself that it would not beat me.

Then my satisfactions changed from negative to positive. In two weeks, after several other dishwashers had quit, I was promoted to assistant cook, or "pit man." I was teamed with a chef, and taught to set up the different orders on plates, with just the right amount of parsley in just the right place, and to cook certain parts of certain orders. In another three weeks, I was training for chef, with pa[y] raises at each step. When summer came, I was a full-time chef, with pit man of my own. I could work quickly handling the differ[ent] orders as they came in. I once turned out a banquet for seventy [ ] steaks cooked to order from rare to well done. I liked the job so [ ]

Margin annotations:

Opening with opposition

Narrowing through details to refutation and thesis

Topic sentence

Middle: general evidence

Wordy: cut *because . . . do.*

Topic sentence

Middle: personal evidence

Wordy: revise to: *. . . and no problem of college expenses.*

Topic sentence

Personal evidence

Wordy: delete *and I, myself*

Topic sentence

Personal evidence

that I hated to give it up for a short vacation before entering college this fall.

Topic sentence: the opposition restated

I admit some of the charges against the work ethic as materialistic. I bought some expensive new stereo equipment. I bought a new ten-speed bicycle, and I put $1,000 into a time-certificate at the bank. The ability to do these things on my own decision with my own money was very satisfying. But I do not believe that this is really materialism.

Thesis restated

The wish to work, and the satisfaction, are actually psychological, not material. I once said to my dad, when he congratulated me on my paycheck, "But I'm really not doing this for the money — I really don't know why I'm doing it." He said, "You're doing it to prove to yourself that you can do a job in the world, and do it well, that you can make it on your own if you have to." That really is the psychological satisfaction in work. You demonstrate to yourself that you are useful and able in the adult world. The paychecks and the raises, although they are materialistic in themselves, are symbols of your ability to please

The clincher

others in a useful way, to be respected for your ability, and to stand on your own feet.

EXERCISES

1. *Below is a list of thesis sentences. Choose one (or its opposite), or make one of your own on the same pattern. Then back off from it at least four or five sentences, and write a funnel-like beginning paragraph leading your reader down to it: your thesis, the last sentence of your beginning funnel.* EXAMPLE *with thesis italicized follows:*

The coal operators will tell you that stripping is cheaper and more efficient than conventional mining. Their 250-cubic-yard drag-lines, their 200-cubic-yard shovels, their 50-ton trucks, can rip the top off a mountain and expose a whole seam of coal in a fraction of the time it takes to sink a shaft. "It is cheaper," they will say, "to bring the surface to the coal than to bring the coal to the surface." And of course they are right; in a sense it is cheaper. But visit Eastern Kentucky and look at the real price we pay for stripped coal. Visit a stripped area, and you will see that, no matter how low the price for a truckload of stripped coal, *the real price for strip-mining has to be reckoned in terms of blighted land, poisoned streams, and stunted human lives.*

1. No matter what the advertisements promise, the X-rated movie usually turns out to be dull and wearisome; it turns out to be two hours of heavy breathing.
2. The computer has contributed to the modern sense of alienation.
3. If the filibuster is supposed to guarantee respect for minority opinion, it usually turns out to be a flagrant waste of time.
4. The new sense of black pride comes from an increasing awareness of black accomplishments in the past.
5. If women are discriminated against in schools and in industry, they are far more discriminated against in politics.

2. *Now try the inverted funnel, in which your topic sentence is some version of the thesis with which you began and your final paragraph broadens its implications outward to leave the reader fully convinced and satisfied. Using the thesis sentences in Exercise 1, write two ending paragraphs for imaginary papers.*

EXAMPLE *with the rephrased thesis (its topic sentence) italicized, and some of the evidence from the paper's middle summarized for emphasis:*

> *So, at last, we should add up the real costs of strip-mining; we should admit that the ultimate price of coal is far too high if we must rape the land, poison the streams, and wreck human lives to mine it.* For after the drag-lines have gone, even after the coal itself has been burned, the bills for strip-mining will keep coming in. So far, following the expedient path, we have laid bare more than 2,600 square miles of our land, and we show no signs of stopping. Every year we strip an additional 50,000 acres. Just as we cut down our forests in the nineteenth century and fouled our air in the twentieth, we still blunder along toward ecological and social disaster. Isn't it time to stop?

3. *Staying with the same topic sentence, develop a full middle paragraph, remembering the four points: (1) the miniature essay, with beginning, middle, and end; (2) coherence; (3) fullness; (4) transition.*

EXAMPLE *with transitional touches italicized:*

> The *streams* tell the story *as drearily as* the *eroded land.* In winter, *they* are red with running silt, and sometimes black with *coal* dust. *In summer, many* are no *streams* at all, merely dry gullies through which the *winter* rains have rushed. Before the *drag-lines stripped* the earth of its skin, the massed roots of grasses, shrubs, and trees held the soil in place and soaked up the water, easing it into the *streams* for a full year's run. Fish fed in the pools below *grassy* banks and among the weeds that slowed the *water* to a leisurely pace. Now the *water* is soon gone, if not *poisoned* with industrial waste, and the land is *gone* with it.

Now you will have a three-paragraph essay that should convey a thorough sense of beginning, middle, end.

4. *Now, to make an even richer, fuller essay, add two or more middle paragraphs, with good transitions, to give a stronger impetus to the implications of your end paragraph. If you had developed the sample paragraphs in these exercises, for example, you could develop separate paragraphs, each with several illustrations, on ruined land, streams, and lives.*

4

Tactics

Now you have the essay's essence: the inner thesis and the outer structure, the idea and its embodiment. Arranging the structure requires some attention to detail, paragraph by paragraph, and different subjects often suggest different tactics in laying out those details to best advantage. Here are some of the ancient *topoi* — cause and effect, comparison and contrast, classification, definition — which are really tactics for arrangement and persuasion.

CAUSE AND EFFECT
Trace Back or Look Ahead.

Because is the impulse of your thinking here: "Such and such is so *because*. . . ." You think back through a train of causes, each one the effect of something prior; or you think your way into the future, speculating about the possible effects of some present cause. In other words, you organize your paragraph in one of two ways:

    I. You state a general effect, then deal with its several causes.
   II. You state a general cause, then deal with its possible effects.

In Arrangement I, you know the effect (a lost football game, or the solar system, let us say), and you speculate as to causes. In Arrangement II, you know the cause (a new restriction, or abolishing nuclear weapons, let us say), and you speculate as to the effects.

ARRANGEMENT I: EFFECT
FOLLOWED BY CAUSES

> An unusual run of bad luck lost the game. Many blamed Fraser's failure to block the tackler who caused the fumble that produced the winning touchdown. But even here, bad weather and bad luck shared the blame. Both teams faced a slippery field, of course. But Fraser was standing in a virtual bog when he lunged for the block and slipped. Moreover, the storm had delayed the bus for hours, tiring and frustrating the team, leaving them short of sleep and with no chance to practice. Furthermore, Hunter's throwing arm was still not back in shape from his early injury. Finally, one must admit, the Acorns were simply heavier and stronger, which is the real luck of the game.

You will probably notice, as you try to explain causes and effects, that they do not always run in a simple linear sequence, one thing following another, like a row of falling dominoes. Indeed, mere sequence is so famously untrustworthy in tracing causes that one of the classical errors of thought has been named *post hoc, ergo propter hoc* ("after this, therefore because of this"). It is wrong, in other words, to suppose that *A* caused *B* because *A* preceded *B*. The two may have been entirely unrelated. But the greatest danger in identifying causes is to fasten upon a single cause while ignoring others of equal significance. Both your paragraph and your persuasiveness will be better if you do not insist, as some did, that only Fraser's failure to block the tackler lost the game.

In the lost ball game, you were interested in explaining causes, but sometimes your interest will lie with effects. When describing a slum problem, for instance, your topic sentence might be *The downtown slum is a screaming disgrace* (the effect), and you might then in a single sentence set aside the causes as irrelevant, as water over the dam, as so much spilt milk: "perhaps caused by inefficiency, perhaps by avarice, perhaps by the indifference of Mayor Richman." Your interests will dictate your proportions of cause and effect. You might well write an entire essay that balances the slum's causes and effects in equal proportions: a paragraph each on inefficiency, avarice, and the mayor's indifference, then a paragraph each on ill health, poor education, and hopelessness.

Here is how a brief essay, in three paragraphs, can work out in dealing with cause and effect alone. I have begun and ended with the *effect* (the peculiar layout of a town). First, I located the *immediate cause* (cattle) as my thesis, and then, in the middle paragraph, I moved through the cause and its *conditions* up to the *effect* again — the town as it stands today:

NORTH OF THE TRACKS

Effect

If you drive out west from Chicago, you will notice something happening to the towns. After the country levels into Nebraska, the smaller towns are built only on one side of the road. When you stop for a rest, and look south across the broad main street, you will see the railroad immediately beyond. All of these towns spread northward

Cause

from the tracks. Why? As you munch your hamburger and look at the restaurant's murals, you will realize that the answer is cattle.

Conditions

These towns were the destinations of the great cattle drives from Texas. They probably had begun at the scattered watering places in the dry land. Then the wagon trails and, finally, the transcontinental

(Description: moving from south to north, from cause to effect)

railroad had strung them together. Once the railroad came, the whole southwest could raise cattle for the slaughterhouses of Chicago. The droves of cattle came up from the south, and all of these towns reflect the traffic: corrals beside the tracks to the south, the road for passengers and wagons paralleling the tracks on the northern side, then, along the road, the row of hotels, saloons, and businesses, with the town spreading northward behind the businesses.

Cause

The cattle business itself shaped these one-sided Nebraska towns. The conditions in which this immediate cause took root were the growing population in the East and the railroad that connected the plains of the West, and Southwest, with the tables of New York. The towns took their hopeful being north of the rails, on the leeward side of the vast cattle drives from the south. The trade in cattle has now changed, all the way from Miami to Sacramento. But the great herds

Effect

of the old Southwest, together with the transcontinental railroad and man's need to make a living, plotted these Western towns north of the tracks.

ARRANGEMENT II: CAUSE
FOLLOWED BY PROBABLE EFFECTS

Arrangement II is the staple of deliberative rhetoric, of all political and economic forecasting, for instance. Your order of presenting cause and effect is reversed. You are looking to the future. You state a known cause (a new restriction on dormitory hours) or a hypothetical cause ("If this restriction is passed"), and then you speculate about the possible, or probable, effects. Your procedure will then be much the same as before. But for maximum persuasiveness, try to keep your supposed effects, which no one can really foresee, as nearly probable as you can. Occasionally, of course, you may put an improbable hypothetical cause to good use in a satiric essay, reducing some proposal to absurdity: "If all restrictions were abolished. . . ." "If no one wore clothes. . . ." Or the improbable *if* may even help clarify a straightforward explanation of real relationships, as in the following excerpt from *Time* magazine's report on Fred Hoyle, the British astronomer and mathematician who has been modifying Newton's gravity and Einstein's relativity. The paragraph states the general condition, proposes its hypothetical cause with an *if*, then moves to the effects, first in temporal order and then in order of human interest:

> **The masses, and therefore the gravity, of the sun and the earth are partly due to each other, partly to more distant objects such as the stars and galaxies. According to Hoyle, if the universe were to be cut in half, local solar-system gravitation would double, drawing the earth closer to the sun. The pressure in the sun's center would increase, thus raising its temperature, its generation of energy, and its brightness. Before being seared into a lump of charcoal, a man on earth would find his weight increasing from 150 to 300 lbs.**

COMPARISON AND CONTRAST
Run Similarities Side by Side.

Comparison and contrast merely continue this basic order of thought, another natural means of organizing a paragraph—or an entire essay. The process is indeed recurrent, as we have seen with the pro-con structure (pp. 18-20), which is nothing less than contrasting two viewpoints for an advantage. Comparison is probably the very basis of thought itself, or at least one of the primary elements. All knowledge involves comparing things for their similarities and noticing their contrasting differences. We group all people together as People, and then tell them apart as individuals.

We instinctively know our friends in this way, for instance. Two of them drift side by side in our thoughts. We are comparing them. They are both boys; they are the same age and stature; we like them both. But one bubbles up like a mountain spring, and the other runs deep. Their appearances, mannerisms, and tastes match their contrasting personalities. One's room is messy; the other's is neat. One races his car; the other collects stamps. We compare the similar categories—looks, habits, hobbies, goals—and contrast the differences. In the process, we have come to know both friends more completely.

Your topic sentence sets the comparison and makes the contrast:

Comparison (Interwoven descriptions bringing out opposing qualities)

> **Opposites seem to attract. My father is tall, blond, and outgoing. My mother is small, and even her dark brown hair, which is naturally wavy, has a certain quiet repose about it. My dad does everything at a cheerful run, whether he is off to a sales conference or off to the golf course with his foursome on Saturday mornings. My mother never seems to hurry. She hums at her work, and the house seems to slip into order without effort. She plays bridge with a few friends, and belongs to a number of organizations, but she is just as happy with a book. When dad bursts in at the end of the day, her face lights up. They grin at each other. They obviously still find each other attractive.**

In the next chapter, we will look at a special mode of comparison, of treating similarities—the analogy.

Develop Differences Point by Point.

Your comparisons present helpful illustrations of your subject by emphasizing similarities. Contrasts, on the other hand, compare similar things to emphasize their differences—West Germany as against East Germany, for example—usually to persuade your reader that one is in some or most ways better than the other.

The problem in paragraphing such "comparative contrasts" is exactly what we have already suggested in comparing poems or singers (Ch. 2) and in the paragraph comparing the outgoing father and quiet mother: the problem of keeping both sides before the reader, of not talking so long about West Germany that your reader forgets all about East Germany. Again, a good tactic is to run your contrasts point by point, and this you may do in one of two ways: (1) by making a topic sentence to cover one point—agriculture, let us say—and then continuing your paragraph in paired sentences, one for the West, one for the East, another for the West, another for the East, and so on; or (2) by writing your paragraphs in pairs, one paragraph for the West, one for the East, using the topic sentence of the first paragraph to govern the second, something like this:

Topic sentence West

West Germany's agriculture is far ahead of the East's. Everywhere about the countryside, one sees signs of prosperity. Trucks and tractors are shiny. Fences are mended and in order. Buildings all seem newly painted, as if on exhibit for a fair. New Volkswagens buzz along the country roads. The annual statistics spell out the prosperous details. . . .

Contrast

East Germany, on the other hand, seems to be dropping progressively behind. The countryside is drab and empty. On one huge commune, everything from buildings to equipment seems to be creaking from rusty hinges. . . . The annual statistics are equally depressing . . .

In an extended contrast, you will probably want to contrast some things sentence against sentence, within single paragraphs, and to contrast others by giving a paragraph to each. Remember only to keep your reader sufficiently in touch with both sides.

Here are two paragraphs from a student's paper neatly contrasted without losing touch:

Topic sentence First subject

In fact, in some respects the commercials are really better than the shows they sponsor. The commercials are carefully rehearsed, expertly photographed, highly edited and polished. They are made with absolute attention to detail and to the clock. One split-second over time, one bad note, one slightly wrinkled dress, and they are done over again. Weeks, even months, go into the production of a single sixty-second commercial.

e contrast

The shows, on the other hand, are slapped together hastily by writers and performers who have less than a week to put together an hour show. Actors have little time to rehearse, and often the pieces of

a show are put together for the first time in front of the camera. Lighting, sound reproduction, and editing are workmanlike, but unpolished; a shadow from an overhead microphone on an actor's face causes no real concern in the control room. A blown line or a muffed cue is "just one of those things that happen." In all, it often takes less time and money to do an hour show than to do the four sixty-second commercials that sponsor it.

CLASSIFICATION

Use the Natural Divisions.

Many subjects fall into natural or customary classifications, as if they were blandly jointed, like a good roast of pork ready for carving, contrasting one joint with the next: freshman, sophomore, junior, senior; Republicans, Democrats; right, middle, left; legislative, executive, judicial. You can easily follow these divisions in organizing a paragraph, or you can write one paragraph for each division, and attain a nicely coherent essay. Similarly, any manufacturing process, or any machine, will already have distinct steps and parts. These customary divisions will help your reader, since he knows something of them already. Describe the Democratic position on inflation, and he will naturally expect your description of the Republican position to follow. If no other divisions suggest themselves, you can often organize your paragraph — or your essay — into a consistent series of parallel answers, or "reasons for," or "reasons against," something like this:

> **A broad liberal education is best:**
> I. **It prepares you for a world of changing employment.**
> II. **It enables you to function well as a citizen.**
> III. **It enables you to make the most of your life.**

Many problems present natural classifying joints. Take the Panama Canal, for instance. Building it divided into three nicely jointed problems, political, geological, and biological, each with its solutions, as the following paragraph shows:

Problem 1

Solution to 1

Problem(s) 2

> **Building the Panama Canal posed problems of politics, geology, and human survival from the beginning. A French company, organized in 1880 to dig the canal, repeatedly had to extend its treaties at higher and higher prices as the work dragged on. Uneasy about the French, the United States made treaties with Nicaragua and Costa Rica to dig along the other most feasible route. This political threat, together with the failure of the French and the revolt of Panama from Colombia, finally enabled the United States to buy the French rights and negotiate new treaties, which, nevertheless, continue to cause political trouble to this day. Geology also posed its ancient problems: how to manage torrential rivers and inland lakes; whether to build a**

Solutions to 2   longer but more enduring canal at sea level, or a shorter, cheaper, and
                  safer canal with locks. Economy eventually won, but the problem of
Problem 3   yellow fever and malaria, which had plagued the French, remained.
Solution to 3   **By detecting and combating the fever-carrying mosquito. William
                  Gorgas solved these ancient tropical problems. Without him, the po-
                  litical and geological solutions would have come to nothing.**

You could easily organize this into three paragraphs of problem and
solution, with topic sentences like these:

> The Panama Canal posed three major problems, the first of which
> was political.
> The second problem was geological, a massive problem of engi-
> neering.
> The third problem, that of human survival, proved the most stub-
> born of all.

In many instances, you can similarly classify sets of causes and effects,
or comparisons, or contrasts; that is, as so often happens in practice, tactics can combine with magnified force.

DEFINITION

Clear Up Your Terms.

Definition is another mode of classification, in which we clear
away hidden assumptions along with unwanted categories. What the
Russians and Chinese call a People's Democracy is the very opposite
of what the Americans and British call democracy, assumed also to be
of and for and by the people. Ideally, your running prose should make
your terms clear to your reader, avoiding those definitions that seem
too stiff and stuffy. Nevertheless, what we mean by *egotism, superiority, education,* or *character* may need laying on the table.

Richard Hofstadter, for instance, found it necessary in his essay
"Democracy and Anti-Intellectualism in America" to devote a number
of paragraphs to defining both *democracy* and *intellectual,* each
paragraph examining the evidence and clarifying one aspect of his
term. Coming early in his essay, after he has set his thesis and sur-
veyed his subject, his section of definition begins with the following
paragraph:

Topic sentence   **But what is an intellectual, really? This is a problem of definition**
as question   **that I found, when I came to it, far more elusive than I had antici-**
                  pated. A great deal of what might be called the journeyman's work of
What it   **our culture — the work of engineers, physicians, newspapermen, and**
is not   **indeed of most professors — does not strike me as distinctively intel-**
                  lectual, although it is certainly work based in an important sense on
                  ideas. The distinction that we must recognize, then, is one originally
What it *is*   **made by Max Weber between living *for* ideas and living *off* ideas.**
                  The intellectual lives for ideas; the journeyman lives off them. The

Con: examples   engineer or the physician — I don't mean here to be invidious — needs
to have a pretty considerable capital stock in frozen ideas to do his
work; but they serve for him a purely instrumental purpose: he lives
off them, not for them. Of course he may also be, in his private role
Pro: examples   and his personal ways of thought, an intellectual, but it is not necessary for him to be in order to work at his profession. There is in fact no
Con: detailed   profession which demands that one be an intellectual. There do seem
opposition   to be vocations, however, which almost demand that one be an anti-
intellectual, in which those who live off ideas seem to have implac-
able hatred for those who live for them. The marginal intellectual
workers and the unfrocked intellectuals who work in journalism, ad-
vertising, and mass communication are the bitterest and most powerful among those who work at such vocations*

    Definitions frequently seem to develop into paragraphs, almost
by second nature. A sentence of definition is usually short and crisp,
seeming to demand some explanation, some illustration and socia-
bility. The definition, in other words, is a natural topic sentence. Here
are three classic single-sentence kinds of definition that will serve
well as topics for your paragraphs:

    I. **Definition by Synonym.**   A quick way to stipulate the single
meaning you want: "Virtue means moral rectitude."

    II. **Definition by Function.**   "A barometer measures atmospheric
pressure" — "A social barometer measures human pressures" — "A
good quarterback calls the signals and sparks the whole team's
spirits."

    III. **Definition by Synthesis.**   A placing of your term in striking
(and not necessarily logical) relationship to its whole class, usually for
the purposes of wit: "The fox is the craftiest of beasts" — "A sheep is a
friendlier form of goat" — "A lexicographer is a harmless drudge" — "A
sophomore is a sophisticated moron."

    Three more of the classic kinds of definition follow, of broader
dimensions than the single-sentence kinds above, but also ready-
made for a paragraph apiece, or for several. Actually, in making
paragraphs from your single-sentence definitions, you have undoubt-
edly used at least one of these three kinds, or a mixture of them all.
They are no more than the natural ways we define our meanings.

    IV. **Definition by Example.**   The opposite of *definition by synthe-
sis*. You start with the class ("crafty beasts") and then name a member
or two ("fox" — plus monkey and raccoon). But of course you would go

---

* *The Michigan Quarterly Review*, 59 (1953), p. 282. Copyright © 1953 by the
University of Michigan.

on to give further examples or illustrations—accounts of how the bacon was snitched through the screen—that broaden your definition beyond the mere naming of class and members.

V. Definition by Comparison. You just use a paragraph of comparison to expand and explain your definition. Begin with a topic sentence something like: "Love is like the sun." Then extend your comparison on to the end of the paragraph (or even separate it, if your cup runneth over, into several paragraphs), as you develop the idea: love is like the sun because it too gives out warmth, makes everything bright, shines even when it is not seen, and is indeed the center of our lives.

VI. Definition by Analysis. This is Hofstader's way, a searching out and explaining of the essentials in terms used generally, loosely, and often in ways that emphasize incidentals for biased reasons, as when it is said that an *intellectual* is a manipulator of ideas.

Here are four good steps to take in reaching a thorough definition of something, assuring that you have covered all the angles. Consider:

1. What it *is not like*
2. What it *is like*.
3. What it *is not*.
4. What it *is*.

This program can produce a good paragraph of definition:

> 1 Love may be many things to many people, but, all in all, we agree
> on its essentials. Love is not like a rummage sale, in which everyone
> 2 tries to grab what he wants. It is more like a Christmas, in which gifts
> and thoughtfulness come just a little unexpectedly, even from rou-
> 3 tine directions. Love, in short, is not a matter of seeking self-satisfac-
> 4 tion; it is first a matter of giving and then discovering, as an unex-
> pected gift, the deepest satisfaction one can know.

The four steps above can also furnish four effective paragraphs, which you would present in the same order of ascending interest and climax. The same tactics also work well in reverse order:

What it *is*
Definition by example

> **Black Power means, for example, that in Lowndes County, Ala-
> bama, a black sheriff can end police brutality. A black tax assessor and
> tax collector and county board of revenue can lay, collect, and chan-
> nel tax monies for the building of better roads and schools serving
> black people. In such areas as Lowndes, where black people have a
> majority, they will attempt to use power to exercise control. This is

Definition by analysis

> what they seek: control. When black people lack a majority, Black
> Power means proper representation and sharing of control. It means
> the creation of power bases, of strength, from which black people can
> press to change local or nation-wide patterns of oppression—instead
> of from weakness.**

It does not mean *merely* putting black faces into office. Black visi-
What it *is not*   bility is not Black Power. Most of the black politicians around the
country today are not examples of Black Power. The power must be
What it *is*   that of a community, and emanate from there. The black politicians
must start from there. The black politicians must stop being represen-
tatives of "downtown" machines, whatever the cost might be in
terms of patronage and holiday handouts.*

* Stokely Carmichael and Charles V. Hamilton, *Black Power, the Politics of Liberation in America* (New York: Random House, 1967), p. 15.

EXERCISES

1. *Write an "effect-and-cause" (Arrangement I. pp. 37–38) paragraph in which you explain reasons for what happened — a won or lost game, the rejection (or acceptance) of a style in music or clothing, the failure or success of a particular book or film, the election of a candidate for office, the passage of a tax or law.*

2. *Write a "cause-and-effect" paragraph in which you outline the probable effects of some proposal (to ban nuclear power, to require military service in a peacetime draft, to prohibit handguns, and so forth).*

3. *Write two paragraphs contrasting something with the first paragraph's topic sentence governing both, and using parallel contrasting terms on the pattern of the East–West Germany paragraphs on p. 40 — high school and college, small town and city, football and baseball (or soccer), military men and women.*

4. *Write a paragraph comparing two people, like the one on p. 39.*

5. *Here are a number of topics that fall conveniently into natural classifying divisions. For each topic, list the divisions that occur to you.*

1. Causes affecting the rate at which a population grows.
2. Levels of government.
3. The "lunatic fringe."
4. The early stages of space technology.
5. Geological eras.
6. Governmental response to the recession.
7. Defrauding insurance companies.
8. Inequities in the tax structure.

6. *Take a problem and classify its solution into its natural divisions, then write a three- or four-paragraph paper following your classification (see p. 41–42). Try, for example, how architects design tall buildings in San Francisco to withstand earthquakes, how medieval man made a suit of armor, how to convert a minibus into a four-person camper.*

7. *Work out a definition of a term like "barometer," "computer," "class," "humanities," "intelligence." Avoid the scent of the dictionary. If you try a larger term, break it down into parts. And establish firm boundaries for your term by considering what is like, not like; what it does, does not do; what it is, is not.*

5

Evidence

All along, you have been bringing in evidence, whatever your tactics, to support your thesis or your topic sentence. Now we need to take a closer look. Have you brought in enough to prove your point? Have you burdened or bored your reader with too much? Where might it have gone wrong? And what is evidence anyway?

DISCERNING AND TESTING EVIDENCE

Seek Specific Examples.

Evidence is simply an example, something specific to illustrate your general thesis. And your thesis itself will suggest what examples you need. If you are supporting the thesis "Welfare breeds irresponsibility," describe several irresponsible welfare recipients — some you know. To illustrate that a character in a novel is unbelievable, describe the inconsistencies you noticed in him when you read it. Your thesis, your big idea, will emerge from the specific things you have seen, in person, in print, or on TV. Now use these things to support your thesis in turn. Make them brief, but sufficient. Three, proverbially, is an ideal number. But remember also that one extended description — a lonely old neighbor, an abandoned building, a high-speed scrape with automotive death — gives extremely interesting and persuasive evidence, especially when introduced with two or three brief examples, a statistic from the paper, a quotation from *Time,* an observation from yesterday morning.

Several examples are always better than one. One, all alone, implies a universality it may not have. It raises the nagging problem you have already worked at in developing your thesis and its contraries: the problem of unexamined assumptions, which lies behind all fallacies in logic and all shaky evidence, the mistake of assuming that *one,* or *some,* equals *all.*

Check Your Assumptions.

Ask yourself, again, if your essay hangs on some unsuspected assumption. Suppose you have said that football builds character. As evidence, you have told how going out for practice has transformed a happy-go-lucky youth into a disciplined man with a part-time job and good grades. But you have assumed, without thinking, that nothing else would have worked as well, that football would work every time, that character consists only in self-discipline, and perhaps that women have no character at all. Your evidence is persuasive, but the hidden assumptions need resurfacing.

First, limit your assumptions by narrowing your thesis:

> **Although no magical guarantee, football strengthens the rugged and disciplined side of character.**

You then concede that some football players are downright wild, and that character includes social responsibility, moral courage, intelligence, compassion. (You can then probably claim some of these back for football too.) Then bring in some more examples. Three different young players, who have matured in different ways, would strengthen your point, and would assume only reasonable virtues for pigskin and practice.

Try an Analogy.

An analogy introduces another kind of specific evidence as you help your reader grasp your subject by showing how it is like something familiar. Your topic sentence asserts the comparison, and then your paragraph unfolds the comparison in detail:

> **School spirit is like patriotism. Students take their school's fortunes as their own, defending and promoting them against those of another school, as citizens champion their country, right or wrong. Their school is not only their alma mater but their fatherland as well. Like soldiers, they will give their utmost strength in field games and intellectual contests for both personal glory and the greater glory of the domain they represent. And, in defeat, they will mourn as if dragged in chains through the streets of Rome.**

Here is E. B. White describing Thoreau's *Walden* by analogy, here a comparison that is really an extended metaphor:

> Thoreau's assault on the Concord society of the mid-nineteenth century has the quality of a modern Western: he rides into the subject at top speed, shooting in all directions. Many of his shots ricochet and nick him on the rebound, and throughout the melee there is a horrendous cloud of inconsistencies and contradictions, and when the shooting dies down and the air clears, one is impressed chiefly by the courage of the rider and by how splendid it was that somebody should have ridden in there and raised all that ruckus.*

That is probably as long as an analogy can effectively run. One paragraph is about the limit. Beyond that, the reader may tire of it. Further, extended analogies are likely to introduce extraneous details, that is, those that do not fit the comparison, leading to a *false analogy* (p. 51). For example, if the brain seems in *some* ways like a computer, be careful not to assume it is in *all* ways like a computer. A judicious selection of comparisons will avoid such a fault.

Cite Authorities Reasonably.

Citing an authority brings in still another kind of specific evidence to back your point. "Einstein said . . ." can silence many an objection, since we believe Einstein knew more about physical fact than anyone. "According to Freud" may win your point on human personality, as may an appeal to Winston Churchill or Matthew Arnold or H. W. Fowler on English usage. Shakespeare, the Bible, and Samuel Johnson can authenticate your claims about the ways of the world and the spirit.

But appeals to authority risk four common fallacies. The first is in appealing to the authority outside of his field, even if his field is the universe. Although Einstein had a powerful intellect, we should not assume he knew all about economics too. Even if a chance remark of Einstein's sounds like the quantum theory of banking, you will do best to quote it only for its own rational merits, using Einstein's having said it only as a bonus of persuasive interest; otherwise, your appeal to his authority will seem naïve in the extreme. The good doctor, of the wispy hair and frayed sweater, was little known for understanding money.

The second fallacy is in misrepresenting what the authority really says. Sir Arthur Eddington, if I may appeal to an authority myself, puts the case: "It is a common mistake to suppose that Einstein's theory of relativity asserts that everything is relative. Actually it says, 'There are absolute things in the world but you must look

---

* "A Slight Sound at Evening," in *The Points of My Compass* (New York: Harper & Row, 1962), p. 17.

deeply for them. The things that first present themselves to your notice are for the most part relative.' "* If you appeal loosely to Einstein to authenticate an assertion that everything is "relative," you may appeal in vain — since *relative* means relative *to* something else, eventually to some constant.

The third fallacy is in assuming that one instance from an authority is typical. Arguments for admitting the split infinitive (see p. 196) to equal status with the unsplit, for instance, often present split constructions from prominent writers. But they do not tell us how many splits a writer avoided, or how he himself feels about the construction. A friend once showed me a split infinitive in the late Walter Lippmann's column after I had boldly asserted that careful writers like Lippmann never split their infinitives. Out of curiosity, I wrote Mr. Lippmann; after all, he might have changed his tune. He wrote back that the split had been simply a slip, that he disliked the thing and tried to revise it out whenever it crept in.

The fourth fallacy is deepest: the authority may have faded. New facts have generated new ideas. Einstein has limited Newton's authority. Geology and radioactive carbon have challenged the literal authority of Genesis. Jung has challenged Freud; and "stagflation," most economists.

The more eminent the authority, the easier the fallacy. Ask these four questions:

1. Am I citing him outside his field?
2. Am I presenting him accurately?
3. Is this instance really typical?
4. Is he still fully authoritative?

Do not claim too much for your authority, and add other kinds of evidence, or other authorities. In short, don't put all your eggs in one basket; write as if you knew the market and the risks. Every appeal to authority is open to logical challenge.

Check Your Conclusions.

What you conclude from your evidence is always open to question. So question yourself, before your final draft. Put your faith in probability. If you say, "Apples are good food," you assume boldly that *all* apples are good, and you are not upset by the bad one in the barrel. You know that bad apples are neither so numerous nor so typical that you must conclude, "Apples are unfit for human consumption." You also know what causes the bad ones. So see that probability supports your generalization by checking the following conditions:

---

* *The Nature of the Physical World* (Ann Arbor: University of Michigan Press, 1958), p. 23.

1. Your samples are reasonably numerous.
2. Your samples are truly typical.
3. Your exceptions are explainable, demonstrably not typical.

Question your statistics. They can deceive badly because they look so solid—especially averages and percentages. "The average student earns ten dollars a week" may conceal the truth that one earns a hundred dollars and nine earn nothing. And a sample of ten students hardly represents thirty thousand. Moreover, each "one" in any statistical count represents a slightly different quantity, as a glance around a class of twenty students makes clear. So use your statistics with understanding, preferably with other specific examples.

Then, finally, ask if your evidence might not support some other conclusion. Some linguists, for example, have concluded that speech is superior to writing because speech has more "signals" than writing. But from the same evidence one might declare speech inferior: writing conveys the same message with fewer signals.

In the end, your evidence depends on common sense. Don't assume that one swallow makes a summer, and also check your generalizations for the following fallacies:

1. **Either-Or.**   You assume only two opposing possibilities: "either we abolish requirements or education is finished." Education will probably amble on, somewhere in between.

2. **Oversimplification.**   As with *either-or,* you ignore alternatives. "A student learns only what he wants to learn" ignores all the pressures from parents and society, which in fact account for a good deal of learning.

3. **Begging the Question.**   A somewhat unhandy term: you assume as proved something that really needs proving. "Free all political prisoners" assumes that none of those concerned has committed an actual crime.

4. **Ignoring the Question.**   The question of whether it is right for a neighborhood to organize against a newcomer shifts to land values and taxes.

5. **Non Sequitur.**   ("It does not follow.") "He's certainly sincere: he must be right." "He's the most popular: he should be president." The conclusions do not reasonably follow from sincerity and popularity.

6. **Post Hoc, Ergo Propter Hoc.**   ("After this, therefore because of this.") The non sequitur of events: "He stayed up late and therefore

won the race." He probably won in spite of late hours, and for other reasons.

7. False Analogy. "You should choose your wife as you would your car." A person is not a machine, so that the analogy is unacceptable.

DEDUCTION AND INDUCTION

Deduction and induction are the two ways of handling evidence, the two directions of reasoning. *De-duction* (combining *de*, "from," and *ducere*, "to lead") leads *away from* a premise, a general assumption, a thesis. *Induction* leads the other way, *into* or towards a general idea. Deductive reasoning sees how the details of evidence fit and what they mean under some governing proposition like, let us say, *Life is essentially good*, or *We must preserve the environment*. Inductive reasoning, the way of science, sees what the details add up to — *this is dying; that is crumbling; the ozone is full of tatters: we must therefore preserve the environment*. But deduction prevails. The scientist must very soon jump from his evidence to a general proposition — a hypothesis — and then test it deductively with more evidence. The essayist usually follows a deductive order, stating his thesis then challenging it and illustrating it with his evidence. An inductive essay is hard to keep going for very long. *Is this the answer? No. Then perhaps this? Well, not quite. Then this? Ah, this is it.* The inductive writer, like the scientist, must soon leap to some meaningful proposition, his previously unstated thesis, and proceed deductively from there. Deduction also works naturally in those areas of *values* and *qualities* where factual induction finds little to grasp.

The inductive order works well only for short essays — or brief parts of longer essays — because you must keep the cat in the bag, and you can't keep him in too long. Your inductive questions may too soon disclose the answer you are saving for last. Here is a successful inductive run of three partial answers before the cat is out, taken from an interview with a man reminiscing about his experiences during the Depression:

Topic question   **What was the worst thing about the Depression? Well, I don't know. I guess for some folks it was losing their savings. For us that wasn't so bad. I only had about $400 in the McLain County Bank when it closed and I got some of that back later, about 10 cents**

Answer 1

Answer 2   **on the dollar. Then too, being out of work was rough for a lot of people. But even that wasn't so bad for me. I lost my job with the coal company in 1931, but we lived on a farm. And with that and some odd jobs I picked up, I managed to keep pretty busy until I got a steady**

Answer 3   **job again. Of course, I know a lot of people didn't have enough to eat or enough to wear during the Depression. For us that wasn't too bad.**

We grew most of our own food, and my wife is pretty handy at sewing, so we got by. Nothing very fancy, you understand, but we managed. No, I guess for us the worst thing about the Depression was we got to feeling after a while that times just weren't ever going to get better. It just went on too long. For us, things got a little rough in 1931 and they stayed pretty rough until I got a job with the Highway Commission in 1938. Seven years is a long time to keep hoping. It just went on so long.

Main answer (thesis)

The deductive essay, however, brings all of the writer's tactics and evidence into play. The deductive order is, after all, what we have been working on from the start. It is much more widely used, and useful, than the inductive one, because it can sustain itself page after page, even through chapters in a whole book. You set down your thesis, your Big Idea, then bring in the evidence to illustrate it in detail and at length, getting rid of the opposition, if any, starting with the least important evidence, working uphill to the most important, using your tactics. The short inductive interview on the Depression could become a full deductive essay with the addition of more evidence, shaped with tactics of cause and effect, comparison, and a touch of definition (what the worst *was not,* and what it *was*):

Topic

For most Americans, the stock-market crash was not the worst thing about the Depression. True, it carried away billions of dollars of investors' money, but relatively few of us felt directly affected. Few of us owned stock, and for most of us the market collapse was something that happened to other people, not to us. Of course, as we found out, the stock-market collapse was only the trigger, and soon more and more Americans found their lives directly affected. By 1932, twenty-five percent of the work force was without jobs. Yet, for many Americans, the worst thing about the Depression was not the bank closures, or being out of work, or even shortages of food and clothing. For many of us, the worst thing about the Depression was that it lasted so long we almost gave up hoping that times would ever get better. George Harris of Wellsburg, West Virginia, is a good example of how the Depression hit most of us.

Thesis

Demonstration

(Narrative: moving with events through time)

In 1931, Mr. Harris had a job with the Green Coal Company as a tender on a boat that pushed coal barges up and down the Ohio River. His income was generally pretty good, and Mr. Harris had managed to buy a small farm just outside town. But cutbacks in industrial production, particularly in the production of steel, soon forced cutbacks in coal mining as well. And in August of 1931, Mr. Harris was laid off. The next year, in 1932, the McLain County Bank closed, and with it went the only savings the Harrises had, $400, although later he did manage to collect ten percent of his lost savings. And so for the next seven years, Mr. Harris bounced from job to job, whatever he could get: a few days here, a few days there. He was thus able to hold onto his small farm, and on it he raised most of the food for the Harris family for the next seven years. Mrs. Harris, too, helped to cut corners by making most of the family's clothes, and by repairing things when they wore out. In this way, taking it one day at a time, and living as simply and as frugally as possible, the Harrises managed to get by until, in 1938, Mr. Harris once again got a secure and well-paying job with the County Road Commission.

Restatement   So the Harrises are a good example of how the Depression hit many Americans. They lost some savings, they lost their jobs, they had to tighten their belts, but they managed to get by. For them, the worst thing about the Depression was not the deprivation; it was simply that the Depression went on year after year. As Mr. Harris says, "Seven years is a long time to keep hoping. It just went on so long."

EXERCISES

1. *After each of the following assertions, write two or three short questions that will challenge its assumptions, questions like "Good for what? Throwing? Fertilizer?" For example: Girls are brighter than boys. "At what age? In chess? In physics?"*

1. Men are superior to women.
2. The backfield made some mistakes.
3. Communism means violent repression.
4. Don't trust anyone over thirty.
5. All men are equal.
6. The big companies are ruining the environment.
7. Travel is educational.
8. Our brand is free of tar.
9. The right will prevail.
10. A long walk is good for you.

2. *Write a paragraph of analogy like the examples on p. 47. Try a comparison like the brain and the computer, government and a multiheaded creature, construction of essays and buildings.*

3. *Each of the following statements contains at least one fallacious citation of authority. Identify it, and explain how it involves one or several of these reasons: "Outside Field," "Not Accurately Presented," "Not Representative," "Out of Date."*

1. According to Charles Morton, a distinguished eighteenth-century theologian and schoolmaster, the swallows of England disappear to the dark side of the moon in winter.
2. Einstein states that everything is relative.
3. "Nucular" is an acceptable pronunciation of "nuclear." President Eisenhower himself pronounced it this way.
4. War between capitalists and communists is inevitable, as Karl Marx shows.
5. Giving LSD to everyone, including children, as Timothy Leary says, will greatly improve modern society.
6. The American economy should be controlled in every detail; after all, economist John Kenneth Galbraith comes out for control.
7. "Smooths are America's finest cigarette," says Joe Namath.

4. *Name and explain the fallacy in each of the following:*

1. Jones is rich. He must be dishonest.
2. He either worked hard for his money, or he is just plain lucky.
3. The best things in life are free, like free love.
4. Sunshine breeds flies, because when the sun shines the flies come out.
5. If they have no bread, let them eat cake. Cake is both tastier and richer in calories.
6. This is another example of American imperialism.
7. Smith's canned-soup empire reaches farther than the Roman empire.
8. *Chips* is America's most popular soap. It is clearly the best.
9. The draft is illegal. It takes young men away from their education and careers at the most crucial period of their lives. They lose thousands of dollars' worth of their time.
10. Women are the most exploited people in the history of the world.
11. Two minutes after the accused left the building, the bomb exploded.
12. The human mind is only an elaborate computer, because both can do complex calculations and make decisions.

5. *Write a paragraph in the inductive order. Start with a question; then, dismissing each partial answer and posing a further question, lead your reader through the evidence to your conclusive point ("What is A? It might be B, and I know that many think it C, but it is really D.") Follow the pattern in the reminiscence of the Depression on pp. 51–52.*

6. *Now take this inductive paragraph and turn the order around, expanding it into a brief deductive essay by stating your thesis at the end of an introductory paragraph, adding more evidence, tactically deployed, and rounding it off in a good end paragraph.*

6

Writing
Good
Sentences

All this time you have been writing sentences, as naturally as breathing, and perhaps with as little variation. Now for a close look at the varieties of the sentence. Some varieties can be shaggy and tangled indeed. But they are all offshoots of the simple active sentence, the basic English genus *John hits Joe,* with action moving straight from subject through verb to object.

This subject-verb-object sentence can be infinitely grafted and contorted, but there are really only two general varieties of it: (1) the "loose, or strung-along," in Aristotle's phrase, and (2) the periodic. English naturally runs "loose." Our thoughts are by nature strung along from subject through verb to object, with whatever comes to mind simply added as it comes. The loose sentence puts its subject and verb early. But we can also use the periodic sentence characteristic of our Latin and Germanic ancestry, where ideas hang in the air like girders until all interconnections are locked by the final word, at the period: *John, the best student in the class, the tallest and most handsome, hits Joe.* A periodic sentence, in other words, is one that suspends its meaning until the end, usually with subject and verb widely separated, and the verb as near the end as possible.

So we have two varieties of the English sentence. The piece-by-piece and the periodic species simply represent two ways of thought: the first, the natural stringing of thoughts as they come; the second, the more careful contrivance of emphasis and suspense.

THE SIMPLE SENTENCE
Use the Simple Active
Sentence, Loosely Periodic.

Your best sentences will be hybrids of the loose and the periodic. First, learn to use active verbs (*John* HITS *Joe*), which will keep you within the simple active pattern with all parts showing (subject-verb-object), as opposed to a verb in the passive voice (*Joe* IS HIT *by John*), which puts everything backwards and uses more words. Then learn to give your native strung-along sentence a touch of periodicity and suspense.

Any change in normal order can give you unusual emphasis, as when you move the object ahead of the subject:

> That I like.
> The house itself she hated, but the yard was grand.
> Nature I loved; and next to Nature, Art.

Most often, we expect our ideas one at a time, in normal succession—*John hits Joe*—and with anything further added, in proper sequence, at the end—*a real haymaker.* Change this fixed way of thinking, and you immediately put your reader on the alert for something unusual. Consequently, some of your best sentences will be simple active ones sprung wide with phrases coloring subject, verb, object, or all three, in various ways. You may, for instance, effectively complicate the subject:

> King Lear, proud, old, and childish, probably aware that his grip on the kingdom is beginning to slip, devises a foolish plan.

Or the verb:

> A good speech usually begins quietly, proceeds sensibly, gathers momentum, and finally moves even the most indifferent audience.

Or the object:

> Her notebooks contain marvelous comments on the turtle in the back yard, the flowers and weeds, the great elm by the drive, the road, the earth, the stars, and the men and women of the village.

COMPOUND AND COMPLEX SENTENCES
Learn the Difference Between Compound and Complex Sentences.

You make a compound sentence by linking together simple sentences with a coordinating conjunction (*and, but, or, nor, for, so*) or with a colon or a semicolon. You make a complex one by hooking lesser sentences onto the main sentence with *that, which, who,* or one of the many other subordinating connectives like *although, because, where, when, after, if.* The compound sentence *coordinates,* treating everything on the same level; the complex *subordinates,* putting everything else somewhere below its one main self-sufficient idea. The compound links ideas one after the other, as in the basic simple sentence; the complex is a simple sentence elaborated by clauses instead of merely by phrases. The compound represents the strung-along way of thinking; the complex frequently represents the periodic.

Avoid Simple-Minded Compounds.

Essentially the compound sentence *is* simple-minded, a set of clauses on a string—a child's description of a birthday party, for instance: "We got paper hats and we pinned the tail on the donkey and we had chocolate ice cream and Randy sat on a piece of cake and I won third prize." *And . . . and . . . and.*

But this way of thinking is always useful for pacing off related thoughts, and for breaking the staccato of simple statement. It often briskly connects cause and effect: "The clock struck one, and down he run." "The solipsist relates all knowledge to his own being, and the demonstrable commonwealth of human nature dissolves before his dogged timidity." The compound sentence is built on the most enduring of colloquial patterns—the simple sequence of things said as they occur to the mind—it has the pace, the immediacy, and the dramatic effect of talk. Hemingway, for instance, often gets all the numb tension of a shell-shocked mind by reducing his character's thoughts all to one level, in sentences something like this: "It was a good night and I sat at a table and . . . and . . . and. . . ."

Think of the compound sentence in terms of its conjunctions— the words that yoke its clauses—and of the accompanying punctuation. Here are three basic groups of conjunctions that will help you sort out and punctuate your compound thoughts.

Group I. *The three common coordinating conjunctions:* and, but, *and* or (nor). *Put a comma before each.*

> **I like her, and I don't mind saying so.**
> **Art is long, but life is short.**
> **Win this point, or the game is lost.**

Group II. *Conjunctive adverbs:* therefore, moreover, however, nevertheless, consequently, furthermore. *Put a semicolon before, and a comma after each.*

> Nations indeed seem to have a kind of biological span like human life, from rebellious youth, through caution, to decay; consequently, predictions of doom are not uncommon.

Group III. *Some in-betweeners—yet, still, so—which sometimes take a comma, sometimes a semicolon, depending on your pace and emphasis.*

> We long for the good old days, yet we never include the disadvantages.
> People long for the good old days; yet they rarely take into account the inaccuracy of human memory.
> The preparation had been halfhearted and hasty, so the meeting was wretched.
> Rome declined into the pleasures of its circuses and couches; so the tough barbarians conquered.

Try Compounding Without Conjunctions.

Though the conjunction usually governs its compound sentence, two powerful coordinators remain—the semicolon and the colon alone. For contrasts, the semicolon is the prince of coordinators:

Semicolon
> The dress accents the feminine; the pants suit speaks for freedom.
> Golf demands the best of time and space; tennis, the best of personal energy.
> The government tries to get the most out of taxes; the individual tries to get out of the most taxes.

The colon similarly pulls two "sentences" together without blessing of conjunction, period, or capital. But it signals amplification, not contrast: the second clause explains the first.

Colon
> A house with an aging furnace costs more than the asking price suggests: twenty dollars more a month in fuel means about one hundred sixty dollars more a year.
> A growing population means more business: more business will exhaust our supply of ores in less than half a century.
> Sports at any age are beneficial: they keep your pulses hopping.

Learn to Subordinate.

You probably write compound sentences almost without thinking. But the subordinations of the complex usually require some thought. Indeed, you are ranking closely related thoughts, arranging the lesser ones so that they bear effectively on your main thought. You must first pick your most important idea. You must then change mere sequence into subordination — ordering your lesser thoughts "sub," or below, the main idea. The childish birthday sentence, then, might come out something like this:

> **After we got paper hats and ate chocolate ice cream, after Randy sat on a piece of cake and everyone pinned the tail on the donkey,** I WON THIRD PRIZE.

You do the trick with connectives — with any word, like *after* in the sentence above, indicating time, place, cause, or other qualification. Now something more ambitious:

> *If* **they try,** *if* **they fail,** THEY ARE STILL GREAT *because* **their spirit is unbeaten.**

You daily achieve subtler levels of subordination with the three relative pronouns *that, which, who,* and with the conjunction *that. That, which,* and *who* connect thoughts so closely related as to seem almost equal, but actually each tucks a clause (subject-and-verb) into some larger idea:

Relative pronoun

> **The car,** *which* **runs perfectly, is not worth selling.**
> **The car** *that* **runs perfectly is worth keeping.**

Subordinating conjunction

> **He thought** *that* **the car would run forever.**
> **He thought [***that* **omitted but understood] the car would run forever.**

But the subordinating conjunctions and adverbs (*although, if, because, since, until, where, when, as if, so that*) really put subordinates in their places. Look at *when* in this sentence of E. B. White's from *Charlotte's Web:*

Adverbs

> **Next morning** *when* **the first light came into the sky and the sparrows stirred in the trees,** *when* **the cows rattled their chains and the rooster crowed and the early automobiles went whispering along the road, Wilbur awoke and looked for Charlotte.**

Here the simple *when,* used only twice, has regimented five subordinate clauses, all of equal rank, into their proper station below that of the main clause, "Wilbur awoke and looked for Charlotte." You can vary the ranking intricately and still keep it straight:

Subordinating conjunctions

> *Although* **some claim** *that* **time is an illusion,** *because* **we have no absolute chronometer,** *although* **the mind cannot effectively grasp time,** *because* **the mind itself is a kind of timeless presence almost oblivious to seconds and hours,** *although* **the time of our solar system may be only an instant in the universe at large,** WE STILL CANNOT QUITE DENY *that* **some progression of universal time is passing over us,** *if* **only we could measure it.**

Complex sentences are, at their best, really simple sentences gloriously delayed and elaborated with subordinate thoughts. The following beautiful and elaborate sentence from the Book of Common Prayer is all built on the simple sentence "draw near":

> Ye who do truly and earnestly repent you of your sins, and are in love and charity with your neighbors, and intend to lead a new life, following the commandments of God, and walking from henceforth in his holy ways, draw near with faith, and take this holy sacrament to your comfort, and make your humble confession to Almighty God, devoutly kneeling.

Even a short sentence may be complex, attaining a remarkably varied suspense. Notice how the simple statement "I allowed myself" is skillfully elaborated in this sentence by the late Wolcott Gibbs of *The New Yorker:*

> Twice in my life, for reasons that escape me now, though I'm sure they were discreditable, I allowed myself to be persuaded that I ought to take a hand in turning out a musical comedy.

Try for Still Closer Connections: Modify.

Your subordinating *if*'s and *when*'s have really been modifying — that is, limiting — the things you have attached them to. But there is a smoother way. It is an adjectival sort of thing, a shoulder-to-shoulder operation, a neat trick with no need for shouting, a stone to a stone with no need for mortar. You simply put clauses and phrases up against a noun, instead of attaching them with a subordinator. This sort of modification includes the following constructions, all using the same close masonry: (1) appositives, (2) relatives understood, (3) adjectives-with-phrase, (4) participles, (5) absolutes.

Appositives.   Those phrases about shoulders and tricks and stones, above, are all in apposition with *sort of thing*, and they are grammatically subordinate to it. *Apposition* means "put to" or "add to" — putting an equivalent beside, like two peas in a pod — hence these phrases are nearly coordinate and interchangeable. They are compressions of a series of sentences ("It is an adjectival sort of thing. It is a neat trick . . . ," and so forth) set side by side, "stone to stone." Mere contact does the work of the verb *is* and its subject *it*. English often does the same with subordinate clauses, omitting the *who is* or *that is* and putting the rest directly into apposition. "The William who is the Conqueror" becomes "William the Conqueror." "The Jack who is the heavy hitter" becomes "Jack the heavy hitter." These, incidentally, are called "restrictive" appositions, because they restrict to a particular designation the nouns they modify, setting this William and this Jack apart from all others (with no separating commas). Similarly, you can make nonrestrictive appositives from nonrestrictive clauses, clauses that simply add information (between commas). "Smith, who is a man to be reckoned with, . . ." becomes "Smith, a man to be reckoned with, . . ." "Jones, who is our man in Liverpool, . . ."

becomes "Jones, our man in Liverpool, . . ." Restrictive or nonrestrictive, close contact makes your point with economy and fitness.

Relatives Understood. You can often achieve the same economy, as I have already hinted, by omitting the relative pronouns *that, which,* and *who* with their verbs, thus gaining a compression both colloquial and classic:

> A comprehension [that is] both colloquial and classic. . . .
> The house, [which was] facing north, had a superb view.
> The specimens [that] he had collected. . . .
> The girl [whom] he [had] left behind. . . .

Adjectives-with-Phrase. This construction is also appositive and adjectival. It is neat and useful:

> The law was passed, *thick with provisions and codicils, heavy with implications.*
> There was the lake, *smooth in the early-morning air.*

Participles. Participles — verbs acting as adjectives — are extremely supple subordinates. Consider this sequence of six simple sentences:

> He had been thrown.
> He had accepted.
> He felt a need.
> He demanded money.
> He failed.
> He chose not to struggle.

Now see how Richard Wright, in *Native Son,* subordinates the first five of these to the sixth with participles. He elaborates the complete thought into a forceful sentence that runs for eighty-nine words with perfect clarity:

> *Having been thrown* by an accidental murder into a position where he had sensed a possible order and meaning in his relations with the people about him; *having accepted* the moral guilt and responsibility for that murder because it had made him feel free for the first time in his life; *having felt* in his heart some obscure need to be at home with people and *having demanded* ransom money to enable him to do it — *having* done all this and *failed,* he chose not to struggle any more.

These participles have the same adjectival force:

> Dead to the world, *wrapped* in sweet dreams, *untroubled* by bills, he slept till noon.

Notice that the participles operate exactly as the adjective *dead* does.
Beware of dangling participles. They may trip you, as they have

tripped others. The participle, with its adjectival urge, may grab the first noun that comes along, with shocking results:

> **Bowing to the crowd, the bull caught him unawares.**
> **Observing quietly from the bank, the beavers made several errors in judgment.**
> **Squandering everything at the track, the money was never repaid.**
> **What we need is a list of teachers broken down alphabetically.**

Move the participle next to its intended noun or pronoun; you will have to supply this word if inadvertence or the passive voice has omitted it entirely. Recast the sentence for good alignment when necessary. You may also save the day by changing a present participle to a past, as in the third example below, or, perhaps better, by activating the sentence, as in the fourth example:

> **The bull caught him unawares as he bowed to the crowd.**
> **Observing quietly from the bank, they saw the beavers make several errors in judgment.**
> **Squandered at the track, the money was never repaid.**
> **Having squandered everything at the track, he never repaid the money.**
> **What we need is an alphabetical list of teachers.**

Gerunds, which look like present participles but act as nouns, are also good economizers. The two sentences "He had been thrown" and "It was unpleasant" can become one, with a gerund as subject: "*Having been thrown* was unpleasant." Gerunds also serve as objects of verbs and prepositions:

> **She hated *going* home.**
> **By *driving* carefully, they increased their mileage.**

Absolutes. The absolute phrase has a great potential of polished economy. It stands grammatically "absolute" or alone, modifying only through proximity, like an apposition. Many an absolute is simply a prepositional phrase with the preposition dropped:

> **He ran up the stairs, [with]** *a bouquet of roses under his arm,* **and rang the bell.**
> **She walked slowly, [with]** *her camera ready.*

But the ablative absolute (*ablative* means "removed") is removed from the main clause, borrowing tense and modifying only by proximity. If you have had some Latin, you will probably remember this construction as some kind of brusque condensation, something like "*The road completed,* Caesar moved his camp." But it survives in the best of circles. Somewhere E. B. White admits to feeling particularly good one morning, just having brought off an especially fine ablative absolute. And it is actually more common than you may suppose. A recent newspaper article stated that "the Prince had fled the country, *his hopes of a negotiated peace shattered.*" The *hopes shattered* pattern (noun plus participle) marks the ablative absolute (also called, because of the noun, a "nominative absolute"). The idea might have been more conventionally subordinated: "since his hopes were shattered" or "with his hopes shattered." But the ablative absolute accomplishes the subordination with economy and style.

Take a regular subordinate clause: "*When* the road *was* completed." Cut the subordinator and reduce the verb. You now have an ablative absolute, a phrase that stands absolutely alone, shorn of both its connective *when* and its full predication *was*: "*The road completed,* Caesar moved his camp." Basically a noun and a participle, or noun and adjective, it is a kind of grammatical shorthand, a telegram: *ROAD COMPLETED CAESAR MOVED* — most said in fewest words, speed with high compression. This is its appeal and its power.

> **The cat stopped,** *its back arched, its eyes frantic.*
> **The whole economy,** *God willing,* **soon will return to normal.**
> *All things considered,* **the plan would work.**

PARALLEL CONSTRUCTION
Use Parallels to Strengthen Equivalent Ideas.

No long complex sentence will hold up without parallel construction. Paralleling can be very simple. Any word will seek its own kind, noun to noun, adjective to adjective, infinitive to infinitive. The simplest series of things automatically runs parallel:

> **shoes and ships and sealing wax**
> **I came, I saw, I conquered**
> **to be or not to be**
> **a dull, dark, and soundless day**
> **mediocre work, cowardly work, disastrous work**

But they very easily run out of parallel too, and this you must learn to prevent. The last item especially may slip out of line, as in this series: "friendly, kind, unobtrusive, and *a bore*" (boring). The noun *bore* has jumped off the track laid by the preceding parallel adjectives. Your train of equivalent ideas should all be of the same grammatical kind to carry their equivalence clearly — to strengthen it: either parallel adjectives, *friendly, kind, unobtrusive,* and *boring,* or all nouns, *a friend, a saint, a diplomat,* and *a bore.* Your paralleling articles and prepositions should govern a series as a whole, or should accompany *every* item:

> **a hat, cane, pair of gloves, and mustache**
> **a hat, a cane, a pair of gloves, and a mustache**
> **by land, sea, or air**
> **by land, by sea, or by air**

Verbs also frequently intrude to throw a series of adjectives (or nouns) out of parallel:

> He thought the girl was *attractive, intelligent,* **and** *knew* **how to make him feel needed.**
> He thought the girl was *attractive, intelligent,* **and** *sympathetic,* **knowing how to make him feel needed.**

Watch the Paralleling of Pairs.

Pairs should be pairs, not odds and ends. Notice how the faulty pairs in these sentences have been corrected:

> She liked *the lawn and gardening* (**the lawn and the garden**).
> They were *all athletic or big men on campus* (**athletes or big men on campus**).
> They wanted *peace without being disgraced* (**peace without dishonor**).
> He was *shy but a creative boy* (**shy but creative**).

Check your terms on both sides of your coordinating conjunctions (*and, but, or*) and see that they match:

> necessary [adj.]
> **Orientation week seems both worthwhile [adjective] and** a neces-sity [noun]. that
> **He prayed that they would leave and** ∧ **the telephone would not ring.**

Learn to Use Paralleling Coordinators.

The sentence above about "Orientation week" has used one of a number of useful (and tricky) parallel constructions: *both-and; either-or; not only-but also; not-but; first-second-third; as well as.* This last one is similar to *and,* a simple link between two equivalents, but it often causes trouble:

> **One should take care of one's physical self [noun]** *as well as* **being [participle] able to read and write.**

Again, the pair should be matched: "one's *physical self* as well as one's *intellectual self,*" or "one's physical *self* as well as one's *ability* to read and write"—though this second is still slightly unbalanced, in rhetoric if not in grammar. The best cure would probably extend the underlying antithesis, the basic parallel:

> **One should take care of one's physical self as well as one's intellectual self, of one's ability to survive as well as to read and write.**

With the *either-or*'s and the *not only-but also*'s, you continue the principle of pairing. The *either* and the *not only* are merely signposts of what is coming: two equivalents linked by a coordinating conjunction (*or* or *but*). Beware of putting the signs in the wrong place — too soon for the turn:

> He (either) is an absolute piker or a fool!

> (Neither) in time nor space. . . .

> He (not only) likes the girl but the family, too.

In these examples, the thought got ahead of itself, as in talk. Just make sure that the word following each of the two coordinators is of the same kind, preposition for preposition, article for article, adjective for adjective — for even with signs well placed, the parallel can skid:

> The students are not only organizing [present participle] social activi-
>   discussing
> ties, but also ~~are interested~~ [passive construction] ~~in~~ political ques-
> tions.

Put identical parts in parallel places; fill in the blanks with the same parts of speech: "not only _____, but also _____." You similarly parallel the words following numerical coordinators:

Numerical coordinates

> However variously he expressed himself, he unquestionably thought, first, *that* everyone could get ahead; second, *that* workers generally were paid more than they earned; and, third, *that* laws enforcing a minimum wage were positively undemocratic.
> For a number of reasons, he decided (1) that he did not like it, (2) that she would not like it, (3) that they would be better off without it. [Note that the parentheses around the numbers operate exactly as any parentheses, and need no additional punctuation.]
> My objections are obvious: (1) it is unnecessary, (2) it costs too much, and (3) it won't work.

In parallels of this kind, *that* is usually the problem, since you may easily, and properly, omit it when there is only one clause and no confusion:

> . . . he unquestionably thought everyone could get ahead.

If second and third clauses occur, as your thought moves along, you may have to go back and put up the first signpost:

>   **that**
> . . . he unquestionably thought ∧ everyone could get ahead, that workers . . . , and that laws. . . .

Enough of *that*. Remember simply that equivalent thoughts demand parallel constructions. Notice the clear and massive strategy in the following sentence from the concluding chapter of Freud's last book, *An Outline of Psychoanalysis*. Freud is not only summing up the previous discussion, but also expressing the quintessence of his life's work. He is pulling everything together in a single sentence.

Each of the parallel *which* clauses gathers up, in proper order, an entire chapter of his book (notice the parallel force in repeating *picture*, and the summarizing dash):

> The picture of an ego which mediates between the id and the external world, which takes over the instinctual demands of the former in order to bring them to satisfaction, which perceives things in the latter and uses them as memories, which, intent upon its self-preservation, is on guard against excessive claims from both directions, and which is governed in all its decisions by the injunctions of a modified pleasure principle — this picture actually applies to the ego only up to the end of the first period of childhood, till about the age of five.

Such precision is hard to match. This is what parallel thinking brings — balance and control and an eye for sentences that seem intellectual totalities, as if struck out all at once from the uncut rock. Francis Bacon's sentences can seem like this (notice how he drops the verb after establishing his pattern):

> For a crowd is not company, and faces are but a gallery of pictures, and talk but a tinkling cymbal, where there is no love.
> Reading maketh a full man; conference a ready man; and writing an exact man.

Commas would work well in the second example (see p. 158):

> Reading maketh a full man; conference, a ready man; and writing, an exact man.

THE LONG AND SHORT OF IT

Your style will emerge once you can manage some length of sentence, some intricacy of subordination, some vigor of parallel, and some play of long against short, of amplitude against brevity. Try the very long sentence, and the very short. Short sentences are meatiest:

> I think; therefore, I am.
> The mass of men lead lives of quiet desperation.
> The more selfish the man, the more anguished the failure.

Experiment with the Fragment.

The fragment is close to conversation. It is the laconic reply, the pointed afterthought, the quiet exclamation, the telling question. Try to cut and place it clearly (usually at beginnings and ends of paragraphs) so as not to lead your reader to expect a full sentence, or to suspect a poor writer:

> But no more.   No, not really.
> First, a look behind the scenes.   Enough of that.

The fragment, of course, usually counts as an error. The reader expects a sentence and gets only a fragment of one: you leave him hanging in air, waiting for the second shoe to fall, or the voice to drop, with the thought completed, at the period. The *rhetorical* fragment — the effective and persuasive one — leaves him satisfied: *Of course.* The *grammatical* fragment leaves him unsatisfied: *When the vote was counted.* A question hangs in the air: *what* happened? who won? who got mad? But the point here about rhetorical fragments is to use their short, conversational staccato as one of your means to vary the rhythm of your long and longer sentences, playing long against short.

Develop a Rhythm of Long and Short.

The conversational flow between long and short makes a passage move. Study the subordinations, the parallels, and the play of short and long in this elegant passage of Virginia Woolf's — after you have read it once for sheer enjoyment. She is writing of Lord Chesterfield's famous letters to Philip Stanhope, his illegitimate son:

Subordinate, long	But while we amuse ourselves with this brilliant nobleman and his views on life we are aware, and the letters owe much of their fascination to this consciousness, of a dumb yet substantial figure on the far-
Short	ther side of the page. Philip Stanhope is always there. It is true that
Long	he says nothing, but we feel his presence in Dresden, in Berlin, in Paris, opening the letters and pouring over them and looking dolefully at the thick packets which have been accumulating year after
Short	year since he was a child of seven. He had grown into a rather
Shorter	serious, rather stout, rather short young man. He had a taste for
Longer	foreign politics. A little serious reading was rather to his liking. And
Long	by every post the letters came — urbane, polished, brilliant, imploring and commanding him to learn to dance, to learn to carve, to consider
Short; longer	the management of his legs, and to seduce a lady of fashion. He did his best. He worked very hard in the school of the Graces, but their service was too exacting. He sat down halfway up the steep stairs
Short	which lead to the glittering hall with all the mirrors. He could not do
Parallel	it. He failed in the House of Commons; he subsided into some small
Long	post in Ratisbon; he died untimely. He left it to his widow to break the news which he had lacked the heart or the courage to tell his father — that he had been married all these years to a lady of low birth, who had borne him children.
Short	The Earl took the blow like a gentleman. His letter to his
Longer	daughter-in-law is a model of urbanity. He began the education of his grandsons. . . .*

Those are some sentences to copy. We immediately feel the rhythmic play of periodic and loose, parallel and simple, long and short. Such orchestration takes years of practice, but you can always begin.

* *The Second Common Reader*, p. 81. Copyright, 1932, by Harcourt Brace Jovanovich, Inc, renewed, 1960, by Leonard Woolf. Reprinted by permission of Harcourt Brace Jovanovich, Inc., the Author's Literary Estate and The Hogarth Press, Ltd.

EXERCISES

1. *Give each of the following sentences a touch of periodicity (that is, suspense) by changing the normal word order, by adding interruptive words or phrases, or by complicating one of the three principal elements of the sentence: the subject, the verb, the object.*

EXAMPLE. *She made her way along the smoldering roof.*

Carefully at first, then with reckless steps, she made her way along the peak of the smoldering roof.

1. Commune residents are often escapees from solidly middle-class families.
2. Old friends are often shocked and embarrassed when they meet after years of separation and find they now have little in common.
3. Some firemen began carrying guns when they were frightened by the chaos of the riots.
4. The bottleneck in education is that the teacher can listen and respond to no more than one student at a time.
5. The car wheezed to a stop.

2. *Write six compound sentences, two with* and, *two with* but, *two with* or (nor). *Try to get as grand a feeling of consequence as possible with your* and's: *"Empires fall, and the saints come marching in."*

3. *Write three compound sentences using conjunctive adverbs, on the pattern: "_____; therefore, _____." Punctuate carefully with semicolon and comma.*

4. *Write three compound sentences in which the link is the semicolon alone. Try for meaningful contrasts.*

EXAMPLE. *The county wants the new expressway; the city wants to renew its streets.*

5. *Write three compound sentences in which the link is a colon. Try to make the second half of the compound explain the first.*

EXAMPLE. *His game was ragged: he went into sand traps four times, and into the trees five.*

6. *Here are some pairs of sentences. Convert them into complex sentences, trying to use a variety of subordinators.*

1. He couldn't go on. He was just too tired.
2. The crime commission recommended a number of such programs. Federal funds have been made available for putting them into operation.
3. We can probably never perfect the process beyond its present state. We should still try.
4. Most schools are just now starting courses in computers for freshmen. To evaluate those programs will take several years.
5. On small farms, labor was not specialized. On medium farms, labor was partially specialized. But large farms carefully divided their workers into teams of specialists.

7. *Streamline the following sentences by using appositives:*

1. The security guard, who must have been a very frightened man, fired point-blank into the crowd.

2. Professor Stanley, who is now associate vice-president and director of business operations, has been named a vice-president at the University of Nebraska.

3. The book, which has been a best seller for several months, will be made into a movie.

4. American social mores have undergone staggering changes since the early 1950's. These changes are so great in quality and number as to constitute a virtual revolution.

5. The Globe Theatre, which was immediately acclaimed the best designed and appointed playhouse in London, was completed in 1599.

8. *Consolidate the following sentences, using adjectival phrases and absolutes rather than subordinate clauses.*

1. The young girl cowered in the corner. There was pure terror in her eyes.

2. This construction is also appositional and adjectival. It is a neat trick for the beginning writer to remember.

3. Its deck was splintered and peeling. Its rigging was nearly all frayed and rotted. The boat obviously hadn't been cared for at all.

4. Griswell had neither eaten nor slept, and when he stumbled into the bar he was trembling with fatigue.

5. The ladder was sagging with his weight, and at last it collapsed.

9. *Keeping an eye out for dangling participles, revise the following sentences by transforming as many verbs as reasonably possible into participles.*

1. Apparently the boxer thought the bell had sounded. He dropped his guard, and he was immediately knocked out.

2. He settled into a Bohemian life in the French quarter. He started publishing in all the appropriate little magazines. And at last he found himself presiding over a colony of artists and writers.

3. The prisoners were obviously angered by the news that no guards were fired. They felt cheated and betrayed. And so on August 4 they seized three guards as hostages to force the warden to reconsider.

4. Dalton Trumbo was blacklisted in Hollywood; he was vilified in the press; and he was forced to write scripts under an assumed name until nearly 1960.

5. The student-designed rocket functioned perfectly. It rose one hundred miles above the earth, flew for ten minutes, traveled some fifty miles down range, and splashed down precisely on target.

10. *Try turning the phrases and subordinate clauses in the following sentences into absolutes.*

1. With examinations coming and with the temperature dropping, students are beginning to show up at the health service with all sorts of nebulous ailments, most of them purely imagined.

2. Ted left the room, leaving his things still scattered over the floor.

3. Even though the tank was filled with gas and the ignition was working perfectly, the engine still wouldn't start.

4. Even though the stock market had collapsed, and fifteen percent of the workers were jobless, Hoover nonetheless felt the economy would eventually right itself without tinkering.
5. When his three minutes were up, he deposited another quarter.

11. *Correct the faulty parallelism in the following sentences from students' papers, and clean up any wordiness you find.*

1. A student follows not only a special course of training, but among his studies and social activities finds a liberal education.
2. Either the critics attacked the book for its triteness, or it was criticized for its lack of organization.
3. This is not only the case with the young voters of the United States but also of the adult ones.
4. Certain things are not actually taught in the classroom. They are learning how to get along with others, to depend on oneself, and managing one's own affairs.
5. Knowing Greek and Roman antiquity is not just learning to speak their language but also their culture.

12. *Write an imitation of the passage from Virginia Woolf on p. 67, choosing your own subject but matching the pattern, lengths, and rhythms of her sentences, sentence for sentence, if you can, At any rate, aim toward effective rhythms of long and short.*

instead a passive smokescreen, and the student sees no one at all to help him:

> **It has been decided that your proposal for independent study is not sufficiently in line with the prescribed qualifications as outlined by the college in the catalog.**

Committees always write this way, and the effect on academic writing, as the professor goes from committee to desk to classroom, is astounding. "It was moved that a meeting would be held," the secretary writes, to avoid pinning the rap on anybody. So writes the professor, so writes the student.

I reluctantly admit that the passive voice has certain uses. In fact, your meaning sometimes demands the passive voice; the agent may be better under cover—insignificant, or unknown, or mysterious. The active "Shrapnel hit him" seems to belie the uncanny impersonality of "He was hit by shrapnel." The broad forces of history similarly demand the passive: "The West was opened in 1848." Moreover, you may sometimes need the passive voice to place your true subject, the hero of the piece, where you can modify him conveniently: "Joe was hit by John, who, in spite of all. . . ." And sometimes it simply is more convenient: "This subject-verb-object sentence can be infinitely contorted." You can, of course, find a number of passive constructions in this book, which preaches against them, because they can also space out a thought that comes too fast and thick. In trying to describe periodic sentences, for instance (p. 55), I changed "until all interconnections lock in the final word" (active) to ". . . are locked by the final word" (passive). The *lock* seemed too tight, especially with *in,* and the locking seemed contrary to the ways buildings *are built.* Yes, the passive has its uses.

But it is wordy. It puts useless words in a sentence. Its dullness derives as much from its extra wordage as from its impersonality. The best way to prune is with the active voice, cutting the passive and its fungus as you go. Notice the effect on these typical and real samples:

> PASSIVE: **Public concern** *has* also *been given* **a tremendous impetus** *by* **the findings of the Hoover Commission on the federal government, and "little Hoover" commissions to survey the organizational structure and functions of many state governments** *have been established.*
>
> ACTIVE: **The findings of the Hoover Commission on federal government** *have* **also greatly stimulated public concern, and many states** *have established* **"little Hoover" commissions to survey their governments.** [27 *words for 38*]
>
> PASSIVE: **The algal mats** *are made up of* **the interwoven filaments of several genera.**
>
> ACTIVE: **The interwoven filaments of several genera** *make up* **the algal mats.** [11 *words for 13*]

PASSIVE: **Many of the remedies** *would* **probably** *be shown to be* **faith cures.**

ACTIVE: **Many of the remedies** *were* **probably faith cures.** [*8 words for 12*]

PASSIVE: **Anxiety and emotional conflict** *are lessened* **when latency sets in. The total personality** *is oriented* **in a repressive, inhibitory fashion so as to maintain the barriers, and what Freud has called "psychic dams," against psychosexual impulses.**

ACTIVE: **When latency sets in, anxiety and emotional conflict** *subside.* **The personality** *inhibits* **itself, maintaining its barriers — Freud's "psychic dams" — against psychosexual impulses.** [*22 words for 36*]

Check the Stretchers.

To be, itself, frequently ought not to be:

> He seems [to be] upset about something.
> She considered him [to be] perfect.
> This appears [to be] difficult.

Above all, keep your sentences awake by not putting them into those favorite stretchers of the passivists, *There is . . . which, It is . . . that,* and the like:

> Moreover, [there is] one segment of the population [which] never seeks employment.
> [There are] many women [who] never marry.
> [There] (is) nothing wrong with it. [Nothing is. . . .]
> [It is] his last book [that] shows his genius best.
> [It is] this [that] is important.

Cut every *it* not referring to something. Next to activating your passive verbs, and cutting the passive *there is*'s and *it is*'s, perhaps nothing so improves your prose as to go through it systematically also deleting every *to be,* every *which, that, who,* and *whom* not needed for utter clarity or for spacing out a thought. All your sentences will feel better.

Beware the Of-and-Which Disease.

The passive sentence frequently breaks out in a rash of *of*'s and *which*'s, and even the active sentence may suffer. Diagnosis: something like sleeping sickness. *With*'s, *in*'s, *to*'s and *by*'s also inflamed. Surgery imperative. Here is an actual case:

> Many biological journals, especially those *which* regularly publish new scientific names, now state *in* each issue the exact date *of* publication *of* the preceding issue. *In* dealing *with* journals *which* do not follow this practice, or *with* volumes *which* are issued individually, the biologist often needs *to* resort *to* indexes . . . *in order to* determine the actual date *of* publication *of* a particular name.

Note *of publication of* twice over, and the three *which*'s. The passage is a sleeping beauty. The longer you look at it, the more useless little attendants you see. Note the inevitable passive voice (*which are issued*) in spite of the author's active efforts. The *of*'s accompany extra nouns, *publication* repeating *publish,* for instance. Remedy: (1) eliminate *of*'s and their nouns, (2) change *which* clauses into participles, (3) change nouns into verbs. You can cut more than a third of this passage without touching the sense (using 39 words for 63):

> **Many biological journals, especially those regularly** *publishing* **new scientific names, now give the date of each preceding issue. With journals not** *following* **this practice, and with some books, the biologist must turn to indexes . . .** *to date* **a particular name.**

I repeat: you can cut most *which*'s, one way or another, with no loss of blood. Participles can modify their antecedents directly, since they are verbal adjectives, without an intervening *which:* "a car *which was* going south" is "a car going south"; a train *which is* moving" is "a moving train." Similarly with the adjective itself: "a song *which was* popular last year" is "a song popular last year"; "a person *who is* attractive" is "an attractive person." Beware of this whole crowd: *who are, that was, which are.*

If you need a relative clause, remember *that. Which* has almost completely displaced it in labored writing. *That* is still best for restrictive clauses, those necessary to definition: "A house that faces north is cool" (a participle would save a word: "A house facing north is cool"). *That* is tolerable; *which* is downright oppressive. *Which* should signal the nonrestrictive clause (the afterthought): "The house, which faces north, is a good buy." Here you need *which.* Even restrictive clauses must turn to *which* when complicated parallels arise. "He preaches the brotherhood of man *that* everyone affirms" elaborates like this: "He preaches the brotherhood of man *which* everyone affirms, *which* all the great philosophies support, but *for which* few can make any immediate concession." Nevertheless, if you need relatives, a *that* will often ease your sentence and save you from the *which*'s.

Verbs and their derivatives, especially present participles and gerunds, can also help to cure a string of *of*'s. Alfred North Whitehead, usually of clear mind, once produced this linked sausage: "Education is the acquisition *of* the art *of* the utilization *of* knowledge." Anything to get around the three *of*'s and the three heavy nouns would have been better: "Education instills the art of using knowledge" — "Education teaches us to use knowledge well." Find an active verb for *is the acquisition of,* and shift *the utilization of* into some verbal form: the gerund *using,* or the infinitive *to use.* Shun the *-tion*'s! Simply change your surplus *-tion*'s and *of*'s — along with your *which* phrases — into verbs, or verbals (*to use, learning*). You will save words, and activate your sentences.

Avoid "The Use Of."

In fact, both *use*, as a noun, and *use*, as a verb, are dangerously wordy words. Since *using* is one of our most basic concepts, other words in your sentence will already contain it.

> He uses rationalization. [He rationalizes.]
> He uses the device of foreshadowing. [He foreshadows.]
> Through [the use of] logic, he persuades.
> His [use of] dialogue is effective.

The utilization of and *utilize* are only horrendous extremes of the same pestilence, to be stamped out completely.

Break the Noun Habit.

Passive writing adores the noun, modifying nouns with nouns in pairs, and even in denser clusters — which then become official jargon. Break up these logjams, let the language flow, make one noun of the pair an adjective:

> *Teacher militancy* **is not as marked in Pittsburgh.** [*Teachers* **are not so** *militant* **in Pittsburgh.** 7 *words for* 8]

Or convert one noun to a verb:

> *Consumer demand* **is falling in the area of services.** [**Consumers** *are* *demanding* **fewer services.** 5 *words for* 9]

Of course, nouns have long served English as adjectives: as in "*rail*road," "*railroad* station," "*court*house," and "*noun* habit." But modern prose has aggravated the tendency beyond belief; and we get such monstrosities as *child sex education course* and *child sex education curriculum publication deadline reminder* — whole strings of nothing but nouns. Education, sociology, and psychology produce the worst noun-stringers, the hardest for you not to copy if you take these courses. But we have all caught the habit. The nouns *level* and *quality*, used as adjectives, have produced a rash of redundancies. A meeting of "high officials" has now unfortunately become a meeting of "high-*level* officials." The "finest cloth" these days is always "finest *quality* cloth." Drop those two redundant nouns and you will make a good start, and will sound surprisingly original. In fact, using the noun *quality* as an adjective has become almost obsessive — *quality food, quality wine, quality service, quality entertainment, high-quality drilling equipment* — blurring all distinctions of *good, fine, excellent, superb, superior,* in one dull and inaccurate cliché. A good rule: DON'T USE NOUNS AS ADJECTIVES. You can drop many an excess noun:

Wordy	**Direct**
advance notice	notice
long in size	long

Wordy	Direct
puzzling in nature	puzzling
of an indefinite nature	indefinite
of a peculiar kind	peculiar
in order to	to
by means of	by
in relation to	with
in connection with	with
1978-model car	1978 car
at this point in time	at this time; now

Wherever possible, find the equivalent adjective:

of great importance	important
highest significance level	highest significant level
government spending	governmental spending
reaction fixation	reactional fixation
teaching excellence	excellent teaching
encourage teaching quality	encourage good teaching

Or change the noun to its related participle:

advance placement	advanced placement
uniform police	uniformed police
poison arrow	poisoned arrow

Or make the noun possessive:

reader interest	reader's interest
veterans insurance	veterans' insurance

Or try a cautious *of:*

color lipstick	color of lipstick
significance level	level of significance

Of all our misused nouns, *type* has become particularly pestilential and trite. Advertisers talk of *detergent-type cleansers* instead of *detergents;* educators, of *apprentice-type situations* instead of *apprenticeships;* newspapermen, of *fascist-type organizations* instead of *fascistic organizations.* We have forgotten that making the individual stand for the type is the simplest and oldest of metaphors: "Give us this day our daily bread." A twentieth-century supplicant might have written "bread-type food."

The active sentence transmits the message by putting each word unmistakably in its place, a noun as a noun, an adjective as an adjective, with the verb—no stationary *is*—really carrying the mail. Recently, after a flood, a newspaper produced this apparently succinct and dramatic sentence: **Dead animals cause water pollution.** (The word *cause*, incidentally, indicates wasted words.) That noun *water* as an adjective throws the meaning off and takes 25 percent more words than the essential active message: **Dead animals pollute water.** As you read your way into the sentence, it seems to say *dead animals cause water* (which is true enough), and then you must readjust your thoughts to accommodate *pollution.* The simplest change is from *water pollution* (noun-noun) to *polluted water* (adjective-noun), clarifying each word's function. But the supreme solution is to make *pollute* the verb it is, and the sentence a simple active message in which no word misspeaks itself. Here are the possibilities, in a scale from most active and clearest to most passive and wordiest, which may serve to chart your troubles if you get tangled in causes and nouns:

> **Dead animals pollute water.**
> **Dead animals cause polluted water.**
> **Dead animals cause water pollution.**
> **Dead animals are a factor in causing the pollution of water.**
> **Dead animals are a serious factor in causing the water pollution situation.**
> **Dead farm-type animals are a danger factor in causing the post-flood clearance and water pollution situation.**

So the message should now be clear. Write simple active sentences, outmaneuvering all passive eddies, all shallow *is*'s, *of*'s, *which*'s, and *that*'s, all overlappings, all rocky clusters of nouns: they take you off your course, delay your delivery, and wreck many a straight and gallant thought.

Avoid Excessive Distinctions and Definitions.

Too many distinctions, too many nouns, and too much Latin make pea soup:

> **Reading is a processing skill of symbolic reasoning sustained by the interfacilitation of an intricate hierarchy of substrata factors that have been mobilized as a psychological working system and pressed into service in accordance with the purpose of the reader.**

This comes from an educator, with the wrong kind of education. He is saying:

> **Reading is a process of symbolic reasoning aided by an intricate network of ideas and motives. [*16 words for 40*]**

Except with crucial assumptions and implications (see pp. 42, 47), try *not* to define your terms. If you do, you are probably either evading the toil of finding the right word, or defining the obvious:

> **Let us agree to use the word signal as an abbreviation for the phrase "the simplest kind of sign." (This agrees fairly well with the customary meaning of the word "signal.")**

That came from a renowned semanticist, an authority on the meanings of words. The customary meaning of a word *is* its meaning, and uncustomary meanings come only from careful punning. Don't underestimate your readers, as this semanticist did.

The definer of words is usually a bad writer. Our semanticist continues, trying to get his signals straight and grinding out about three parts sawdust to every one of meat. In the following excerpt, I have bracketed his sawdust. Read the sentence first as it was written: then read it again, omitting the bracketed words:

> The moral of such examples is that all intelligent criticism [of any instance] of language [in use] must begin with understanding [of] the motives [and purposes] of the speaker [in that situation].

Here, each of the bracketed phrases is already implied in the others. Attempting to be precise, the writer has beclouded himself. Naturally, the speaker would be "in that situation"; naturally, a sampling of language would be "an instance" of language "in use." *Motives* may not be *purposes*, but the difference here is insignificant. Our semanticist's next sentence deserves some kind of immortality. He means "Muddy language makes trouble":

> Unfortunately, the type of case that causes trouble in practice is that in which the kind of use made of language is not transparently clear. . . .

Clearly, transparency is hard. Writing is hard. It requires constant attention to meanings, and constant pruning. Count your words, and make your words count.

EXERCISES

1. *Clear up the blurred ideas, and grammar, in these sentences from students' papers and official prose, making each word say what it means, and counting your words to make sure your version has fewer.*

1. Tree pruning may be done in any season of the year. [11 words]
2. After reading a dozen books, the subject is still as puzzling as ever. [13]
3. The secret teller vote used in the past was this time a recorded teller vote. [15]
4. The courses listed herein are those which meet the college-level requirements which were stated above. [16]
5. Records can be used in the Audio Room by individual students for their suggested listening assignments. [16]
6. My counter was for refunds for which the customer had already paid for. [13]
7. Entrance was gained by means of the skylight. [8]
8. The reason we give this test is because we are anxious to know whether or not you have reflexes that are sufficiently fast to allow you to be a safe worker. [31]

2. *Find in your textbooks two or three passages suffering from the passive voice, the* of-and-which *disease, the* the-use-of *contagion, and the noun habit ("which shows the effect of age and intelligence level upon the use of the reflexes and the emergence of child behavior difficulties") and rewrite them in clear English.*

3. *Recast these sentences in the active voice, clearing out all passive constructions, saving as many words as you can, and indicating the number saved:*

1. The particular topic chosen by the instructor for study in his section of English 2 must be approved by the Steering Committee. [Start with "The Steering Committee," and don't forget the economy of an apostrophe-*s*. I managed 14 words for 22.]
2. Avoidance of such blunders should not be considered a virtue for which the student is to be commended, any more than he would be praised for not wiping his hands on the tablecloth or polishing his shoes with the guest towels. [Begin "We should not"; try *avoiding* for *avoidance*. I dropped *virtue* as redundant and scored 27 for 41.]
3. The first respect in which too much variation seems to exist is in the care with which writing assignments are made. ["First, care in assigning" — 8 for 21.]
4. The remaining variations that will be mentioned are concerned not with the assignment of papers but with the marking and grading of them. ["Finally, I shall mention" — 14 for 23.]
5. The difference between restrictives and nonrestrictives can also be better approached through a study of the different contours that mark the utterance of the two kinds of elements than through confusing attempts to differentiate the two by meaning. ["One can differentiate restrictives" — I managed 13 for 38. The writer is dead wrong, incidentally: meaning is the true differentiator. See pp. 152–53.]

4. *Eliminate the italicized words in the following passages, together with all their accompanying wordiness, indicating the number of words saved (my figures again are merely guides; other solutions that come close are quite good).*

1. *There is* a certain tendency to defend one's own position *which* will cause the opponent's argument to be ignored. [13 for 19]
2. *It is* the other requirements *that* present obstacles, some *of which* may prove insurmountable in the teaching of certain subjects. [11 for 20]
3. In the sort of literature-centered course being discussed here, *there is* usually a general understanding *that* themes will be based on the various literary works *that* are studied, the theory being *that* both the instruction in literature and *that* in writing will be made more effective by this interrelationship. [21 for 49]
4. The person *whom* he met was an expert *who was* able to teach the fundamentals quickly. [13 for 16]
5. They will take a pride *which is* wholly justifiable in being able to command a prose style *that is* lucid and supple. [13 for 22]

5. *To culminate this chapter, clear up the wordiness, especially the italicized patches, in these two official statements, one from an eminent linguist, one from an eminent publisher.*

1. The work *which is* reported *in this* study *is* an investigation *of* language *within* the social context *of* the community *in which it is spoken. It is* a study *of* a linguistic structure *which is* unusually complex, but no more than the social structure *of* the city *in which it* functions. [I tried two versions, as I chased out the *which*'s; 29 for 52, and 22 for 52.]

2. Methods *which are* unique to the historian *are illustrated* throughout the volume *in order* to show how history *is written* and how historians work. The historian's approach to his subject, *which* leads to the asking of provocative questions and to a new understanding of complex events, situations, and personalities *is probed.* The manner *in which* the historian reduces masses of chaotic fact — and occasional fancy — to reliable meaning, and the way *in which* he formulates explanations and tests them *is examined and clarified* for the student. *It is its* emphasis on historical method *which* distinguishes this book from other source readings in western civilization. The problems *which are examined* concern *themselves with* subjects *which are dealt with by* most courses in western civilization. [66 for 123. The all-time winner from a student is 45 words.]

Words

Here is the word. Sesquipedalian or short, magniloquent or low, Latin or Anglo-Saxon, Celtic, Danish, French, Spanish, Indian, Hindustani, Dutch, Italian, Portuguese, Choctaw, Swahili, Chinese, Hebrew, Turkish, Greek—English contains them all, a million words at our disposal, if we are disposed to use them. Although no language is richer than English, our expository vocabularies average probably fewer than eight thousand words. We could all increase our active vocabularies; we all have a way to go to possess our inheritance.

VOCABULARY

Build Your Stock Systematically.

If you can increase your hoard, you increase your chances of finding the right word when you need it. Read as widely as you can, and look words up the second or third time you meet them. I once knew a man who swore he learned three new words a day from his reading by using each at least once in conversation. I didn't ask him about *polyphiloprogenitive* or *antidisestablishmentarianism*. It depends a little on the crowd. But the idea is sound. The bigger the vocabulary, the more various the ideas one can get across with it—the more the shades and intensities of meaning.

The big vocabulary also needs the little word. The vocabularian often stands himself on a Latin cloud and forgets the Anglo-Saxon ground—the common ground between him and his audience. So do not forget the little things, the *stuff, lint, get, twig, snap, go, mud, coax.* Hundreds of small words not in immediate vogue can refresh your vocabulary. The Norse and Anglo-Saxon adjectives in -*y* (*muggy, scrawny, drowsy*) for instance, rarely appear in sober print. The minute the beginner tries to sound dignified, in comes a misty layer of words a few feet off the ground and nowhere near heaven, the same two dozen or so, most of them verbs. One or two will do no harm, but any accumulation is fatal—words like *depart* instead of *go:*

accompany — go with	place — put
appeared — looked *or* seemed	possess — have
arrive — come	prepare — get ready
become — get	questioned — asked
cause — make	receive — get
cease — stop	relate — tell
complete — finish	remain — stay
continue — keep on	remove — take off
delve — dig	retire — go to bed
discover — find	return — go back
indicate — say	secure — get
locate — find	transform — change
manner — way	verify — check

Through the centuries, English has added Latin derivatives alongside the Anglo-Saxon words already there, keeping the old with the new: after the Anglo-Saxon *deor* (now *deer*) came the *beast* and then the *brute*, both from Latin through French, and the *animal* straight from Rome. We have the Anglo-Saxon *cow, sheep,* and *pig* furnishing (through French) Latin *beef, mutton,* and *pork.* Although we use more Anglo-Saxon in assembling our sentences (*to, by, with, though, is*), well over half our total vocabulary comes one way or another from Latin. The things of this world tend to be Anglo-Saxon (*man, house, stone, wind, rain*); the abstract qualities, Latin and French (*value, duty, contemplation*).

Most of our big words are Latin and Greek. Your reading acquaints you with them; your dictionary will show you their prefixes and roots. Learn the common prefixes and roots (see Exercise 3 at the end of this chapter), and you can handle all kinds of foreigners at first encounter; *con-cession* (going along with), *ex-clude* (lock out), *pre-fer* (carry before), *sub-version* (turning under), *trans-late* (carry across), *claustro-phobia* (dread of being locked in), *hydro-phobia* (dread of water), *ailuro-philia* (love of cats), *megalo-cephalic* (big-headed), *micro-meter* (little measurer). You can even, for fun, coin a word to suit the occasion: *megalopede* (big-footed). You can remember that *in-tramural* means "within the (college) walls," and that "intermural sports," which is the frequent mispronunciation and misspelling, would mean something like "wall battling wall," a physical absurdity.

Besides owning a good dictionary, you should refer, with caution, to a thesaurus, a treasury of synonyms ("together-names"), in which you can find the word you couldn't think of; the danger lies in raiding this treasury too enthusiastically. Checking for meaning in a dictionary will assure that you have expanded, not distorted, your vocabulary.

ABSTRACT AND CONCRETE

Learn Their Powers, Separate and Combined.

Every good stylist has perceived, in one way or another, the distinction between the abstract and the concrete. Tangible things — things we can touch — are "concrete"; their qualities, along with all our emotional, intellectual, and spiritual states, are "abstract." The rule for a good style is to be as concrete as you can, to illustrate tangibly your general propositions, to use *shoes* and *ships* and *sealing wax* instead of *commercial concomitants*.

But abstraction, a "drawing out from," is the very nature of thought. Thought moves from concrete to abstract. In fact, *all* words are abstractions. *Stick* is a generalization of all sticks, the crooked and the straight, the long and the short, the peeled and the shaggy. No word fits its object like a glove, because words are not things: words represent ideas of things. They are the means by which we class eggs and tents and trees so that we can handle them as ideas — not as actual things but as *kinds* or *classes* of things.

Abstract words can attain a power of their own, as the rhetorician heightens attention to their meanings. This ability, of course, does not come easily or soon. I repeat, you need to be as concrete as you can, to illustrate tangibly, to pin your abstractions down to specifics. But once you have learned this, you can move on to the rhetoric of abstraction, which is a kind of squeezing of abstract words for their specific juice.

Lincoln does exactly this when he concentrates on *dedication* six times within the ten sentences of his dedication at Gettysburg: "We have come to *dedicate*. . . . It is rather for us to be here *dedicated*. . . ." Similarly, Eliot refers to "faces/Distracted from distraction by distraction" (*Four Quartets*). Abstractions can, in fact, operate beautifully as specifics: "As a knight, Richard the Lion-Hearted was a *triumph;* as a king, he was a *disaster*." Many rhetorical patterns likewise concentrate on abstract essences:

> . . . tribulation works patience, and patience experience, and experience hope. (Rom. v.3–4)
> The humble are proud of their humility.
> Care in your youth so you may live without care.

An able writer like Samuel Johnson can make a virtual poetry of abstractions, as he alliterates and balances them against each other (I have capitalized the alliterations and italicized the balances):

> Dryden's performances were always hasty, either *Excited* by some *External occasion*, or *Extorted* by some *domestic necessity;* he *Composed without Consideration* and *Published without Correction.*

Notice especially how *excited* ("called forth") and *extorted* ("twisted out"), so alike in sound and form, so alike in making Dryden write, nevertheless contrast their opposite essential meanings.

So before we disparage abstraction, we should acknowledge its rhetorical power; and we should understand that it is an essential distillation, a primary and natural and continual mental process. Without it, we could not make four of two and two. So we make abstractions of abstractions to handle bigger and bigger groups of ideas. *Egg* becomes *food*, and *food* becomes *nourishment*. We also classify all the psychic and physical qualities we can recognize: *candor, truth, anger, beauty, negligence, temperament*. But because our thoughts drift upward, we need always to look for the word that will bring them nearer earth, that will make our abstractions seem visible and tangible, that will make them graspable—mentioning a *handle*, or a *pin*, or an *egg*, alongside our abstraction, for instance.

But the writer's ultimate skill perhaps lies in making a single object represent its whole abstract class. I have paired each abstraction below with its concrete translation:

> *Friendliness* is the salesman's best asset.
> A *smile* is the salesman's best asset.
>
> *Administration of proper proteins* might have saved John Keats.
> A *good steak* might have saved John Keats.
>
> To *understand* the world by *observing all of its geological details....*
> To *see* the world in *a grain of sand. . . .*

METAPHOR

Bring Your Words to Life.

As you have probably noticed, I frequently use metaphors—the most useful way of making our abstractions concrete. The word is Greek for "transfer" (*meta* equals *trans* equals *across; phor* equals *fer* equals *ferry*). Metaphors illustrate our general ideas at a single stroke. Many of our common words are metaphors, *grasp* for "understanding," for instance, which compares the mind to something with hands, *transferring* the physical picture of the clutching hand to the invisible mental act.

Metaphor seems to work at about four levels, each with a different clarity and force. Suppose you wrote "he swelled and displayed his finery." You have transferred to a man the qualities of a peacock to make his appearance and personality vivid. You have chosen one of the four ways to make this transfer:

I. SIMILE: He was like a peacock.
He displayed himself as a peacock does.
He displayed himself as if he were a peacock.

II. PLAIN METAPHOR: He was a peacock.

III. IMPLIED METAPHOR: He swelled and displayed his finery.
He swelled and ruffled his plumage.
He swelled, ruffling his plumage.

IV. DEAD METAPHOR: He strutted.

I. Simile. The simile is the most obvious form the metaphor can take, and hence would seem elementary. But it has powers of its own, particularly where the writer seems to be trying urgently to express the inexpressible, comparing his subject to several different possibilities, no one wholly adequate. In *The Sound and the Fury*, Faulkner thus describes two jaybirds (my italics):

> [they] whirled up on the blast *like gaudy scraps of cloth or paper* and lodged in the mulberries, . . . screaming into the wind that *ripped* their harsh cries onward and away *like scraps of paper or of cloth* in turn.

The simile has a high poetic energy. D. H. Lawrence uses it frequently, as here in *The Plumed Serpent* (my italics):

> The lake was quite black, *like a great pit*. The wind suddenly blew with violence, with a strange ripping sound in the mango trees, *as if some membrane in the air were being ripped*.

II. Plain Metaphor. The plain metaphor makes its comparison in one imaginative leap. It is shorthand for "as if he were a peacock"; it pretends, by exaggeration (*hyperbole*), that he *is* a peacock. We move instinctively to this kind of exaggerated comparison as we try to convey our impressions with all their emotional impact. "He was a maniac at Frisbee," we might say, or "a dynamo." The metaphor is probably our most common figure of speech: *the pigs, the swine, a plum, a gem, a phantom of delight, a shot in the arm*. It may be humorous or bitter; it may be simply and aptly visual: "The road was a ribbon of silver." Thoreau extends a metaphor through several sentences in one of his most famous passages:

> Time is but a stream I go a-fishing in. I drink at it; but while I drink I see the sandy bottom and detect how shallow it is. Its thin current slides away, but eternity remains. I would drink deeper; fish in the sky, whose bottom is pebbly with stars.

III. Implied Metaphor. The implied metaphor is even more widely used. It operates most often among the verbs, as in *swelled, displayed,* and *ruffled,* the verbs suggesting "peacock." Most ideas can suggest analogues of physical processes or natural history. Give your television system *tentacles* reaching into every home, and you have compared TV to an octopus, with all its lethal and wiry suggestions. You can have your school spirit *fall below zero,* and you have implied that your school spirit is like temperature, registered on a thermometer in a sudden chill. In the following passage about Hawthorne's style, Malcolm Cowley develops his explicit analogy first into a direct simile (*like a footprint*) and then into a metaphor implying that phrases are people walking at different speeds:

> He dreamed in words, while walking along the seashore or under the pines, till the words fitted themselves to his stride. The result was that his eighteenth-century English developed into a natural, a *walked,* style, with a phrase for every step and a comma after every phrase like a footprint in the sand. Sometimes the phrases hurry, sometimes they loiter, sometimes they march to drums.°

IV. Dead Metaphor. The art of resuscitation is the metaphorist's finest skill. It comes from liking words and paying attention to what they say. Simply add onto the dead metaphor enough implied metaphors to get the circulation going again: *He strutted, swelling and ruffling his plumage. He strutted* means by itself "walked in a pompous manner." By bringing the metaphor back to life, we keep the general meaning but also restore the physical picture of a peacock puffing up and spreading his feathers. We recognize *strut* concretely and truly for the first time. We know the word, and we know the man. We have an image of him, a posture strongly suggestive of a peacock.

Perhaps the best dead metaphors to revive are those in proverbial clichés. See what Thoreau does (in his *Journal*) with *spur of the moment:*

> I feel the spur of the moment thrust deep into my side. The present is an inexorable rider.

Or again, when in *Walden* he speaks of wanting "to improve the nick of time, and notch it on my stick too," and of not being *thrown off the track* "by every nutshell and mosquito's wing that falls on the rails." In each case, he takes the proverbial phrase literally and physically, adding an attribute or two to bring the old metaphor back alive.

You can go too far, of course. Your metaphors can be too thick and vivid, and the obvious pun brings a howl of protest. I have myself advised scholars against using metaphors because they are so often overworked and so often tangled in physical impossibilities, becom-

---

° *The Portable Hawthorne* (New York: The Viking Press, 1948).

ing "mixed" metaphors. "The violent population explosion has paved the way for new intellectual growth" looks pretty good — until you realize that explosions do not pave, and that new vegetation does not grow up through solid pavement. The metaphor, then, is your most potent device. It makes your thought concrete and your writing vivid. It tells in an instant how your subject looks to you. But it is dangerous. It should be quiet, almost unnoticed, with all details agreeing, and all absolutely consistent with the natural universe.

ALLUSION

Illuminate the Dim with a Familiar Light.

Allusions also illustrate your general idea by referring it to something else, making it take your reader as Grant took Richmond, making you the Mickey Mantle of the essay, or the Mickey Mouse. Allusions depend on common knowledge. Like the metaphor, they illustrate the remote with the familiar — a familiar place, or event, or personage. "He looked . . . like a Japanese Humphrey Bogart," writes William Bittner of French author Albert Camus, and we instantly see a face like the one we know so well (a glance at Camus' picture confirms how accurate this unusual allusion is). Perhaps the most effective allusions depend on a knowledge of literature. When Thoreau writes that "the winter of man's discontent was thawing as well as the earth," we get a secret pleasure from recognizing this as an allusive borrowing from the opening lines of Shakespeare's *Richard III*: "Now is the winter of our discontent/Made glorious summer by this sun of York." Thoreau flatters us by assuming we are as well read as he. We need not catch the allusion to enjoy his point, but if we catch it, we feel a sudden fellowship of knowledge with him. We now see the full metaphorical force, Thoreau's and Shakespeare's both, heightened as it is by our remembrance of Richard Crookback's twisted discontent, an allusive illustration of all our pitiful resentments now thawing with the spring.

Allusions can also be humorous. The hero of Peter De Vries's "The Vale of Laughter," alluding to Lot's wife looking back on Sodom (Gen. xix.26) as he contemplates adultery for a moment, decides on the path toward home and honor:

> If you look back, you turn into a pillar of salt. If you look ahead, you turn into a pillar of society.

DICTION

Reach for Both the High and the Low.

"What we need is a mixed diction," said Aristotle, and his point remains true twenty-three centuries and several languages later. The aim of style, he says, is to be clear but distinguished. For clarity, we need common, current words; but, used alone, these are commonplace, and as ephemeral as everyday talk. For distinction, we need words not heard every minute, unusual words, large words, foreign words, metaphors; but, used alone, these become bogs, vapors, or at worst, gibberish. What we need is a diction that weds the popular with the dignified, the clear current with the sedgy margins of language and thought.

Not too low, not too high; not too simple, not too hard — an easy breadth of idea and vocabulary. English is peculiarly well endowed for this Aristotelian mixture. The long abstract Latin words and the short concrete Anglo-Saxon ones give you all the range you need. For most of your ideas, you can find Latin and Anglo-Saxon partners. In fact, for many ideas, you can find a whole spectrum of synonyms from Latin through French to Anglo-Saxon, from general to specific — from *intrepidity* to *fortitude* to *valor* to *courage* to *bravery* to *pluck* to *guts*. Each of these *denotes* or specifies the same thing: being brave. But each has a different *connotation*, or aura of meaning (see Glossary, p. 180). You can choose the high word for high effect, or you can get tough with Anglo-Saxon specifics. But you do not want all Anglo-Saxon, and you must especially guard against sobriety's luring you into all Latin. Tune your diction agreeably between the two extremes.

Indeed, the two extremes generate incomparable zip when tumbled side by side, as in *incomparable zip, inconsequential snip, megalomaniacal creep*, and the like. Rhythm and surprise conspire to set up the huge adjective first, then to add the small noun, like a monumental kick. Here is a passage from Edward Dahlberg's *Can These Bones Live*, which I opened completely at random to see how the large fell with the small (my italics):

> Christ walks on a *visionary sea;* Myshkin . . . has his ecstatic premonition of infinity when he has an *epileptic fit.* We know the inward size of an artist by his *dimensional thirsts.* . . .

This mixing of large Latin and small Anglo-Saxon, as John Crowe Ransom has noted, is what gives Shakespeare much of his power:

> This my hand will rather
> The multitudinous seas incarnadine,
> Making the green one red.

The short Anglo-Saxon *seas* works sharply between the two magnificent Latin words, as do the three short Anglo-Saxons that bring the big passage to rest, contrasting the Anglo-Saxon *red* with its big Latin kin, *incarnadine*. William Faulkner, who soaked himself in Shakespeare, gets much the same power from the same mixture. He is describing a very old Negro woman in *The Sound and the Fury* (the title itself comes from Shakespeare's *Macbeth*, the source of the *multitudinous seas* passage). She has been fat, but now she is wrinkled and completely shrunken except for her stomach:

> . . . a paunch almost dropsical, as though muscle and tissue had been courage or fortitude which the days or the years had consumed until only the indomitable skeleton was left rising like a ruin or a landmark above the somnolent and impervious guts. . . .

The impact of that short, ugly Anglo-Saxon word *guts*, with its slang metaphorical pun, is almost unbearably moving. And the impact would be nothing, the effect slurring, without the grand Latin preparation.

A good diction takes work. It exploits the natural, but does not come naturally. It demands a wary eye for the way meanings sprout, and the courage to prune. It has the warmth of human concern. It is a cut above the commonplace, a cut above the inaccuracies and circumlocutions of speech, yet within easy reach. Clarity is the first aim; economy, the second; grace, the third; dignity, the fourth. Our writing should be a little strange, a little out of the ordinary, a little beautiful, with words and phrases not met every day but seeming as right and natural as grass. A good diction takes care and cultivation.

It can be overcultivated. It may seem to call attention to itself rather than to its subject. Suddenly we are aware of the writer at work, and a little too pleased with himself, reaching for the elegant cliché and the showy phrase. Some readers find this very fault with my own writing, though I do really try to saddle my maverick love of metaphor. If I strike you in this way, you can use me profitably as a bad example along with the following passage. I have italicized elements that individually may have a certain effectiveness, but that cumulatively become mannerism, as if the writer were watching himself gesture in a mirror. Some of his phrases are redundant; some are trite. Everything is somehow cozy and grandiose, and a little too nautical:

> *There's* little excitement *ashore* when merchant ships from *faraway* India, Nationalist China, or Egypt *knife through* the *gentle swells* of Virginia's Hampton Roads. This *unconcern* may simply reflect the *nonchalance* of people who live by *one of the world's great seaports.* Or perhaps *it's just* that *folk* who *dwell* in the *home towns* of atomic submarines and Mercury astronauts are not likely to be impressed by a visiting freighter, *from however distant a realm.* . . .
> *Upstream a bit* and also *to port,* the mouth of the Elizabeth River leads to Portsmouth and a major naval shipyard. *To starboard lies* Hampton, where at Langley Air Force Base the National Aeronautics and Space Administration prepares to send a man *into the heavens.*

EXERCISES

1. *As a warmup, clear the preceding example of its overdone phrases.*
2. *Revise the following sentences to make them more vivid and dis-*

tinct by replacing as many of the abstract terms as possible with concrete terms.

1. Unhappy because of their lack of recognition, the Wright brothers temporarily quit flying in October, 1905.
2. Of the students who go to college outside their own state, seventy percent do not go back after completing their studies.
3. A sizable proportion of those people who use long-distance movers are large-corporation employees whose moving expenses are entirely underwritten by their companies.
4. His great-grandfather once ran successfully for high public office, but he never served because his opponent mortally wounded him in a gunfight.
5. There was a severe disturbance in Jackson prison one day in the spring—convicts, armed with makeshift weapons, took some of the prison personnel hostage.
6. Her husband had one extramarital relationship after another and finally disappeared with a hotel dining room employee in one of our larger midwestern cities.
7. Rejected by the military because of an impairment of his vision, Ernest became a journalist with a midwestern newspaper.
8. Disadvantaged people are often maltreated by the very social-service agencies ostensibly designed to help them.
9. The newspaper reported that a small foreign car had overturned on the expressway just north of town.
10. The new contract offers almost no change in the fringe-benefit package.

3. *Look up in your dictionary six of the Latin and Greek constituents listed below. Illustrate each with several English derivatives closely translated, as in these two examples:* con (with)—convince (conquer with), conclude (shut with), concur (run with); chron- (time)—chronic (lasting a long time), chronicle (a record of the time), chronometer (time-measurer).

LATIN: *a- (ab-), ad-, ante-, bene-, bi-, circum-, con-, contra-, di- (dis-), e- (ex-), in- (two meanings), inter-, intra-, mal-, multi-, ob-, per-, post-, pre-, pro-, retro-, semi-, sub- (sur-), super-, trans-, ultra-.*

GREEK: *a- (an-), -agogue, allo-, anthropo-, anti-, apo-, arch-, auto-, batho-, bio-, cata-, cephalo-, chron-, -cracy, demo-, dia-, dyna-, dys-, ecto-, epi-, eu-, -gen, geo-, -gon, -gony, graph-, gyn-, hemi-, hepta-, hetero-, hexa-, homo-, hydr-, hyper-, hypo-, log-, mega-, -meter, micro-, mono-, morph-, -nomy, -nym, -pathy, penta-, -phagy, phil-, -phobe (ia), -phone, poly-, pseudo-, psyche-, -scope, soph-, stereo-, sym- (syn-), tele-, tetra-, theo-, thermo-, tri-, zoo-.*

4. *Revise the following sentences so as to clear up the illogical or unnatural connections in their metaphors and similes.*

1. The violent population explosion has paved the way for new intellectual growth.
2. The book causes a shock, like a bucket of icy water suddenly thrown on a fire.

3. The whole social fabric will become unstuck.
4. The tangled web of Jack's business crumbled under its own weight.
5. His last week had mirrored his future, like a hand writing on the wall.
6. The recent economic picture, which seemed to spell prosperity, has wilted beyond repair.
7. They were tickled to death by the thunderous applause.
8. Stream of consciousness fiction has gone out of phase with the new castles in the air of fantasy.
9. The murmured protests drifted from the convention floor to the podium, cracking the facade of his imperturbability.
10. Richard was ecstatic with his success. He had scaled the mountain of difficulties and from here on out he could sail with the breeze.

5. *Write a sentence for each of the following dead metaphors, bringing it to life by adding implied metaphorical detail, as in "She* bridled, *snorting and tossing her mane," or by adding a simile, as in "He was* dead *wrong, laid out like a corpse on a slab."*

dead center, pinned down, sharp as a tack, stick to, whined, purred, reflected, ran for office, yawned, take a course.

6. *Write a sentence for each of the following, in which you allude either humorously or seriously to:*

1. A famous—or infamous—person (Caesar, Napoleon, Barnum, Lincoln, Stalin, Picasso, Bogart)
2. A famous event (the Declaration of Independence, the Battle of Waterloo, the landing on Plymouth Rock, the Battle of the Bulge, the signing of the Magna Carta, Custer's Last Stand, the Watergate break-in)
3. A notable place (Athens, Rome, Paris, London Bridge, Jerusalem, the Vatican)
4. This famous passage from Shakespeare, by quietly borrowing some of its phrases:

> To be, or not to be—that is the question:
> Whether 'tis nobler in the mind to suffer
> The slings and arrows of outrageous fortune,
> Or to take arms against a sea of troubles,
> And by opposing end them.

7. *Write a pararaph in which you mix your diction as effectively as you can, with the big Latin word and the little Anglo-Saxon, the formal word and just the right touch of slang, working in at least two combinations of the extremes, on the pattern of* multitudinous seas, diversionary thrust, incomparable zip, *underlining these for your instructor's convenience.*

8. *Write a* TERRIBLE ESSAY. *Have some fun with this perennial favorite, in which you reinforce your sense for clear, figurative, and meaningful words by writing the muddiest and wordiest essay you can invent, gloriously working out all your bad habits. Organize in the usual way, with a thesis, a good beginning, middle, and end, but parody the worst kind of sociological and bureaucratic prose. Here are the rules:*

1. Put EVERYTHING in the passive voice.
2. Modify nouns *only* with nouns, preferably in strings of three or four, never with adjectives: *governmental spending* becomes *government level spending;* an *excellent idea* becomes *quality program concept.*
3. Use only big abstract nouns—as many *-tion's* as possible.
4. Use no participles: not *dripping faucets* but *faucets which drip;* and use as many *which's* as possible.
5. Use as many words as possible to say the least.
6. Work in as many trite and wordy expressions as possible: *needless to say, all things being equal, due to the fact that, in terms of, as far as that is concerned.*
7. Sprinkle heavily with *-wise*-type and *type*-type expressions, and say *hopefully* every three or four sentences.
8. Compile and use a basic terrible vocabulary: *situation, aspect, function, factor, phase, process, procedure, utilize, the use of,* and so on. The class may well cooperate in this.

9. *Refine your sense of diction and meanings still further by writing an* IRONIC ESSAY, *saying the opposite of what you mean, as in "The party was a dazzling success," "The Rockheads are the solidest group in town," "Our team is the best in the West."*

Research

Now to consolidate and advance. Instead of eight or nine hundred words, you will write three thousand. Instead of a self-propelled debate or independent literary analysis, you will write a scholarly argument. You will also learn to use the library, and to take notes and give footnotes. You will learn the ways of scholarship. You will learn to acknowledge your predecessors as you distinguish yourself, to make not only a bibliography, but a contribution.

The research paper is very likely not what you think it is. *Research* is searching again. You are looking, usually, where others have looked before; but you hope to see something they have not. Research is not combining a paragraph from the *Encyclopaedia Britannica* and a paragraph from *The Book of Knowledge* with a slick pinch from *Time*. That's robbery. Nor is it research even if you carefully change each phrase and acknowledge the source. That's drudgery. Even in some high circles, I am afraid, such scavenging is called research. It is not. It is simply a cloudier condensation of what you have done in school as a "report" — sanctioned plagiarism to teach something about ants or Ankara, a tedious compiling of what is already known. That such material is new to you is not the issue: it is already in the public stock.

CHOOSING YOUR SUBJECT

Pick Something That Interests You.

First get yourself a subject. You need not shake the world. Such subjects as "Subsidized College Football," "Small College Versus Big University," "Excluding the Press from Trials," or the changing valuation of a former best seller well suit the research paper. Bigger subjects, of course, will try your mettle: nuclear power, abortion, federal funding, endangered species as against public need. The whole question of governmental versus private endeavor affords many lively issues for research and decision, perhaps in your own locality and your own local newspaper.

You can stir your own interests and turn up a number of good ideas for research by reading the newspapers — *The Christian Science Monitor* is especially fruitful — and by browsing the current magazines such as *Time, Newsweek, Psychology Today, Scientific American, Atlantic Monthly, Saturday Review*, and many another. Other good sources are interviews on TV, film documentaries, and even arguments in the coffee shop or bar.

Work with a Thesis.

Once you have spotted a subject that interests you, lean toward your inclination about it and write it into a tentative thesis sentence. Though tentative, any stand *for* or *against* will save you time in further searching, and help you establish manageable bounds.

Since you will be dealing mostly with facts in the public stock and with ideas with other people's names on them, what can you do to avoid copycatting? You move from facts and old ideas to new ideas. In other words, you begin by inquiring what is *already* known about a subject, then, as you collect inferences and judgments, you begin to perceive fallacies, to form conclusions of your own, to reinforce or to change your working thesis. Here the range is infinite. Every old idea needs new assertion. Every new assertion needs judgment. Here you are in the area of values, where everyone is in favor of virtue but in doubt about what is virtuous. Your best area of research is in some controversial issue, where you can add, and document, a new judgment of "right" or "wrong." I have put it bluntly to save you from drowning in slips of paper.

Unless you have a working hypothesis to keep your purpose alive as you collect, or at least a clear question to be answered, you may collect forever, forever hoping for a purpose. If you have a thesis, you will learn — and then overcome — the temptations of collecting only the supporting evidence and ignoring the obverse facts and whispers of conscience. If further facts and good arguments persuade you to the other side, so much the better. You will be the stronger for it.

Persuade Your Reader You Are Right.

You do not search primarily for facts. You do not aim to summarize everything ever said on the subject. You aim to persuade your reader that the thesis you believe in is right. You persuade him by (1) letting him see that you have been thoroughly around the subject and that you know what is known of it and thought of it, (2) showing him where the wrongs are wrong, and (3) citing the rights as right. *Your* opinion, *your* thesis, is what you are showing; all your quotations from all the authorities in the world are subservient to *your* demonstration. You are the reigning authority. You have, for the moment, the longest perspective and the last word. So, pick a thesis, and move into the library.

USING THE LIBRARY

Start with the Encyclopedias.

Find the *Encyclopaedia Britannica*, and you are well on your way. The *Britannica* will survey your subject and guide you to your sources. It is not, usually, a basic source in itself, but each article will refer you, at the end, to several authorities. If someone's initials appear at the end, look them up in the contributors' list. The author of the article is an authority himself; you should mention him in your paper, and also look him up to see what books he has written on the subject. Furthermore, the contributors' list will name several works, which will swell your bibliography and aid your research. The index will also refer you to data scattered through all the volumes. Under "Medicine," for instance, it directs you to such topics as "Academies," "Hypnotism," "Licensing," "Mythology," and so on. The *Encyclopedia Americana, Collier's Encyclopedia,* and *Chambers's Encyclopaedia,* though less celebrated, will here and there challenge *Britannica's* reign, and the one-volume *Columbia Encyclopedia* is a fine shorter reference.

The World Almanac and Book of Facts, a paperbacked lode of news and statistics (issued yearly since 1868), can provide a factual nugget for almost any subject. Other good ones are *Webster's Biographical Dictionary* and *Webster's New Geographical Dictionary;* their concise entries lead quickly to thousands of people and places. And don't overlook the atlases: *The Times Atlas of the World, The National Atlas of the United States.* Another treasure-trove is *The Oxford English Dictionary* (twelve volumes and supplement—abbreviated

OED in footnotes), which gives the date a word, like *highwayman*, first appeared in print, and traces changing usages through the years.

Explore your library's reference works. You will find many encyclopedias, outlines, atlases, and dictionaries providing more intensive coverage than the general works on the arts, history, philosophy, literature, the social sciences, the natural sciences, business, and the technologies. Instructors in subjects you may be exploring can guide you to the best references.

Next Find the Card Catalog.

The catalog's 3 × 5 cards list all the library's holdings — books, magazines, newspapers, atlases — and alphabetize (1) authors, (2) publications, and (3) general subjects, from *A* to *Z*. You will find *John Adams* and *The Anatomy of Melancholy* and *Atomic Energy*, in that order, in the *A* drawers. Page 98 illustrates the three kinds of cards (filed alphabetically) on which the card catalog will list the same book — by author, by subject, and by title.

You will notice that the bottom of the card shows the Library of Congress's cataloging number (Q175.W6517) and the number from the older, but still widely used, Dewey Decimal System (501). Your library will use one or the other to make its own "call number," typed in the upper left hand corner of its cards — the number you will put on your slip when you sign out the book.

Learn the Catalog's Inner Arrangements.

Since some alphabetical entries run on, drawer after drawer — *New York City, New York State, New York Times*, for instance — knowing the arrangements *within* these entries will help you find your book.

1.   Not only men and women but organizations and institutions can be "authors" if they publish books or magazines.

> **Parke, Davis & Company, Detroit**
> **The University of Michigan**
> **U.S. Department of State**

2.   Initial *A, An, The*, and their foreign equivalents (*Ein, El, Der, Une*, and so forth) are ignored in alphabetizing a title: *A Long Day in a Short Life* is alphabetized under *L*. But French surnames are treated as if they were one word: *De la Mare* as if *Delamare, La Rochefoucauld* as if *Larochefoucauld*.

3.   Cards are usually alphabetized *word by word: Stock Market* comes before *Stockard* and *Stockbroker*. "Short before long" is an-

CATALOG CARDS

LIBRARY OF CONGRESS MODEL

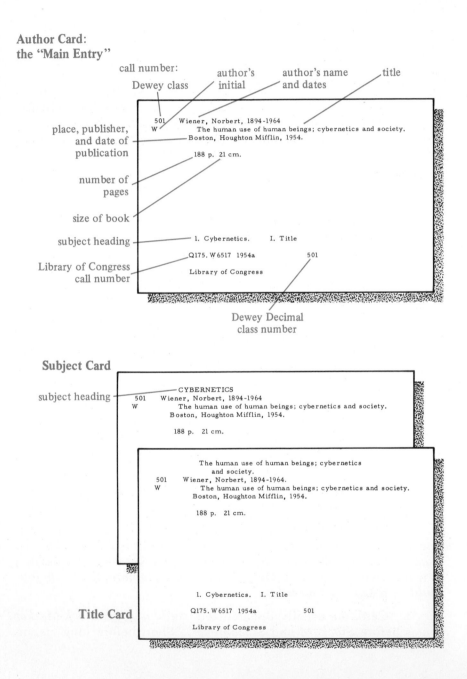

**Author Card:
the "Main Entry"**

call number:
Dewey class · author's initial · author's name and dates · title

place, publisher, and date of publication

number of pages

size of book

subject heading

Library of Congress call number

> 501 Wiener, Norbert, 1894-1964
> W   The human use of human beings; cybernetics and society.
>   Boston, Houghton Mifflin, 1954.
>
>   188 p. 21 cm.
>
>
>   1. Cybernetics.   I. Title
>
>   Q175. W 6517 1954a   501
>
>   Library of Congress

Dewey Decimal class number

Subject Card

subject heading

> CYBERNETICS
> 501 Wiener, Norbert, 1894-1964
> W   The human use of human beings; cybernetics and society.
>   Boston, Houghton Mifflin, 1954.
>
>   188 p.   21 cm.

Title Card

> The human use of human beings; cybernetics and society.
> 501 Wiener, Norbert, 1894-1964.
> W   The human use of human beings; cybernetics and society.
>   Boston, Houghton Mifflin, 1954.
>
>   188 p.   21 cm.
>
>
>
>   1. Cybernetics.   I. Title
>
>   Q175. W 6517 1954a   501
>
>   Library of Congress

other way of putting it, meaning that *Stock* and all its combinations with separate words precede the longer words beginning with *Stock-*. Whether a compound word is one or two makes the apparent disorder. Hyphenations are treated as two words. The sequence would run thus:

> **Stock**
> **Stock-Exchange Rulings**
> **Stock Market**
> **Stockard**

4. Cards on one subject are arranged alphabetically by author. Under *Anatomy*, for instance, you will run from "Abernathy, John" to "Yutzy, Simon Menno," and then suddenly run into a title—*An Anatomy of Conformity*—which happens to be the next large alphabetical item after the subject *Anatomy*.

·5. Identical names are arranged in the order (a) person, (b) titles and places, as they fall alphabetically.

> **Washington, Booker T.**
> **Washington, George**
> **Washington (State)**
> **Washington, University of**
> **Washington, D.C.**
> *Washington Square* **[by Henry James]**

"Washington," the state, precedes the other "Washingtons" because "State" (which appears on the card only in parentheses) is not treated as part of its name. The University of Washington precedes "Washington, D.C." because no words or letters actually follow the "Washington" of its title.

6. Since *Mc, M',* and *Mac* are all filed as if they were *Mac*, they go by the letter following them: *M'Coy, McDermott, Machinery, MacKenzie.*

7. Other abbreviations are also filed as if spelled out: *Dr. Zhivago* would be filed as if beginning with *Doctor; St. Joan* as if with *Saint; Mrs. Miniver* as if with *Mistress*—except that many libraries now alphabetize *Mr.* and *Mrs.* as spelled, and *Ms.* has found its place in the alphabetizing.

8. Saints, popes, kings, and people are filed, in that order, by name and not by appellation (do not look under *Saint* for St. Paul, nor under *King* for King Henry VIII). The order would be:

> **Paul, Saint**
> **Paul VI, Pope**
> **Paul I, Emperor of Russia**
> **Paul, Jean**

9.   An author's books are filed first by collected works, then by individual titles. Different editions of the same title follow chronologically. Books *about* an author follow the books *by* him.

That is the system. Now you can thumb through the cards filed under your subject — "Cancer," or "Television," or "Melville" — to see what books your library has on it, and you can look up any authorities your encyclopedia has mentioned. Two or three of the most recent books will probably give you all you want, because each of these will refer you, by footnote and bibliography, to important previous works.

Find the Indexes to Periodicals and Newspapers.

Indexes to periodicals do for articles what the card catalog does for books. Some index by subjects only, others by subjects and authors. Begin with the *Reader's Guide to Periodical Literature* — an index of articles (and portraits and poems) in more than one hundred magazines. Again, take the most recent issue, look up your subject, and make yourself a bibliographical card for each title — spelling out the abbreviations of titles and dates according to the key just inside the cover. If you don't spell them out fully, your cards may be mysteries to you when you sit down to write. You can drop back a few issues and years to collect more articles; and if your subject belongs to the recent past (after 1907), you can drop back to the right year and track your subject forward. (*Poole's Index to Periodical Literature* provides similar guidance to American and English periodicals from 1802 to 1906.)

You can do the same with the *New York Times Index*, beginning with 1913. It will probably lead you to news that appeared in any paper. The *Social Sciences Index* and the *Humanities Index* do for scholarly journals what the *Reader's Guide* does for the popular ones. (These two *Indexes* were the *International Index* [until 1965] and the *Social Sciences and Humanities Index* [until 1974].) If you are searching for an essay that may be in a book rather than a magazine, your guide is the *Essay and General Literature Index*. Add to these the *Book Review Digest* (since 1905), the *Biography Index* (which nicely collects scattered references), and the *Current Biography Index*, and you will probably need no more. But if you should need more, consult Constance M. Winchell's *Guide to Reference Books*, which is also a valuable guide to encyclopedias and dictionaries.

MAKING YOUR CARDS

Before you start toward the library, get some 3 × 5 cards for your bibliography. Plan on some ten or fifteen sources for your three thousand words of text. As you pick up an author or two, and some titles, start a bibliographical card for each: *one card for each title*. Leave space to the left to put in the call number later, and space at the top for a label of your own, if needed. Put the author (last name first) on one line, and the title of his work on the next, leaving space to fill in the details of publication when you get to the work itself—for books, place of publication, publisher, and date; for magazine articles, volume number, date, and pages. Italicize (that is, underscore) titles of books and magazines; put titles of articles *within* books and magazines in quotation marks. The card catalog will supply the call numbers, and much of the other publishing data you need; but check and complete all your publishing data when you finally get the book or magazine in your hands, putting a light ✔ in pencil to assure yourself that your card is authoritative, that quotations are word for word and all your publishing data accurate, safe to check your finished paper against. Get the author's name as it appears on the title page, adding details in brackets, if helpful: Smith, D[elmar] P[rince]. Get all the information, to save repeated trips to the library. The completed cards and bibliography with our sample paper (pp. 116 and 128–29) will show you what you need.

Take Brief Notes.

Some people abhor putting notes on bibliographical cards. A separate card for bibliography and other cards for notes—written only on one side for ease of manipulation and viewing—are certainly more orderly and thorough. But the economy of taking notes directly on biographical cards is, I have found, well worth the slight clutter. Limiting yourself to what you can put on the front and back of one bibliographical card will restrain your notes to the sharp and manageable. You can always add another note card if you must. If you find one source offering a number of irresistible quotations, put each one separately on a 3 × 5 card (with author's name on each), so you can rearrange them later for writing.

However you do it, keep your notes brief. Read quickly, with an eye for the general idea and the telling point. Holding a clear thesis in mind will guide and limit your note taking. Some of your sources will need no more than the briefest summary: "Violently opposed, recommends complete abolition." This violent and undistinguished author will appear in your paper only among several others in a single footnote to one of your sentences: "Opposition, of course, has been tenacious and emphatic.[2]"

Suppose you are writing a paper recommending a shift from nuclear to solar power (as the student in our sample did, pp. 114–29). You find that Edmund Faltermayer favors nuclear power. Here is a perfect piece of opposition, a *con*, to set your thesis against, to explain and qualify. But don't copy too much. Summarize the author's point, jot down some facts you might use, and copy down directly, within distinct quotation marks, only the most quotable phrase: "The system *did* stick together" (see the second note card in our sample, p. 116).

Take care with page numbers. When your passage runs from one page to the next—from 29 over onto 30, for instance—put "(29–30)" after it, *but also mark the exact point where the page changed.* You might want to use only part of the passage and then be uncertain as to which of the pages contained it. An inverted L-bracket and the number "30" after the last word of page 29, will do nicely: "All had⌐30 occurred earlier." Do the same even when the page changes in mid-word with a hyphen: "having con-⌐21 vinced no one."

When preparing a research paper on a piece of literature, you would also make a bibliographical card for the edition you are using, and would probably need a number of note cards for summaries and quotations from the work itself—one card for each item, for convenience in sorting.

Take Care Against Plagiarism.

If you borrow an idea, footnote your source. If you have an idea of your own and then discover that someone has beaten you to it, swallow your disappointment and footnote your predecessor. Or you can get back some of your own by saying, in a footnote, "I discover that James Smith agrees with me on this point," explaining, if possible, what Smith has overlooked, or his differing emphasis, and again giving a full citation of Smith's article for all future reference. A danger lies in copying out phrases from your source as you summarize what it says, and then incorporating them in your essay, without remembering that those phrases are not yours. The solution is, again, to take down and mark quotations accurately in your notes, to summarize succinctly *in your own words,* as far away from the original as possible, and always to credit your sources.

YOUR FIRST DRAFT

Plot Your Course.

Formal outlines, especially those made too early in the game, can take more time than they are worth, but a long paper with notes demands some planning. First, draft a beginning paragraph, incorporating your thesis. Then read through your notes, arranging them roughly in the order you think you will use them, getting the opposition off the street first. If your thesis is strongly argumentative, you can sort into three piles: *pro's, con's,* and *in-between's* (often simple facts).

Now, by way of outline, you can simply make three or four general headings on a sheet of paper, with ample space between, in which you can jot down your sources in the order, *pro* and *con*, that is best for your argument. Our paper on energy would block out something like this:

I. The nuclear problems

<table>
<tr><td>PRO</td><td>CON</td></tr>
<tr><td></td><td>Nuclear power sufficient
  Putnam
  Thirring
  Bailey
  Teller
  "Energy Crisis"--
    Seaborg</td></tr>
<tr><td>"Energy Crisis"--Nader
Pollution
Waste and breeders
L. J. Carter
Clark</td><td></td></tr>
<tr><td></td><td>Breeders produce renew-
  able fuel
  Faltermayer
  Rickard
  Nuplexes
  Fusion
  Synthetic fossil fuels</td></tr>
</table>

II. But solar power is both re-
    newable and safe
      Bolton--electricity
      Windmills, etc.
      Gasohol
      Van Geldern--methane
      Commoner
        Gas pipelines vs. electric
         networks
        Methane for power and heat
        Cogenerators
        Economy

Outline More Fully, If You Wish.

You can easily refine this rough blocking into a full topic outline, one that displays your points logically, not necessarily in the actual sequence of your writing. The principle of outlining is to rank equivalent headings — keeping your headings all as nouns, or noun phrases, to make the ranks apparent. You simply mark heads and subheads by alternating numbers and letters as you proceed downhill, from roman numeral *I* through capital *A* to arabic *1* and lowercase *a*, until you reach, if you need them, parenthesized *(1)* and *(a)*, and even lowercase roman numerals, *i, ii, iii,* as your very smallest subdivisions. You indent equal heads equally, aligning equivalents under equivalents, roman under roman, capital under capital, and so on. Every *A* should have its *B*, at least; and every *1* its *2*. If you have just a single heading, drop it, or absorb it into the larger heading above it.

But, *begin to write soon.* You have already begun to write, of course, in getting your thesis down on paper, and then drafting a first paragraph to hold it. Now that you have blocked out your argument, however roughly, plunge into your first draft.

Put In Your References As You Go.

Your first draft should have all your footnotes, abbreviated, right in the text. Otherwise you will lose your place, and go mad with numbers. Put the notes at the *end* of the last pertinent sentence. Make your quotations in full, all distinctly set within quotation marks, and include the author's surname and the page number with each citation. You will change these in your final draft, of course, filling in the names or leaving them out of the note altogether if they appear in the text. But it will help you in checking against your cards to have an author's name and a page number for each citation. *Don't number your footnotes yet.* When your draft is finished, add the numbers in pencil, so you can change them; circle them in red pencil, so you can see them. As you type along, mark your footnotes with triple parentheses: (((. . .)))—the easiest distinction you can make. Our student's first draft would look like this:

```
Plutonium is lethal for 250,000 years, even though,

according to the heading of one of Faltermayer's

charts, "With Reactor Wastes, the Worst Is Over in

Six Centuries"--only six hundred years of threaten-

ing disaster after each new burial. (((Faltermayer,

"Burying Nuclear Trash Where It Will Stay Put,"

Fortune, 26 Mar. 1979, p. 102.))) Although breathing

plutonium dust is lethal, . . .
```

YOUR FINAL DRAFT

Reset Your Long Quotations.

Your final draft will change in many ways, as the rewriting polishes up your phrases and turns up new and better ideas. But some changes are merely in presentation. The triple parentheses of your first draft will disappear, along with the quotation marks around the *long* quotations, since you will single-space and indent, *without quotation marks,* all quotations of more than fifty words, to simulate the appearance of a printed page. You will do the same with shorter quotations, if you want to give them special emphasis, and also with passages of poetry. If your quotation begins as a paragraph, indent its first line farther, to reproduce the paragraphing. Check the rules about quotation marks on pp. 160–63.

Allow Spaces for Notes at the Foot of the Page.

Some instructors like footnotes gathered all together in a section at the end, as they would be in a manuscript prepared for the printer. But many prefer them at the foot, where the reader can see them, as if on a printed page. From your preliminary draft, you can see about how many footnotes will fall on your page, and about how much space to allow at the bottom. Allow plenty. You will begin your notes three spaces below your text (you have been double-spacing your text). Do *not* type a solid line between text and notes: this indicates a footnote continued from the preceding page. Single-space each note, but double-space between notes. Indent as for a paragraph. Type the number, then roll down about half the height of a capital letter and type your note:

[11] Faltermayer, pp. 102, 104.

After the first line, notes return to the left margin, as in paragraphs.

Footnotes carry only information not mentioned in the text. At first mention in text or note, give your author's full name, in normal order—"Edmund Faltermayer"—and use only his last name thereafter. (Your alphabetized bibliography will give last name first.) If your text names the author, the note carries only the title of his work, the publishing data, and the page number. If your text names the author and his work, the note carries only the publishing data and the page number. Once you have cited a source, you can put the page numbers of further citations directly into your text, within parentheses. Note, in the first example on the next page, where the quotation marks go and how the period, or comma, *follows* the parenthesis.

Faltermayer points out that even in the na-

tion's worst nuclear accident "the system <u>did</u> stick

together" (p. 114).

Faltermayer (p. 114) believes safeguards are

adequate.

At the end of a long indented, single-spaced quotation from a work already cited, the page number in parentheses *follows* the period (see the inset quotations in our sample paper):

. . . and the people in it. (p. 52)

Make and Punctuate Your Footnotes Meticulously.

The three principal kinds of references produce three forms of footnotes:

BOOK

[1] Hans Thirring, <u>Energy for Man: Windmills to Nuclear Power</u> (Bloomington, Indiana: Indiana University Press, 1958), p. 391.

QUARTERLY MAGAZINE

[2] Fritz Seitz, "Now or Never: Solar Alternatives," <u>The New World Quarterly</u>, 40 (1981), 548–49.

When giving the volume number, "40," you omit the "p." or "pp." before page numbers, which I prefer in full. If you choose to abbreviate them, do it thus: "548–49," not "548–9"; "27–29," not "27–9"; but "107–8," not "107–08." Convert all Roman volume numbers into Arabic: "XL" becomes "40."

POPULAR MAGAZINE OR NEWSPAPER

[3] Norman R. Collins, "More Frenzied Solutions," <u>News Chronicle</u>, 20 Apr. 1975, p. 4.

Ignore volume number, if any. As in this last example, give the full date for a popular magazine, instead of volume number and year, and *use no parentheses.* Newspaper articles sometimes need more detail:

> [4] "The Trouble with Atoms" (editorial), <u>New York Times</u>, 10 Apr. 1984, sec. 4, p. 8.

Notice the comma here: omitted after "Atoms" and inserted after the parenthesis. Do the same with any parenthetical explanation of a title. With this newspaper, you need to give the section number because each section begins numbering anew.

Here are some further complications:

A quotation from a quotation

> [5] Abraham B. Caldwell, "The Case for Steam," <u>American Questioner</u>, 20 June 1979, p. 37, quoted in Albert N. Mendenhall, <u>Modern Commentary</u> (Princeton: Little House, 1979), p. 308.

You have found the quotation in Mendenhall's book.

Multiple authorship

> [6] Corwin L. Rickard and Richard C. Dahlberg, "Nuclear Power: A Balanced Approach," <u>Science</u>, 10 Nov. 1978, p. 582.

Multiple authorship simply follows the printed order of the names (not in an alphabetical rearrangement).

Article in edited collection

> [7] D. C. Hill, "Who Is Communicating What?" in <u>Essays for Study</u>, ed. James L. McDonald and Leonard P. Doan (New York: Appleton Hall, 1973), p. 214; reprinted from <u>Era</u>, 12 (1972).

McDonald and Doan have edited the collection, or casebook. A title ending in a question mark should not take a comma.

Series of books

> [8] David R. Small, "The Telephone and Urbanization," in <u>Annals of American Communication</u>, ed. Walter Beinholt (Boston: Large, Green and Co., 1969), III, 401.

The *Annals of American Communication* is a series of bound books, not a magazine: the volume number is in Roman numerals, and it *follows* the parenthesis. Had this been a magazine, the entry would have omitted the "in," the editor, and the place of publication, to read ". . . *Annals of American Communication*, 3 (1969), 401."

Selection in encyclopedia

> [9] Arnold Peters, "Medicine," <u>Encyc. Brit.</u>: <u>Macropaedia</u>, 1979 ed.

Abbreviate familiar titles, so long as they remain clear. You need neither volume nor page numbers in alphabetized encyclopedias; and only the number (*or* the year of publication) of the edition you are citing, without parentheses. Here the article was initialed "A.P.," and you have looked up the author's name in the contributor's list.

^{10}"Prunes," Encyc. Brit., 11th ed.

Here the article was not initialed.

Single and
double
quotation
marks
^{11}George L. Gillies, "Robert Herrick's 'Corinna,'" Speculation, 2 (1881), 490.

This citation (purely hypothetical) shows where to put the comma when the title of a magazine article ends in a quotation, and you have to use both single and double quotation marks. Gillies's original title would have looked like this: Robert Herrick's "Corinna."

A "classical"
play
^{12}Romeo and Juliet II.iii.94, in An Essential Shakespeare, ed. Russell Fraser (New York: Prentice-Hall, 1972).

Note the absence of the comma after the play's title, and the periods and close spacing between Act.scene.line. Subsequent references would go directly in your text within parentheses: "(IV.iii.11–12)." Or, if you are quoting several of Shakespeare's plays: "(*Romeo* IV.iii.11–12)." See further instructions below (p. iii).

Omitted
details
^{13}P[aul] F[riedrich] Schwartz, A Quartet of Thoughts (New York: Appleton Hall, 1943), p. 7.

^{14}[George H. Lewes], "Percy Bysshe Shelley," Westminster Review, 35 (April 1841), 303–44.

These two footnotes show how to use brackets to add details not actually appearing in the published work. Of course, famous initials are kept as initials, as with T. S. Eliot, H. G. Wells, or D. H. Lawrence. You also need brackets to replace parentheses when your comments in a footnote require a parenthesis around your entire source:

Brackets
^{15}. . . (cited in John E. Basset, William Faulkner: An Annotated Checklist of Criticism [New York: David Lewis, 1972], p. 35).

Pamphlets and other oddities just require common sense:

^{16}"The Reading Problem," mimeographed pamphlet, Concerned Parents Committee, Center City, Arkansas, 25 Dec. 1975, p. 8.

^{17}U. S. Congress, House Committee on Health, Education, and Welfare, Racial Integration, 101st

Cong., 2nd sess., 1969, H. Rep. 391 to accompany H. R. 6128, pp. 16–22.

You must play such pamphlets by instinct, including all the details, briefly, that would help someone else hunt them down.

Recordings, films, and tapes also require some ingenuity. Do not cite microfilms and other reproductions of things in print. Simply cite the book, article, or newspaper as if you had it in hand. But other media are forms of publication in themselves, to be cited as clearly as possible if you use them. The American Library Association recommends the following ways of citation.*

DISC

18 Eugene O'Neill, Long Day's Journey into Night [Sound Recording] (Caedmon, [1972], 3 discs TRS350), Disc 3, Side 2.

CASSETTE

19 "Ree-deep, ribbid": Herpetologist Charles Bogard Studies the Frog and Its Call [Sound Recording] (Center for Cassette Studies, 1971), Cassette 010 13460.

Other non-print items follow the same pattern, with the square brackets containing "[Motion Picture]" or "[Filmstrip]" to indicate the kind.

These examples, together with the footnotes in our sample research paper, should cover most footnoting problems, or suggest how you can meet them.

Abbreviate Your References After the First Full Citation.

Three old favorite abbreviations are now mercifully out of style. DO NOT USE:

ibid. —*ibidem* ("in the same place"), meaning the title cited in the note directly before. Instead, USE THE AUTHOR'S LAST NAME, AND GIVE THE PAGE.

loc. cit. —*loco citato* ("in the place cited"). SIMPLY REPEAT THE PAGE NUMBER.

op. cit. —*opere citato* ("in the work cited"), meaning a title

---

* Eugene B. Fleischer, *Style Manual for Citing Microform and Nonprint Media* (Chicago: American Library Association, 1978).

referred to again after other notes have intervened. Again, USE THE AUTHOR'S LAST NAME INSTEAD, AND GIVE THE PAGE: "Wald, p. 97."

If you have two Walds, simply include their initials. If Wald has two articles or books on nuclear power, devise two convenient short titles for subsequent references:

> 2 Wald, <u>Reactors</u>, p. 97.
>
> 3 Wald, "Waste," p. 301.

Two are still used and especially useful (do *not* italicize them):

cf.—*confer* ("bring together," or "compare"); do not use for "see."

et al.—*et alii* ("and others"); does not mean "and all"; use after the first author in multiple authorships. "Ronald Elkins et al."

Two more Latin terms, also not italicized, are equally handy:

passim—(not an abbreviation, but a Latin word meaning "throughout the work; here and there") use when a writer makes the same point in many places within a single work; use also for statistics you have compiled from observations and tables scattered throughout his work.

sic—a Latin word meaning "so"; "this is so"; always in brackets—[sic]—because used only within quotations following some mispelling or other surprising detail to show that it really was there, was "so" in the original, and that the mistake is not yours.

Other useful abbreviations for footnotes are:

c. or ca.	*circa*, "about" (c. 1709)
Ch., Chs.	chapter, chapters
ed.	edited by, edition, editor
f., ff.	and the following page, pages
l., ll.	line, lines
ms., mss.	manuscript, manuscripts
n.d.	no date given
n.p.	no place of publication given
p., pp.	page, pages
rev.	revised
sec., secs.	section, sections
tr., trans.	translated by
vol., vols.	volume, volumes

A footnote using some of these might go like this (you have already fully cited Weiss and Dillon):

16 See Donald Allenberg et al., <u>Population in
Early New England</u> (Boston: Large, Green and Co.,
1974), pp. 308ff.; cf. Weiss, p. 60. Dillon,
passim, takes a position even more conservative than
Weiss's. See also A. H. Hawkins ed., <u>Statistical
Surveys</u> (Chicago: Nonesuch Press, 1960; rev. 1973),
pp. 71–83 and Ch. 10. Records sufficient for broad
comparisons begin only ca. 1850.

Abbreviate Books of the Bible, Even the First Time.

The Bible and its books, though capitalized as ordinary titles, are
never italicized. Biblical references go directly into your text, within
parentheses — no footnote, no commas, *lowercase* Roman numerals for
chapter, Arabic for verse: "Mark xvi.6"; "Jer. vi.24"; "II Sam.
xviii.33." No comma — only a space — separates name from numbers;
periods separate the numbers, *with no spacing*. The dictionary gives
the accepted abbreviations: Gen., Exod., Lev., Deut. Make biblical
references like this (the first two are indirect quotations):

There is still nothing new under the sun (Eccl. i.9);

man still does not live by bread alone (Matt. iv.4).

As Ecclesiastes tells us, "there is no new thing

under the sun" (i.9).

Abbreviate Plays and Long Poems After the First Time.

Handle plays and long poems like biblical citations, after an initial footnote that identifies the edition (see p. 108). Italicize the title
(underscore the title with your typewriter): "*Merch.* II.iv.72–75" (this
is *The Merchant of Venice*, Act II, Scene iv, lines 72–75); "*Caesar*
V.iii.6," "*Ham.* I.i.23," "*Iliad* IX.93," "*P.L.* IV.918" (*Paradise Lost*,
Book IV, line 918). Use the numbers alone if you have already mentioned the title, or have clearly implied it, as in repeated quotations
from the same work.

Match Your Bibliography to Your Footnotes.

When your paper is finally typed, arrange the cards of the works
cited in your footnotes in alphabetical order (by authors' last names or,
with anonymous works, by first words of titles — ignoring initial *The*,
A, or *An*). You will not have used all your notes, nor all the articles you

have carded. In typing your bibliography, pass over them in decent silence. *Include no work not specifically cited.* Your bibliographical entries will be just like your footnotes except that (1) you will put the author's last name first; (2) you will give the total span of pages for magazine articles — none at all for books; (3) you will reverse indentation so that the author's name will stand out; and (4) you will punctuate differently — putting periods after the alphabetized name, the title, and (no parentheses) the book's place and date of publication, with two letter-spaces after each period. See the bibliography concluding our sample paper (p. 128). Here are some special cases:

Article in edited collection

> Hill, D. C.   "Who Is Communicating What?" in <u>Essays</u>
> <u>for Study</u>, ed. James L. McDonald and Leonard P.
> Doan.   New York: Appleton Hall, 1973.   Pp. 211-
> 19.   Reprinted from <u>Era</u>, 12 (1972), 9-18.

Notice the capitalized "Pp. 211–219." Since this article is in a book, the publishing data have required a period after "1973." When listing other works by the same author, use a solid line (your underscorer) and a period:

More than one entry for same author

> Jones, Bingham.   <u>The Kinescopic Arts and Sciences</u>.
> Princeton: Little House, 1970.

> _____.   "Television and Vision: The Case
> for Governmental Control." <u>Independent Review</u>, 7
> (1969), 18-31.

Alphabetize by the name of the *author*, not the editor of collections.

Author in collection

> Small, David R.   "The Telephone and Urbanization,"
> in <u>Annals of American Communication</u>, ed. Walter
> Beinholt.   Boston: Large, Green and Co., 1969.
> III, 398-407.

But alphabetize by the name of the editor, when you have referred to his Introduction and notes:

Editor cited

> Cowley, Malcolm.   <u>The Portable Hawthorne</u>, ed., with
> Introduction and Notes.   New York: Viking Press,
> 1948.

With two or more authors, alphabetize by the first author's last name, but keep the other names in normal order.

Multiple authorship

> Rankin, Claude P., Bliss Brooke, and Alice Q. Adams.
> <u>A Statistical Approach to Poverty</u>.   Quincy,
> Mass.: Quantum, Inc., 1983.

Alphabetize by the first significant word in anonymous works ("Trouble" in the first example following):

Anonymous works

"The Trouble with Atoms." Editorial. <u>New York Times</u>, 10 Apr. 1984, sec. 4, p. 8.

<u>Valley Forge</u> [Motion Picture]. (New York: Steve Krantz Productions. Released by Encyclopaedia Britannica Educational Corp., 1972).

For the most part, I have followed the 1977 edition of *The MLA Handbook for Writers of Research Papers, Theses, and Dissertations* (compiled by the Modern Language Association of America), describing the customs for work in literature and the humanities. The social and natural sciences use slightly different conventions. An article would look like this in a botanical bibliography (no quotation marks, no parentheses, fewer capitals):

Entry in scientific bibliography

Mann, K. H. 1973. Seaweeds: their productivity and strategy for growth. <u>Science</u> 182:975–81.

This article might be cited in the text as (Mann, 1973); or simply as, say, (14), if the bibliographic entries are not alphabetized but numbered (for example, "14. K. H. Mann, *Science.* 182:975–81" — title of article omitted). Footnotes would be reserved for the author's additional comments. For papers in the social and natural sciences, consult your instructor about the correct style, or style manual, to follow.

A good general manual is the current edition of Kate L. Turabian, *A Manual for Writers of Term Papers, Theses, and Dissertations* (Chicago and London: The University of Chicago Press). A larger reference popular with scholars is *A Manual of Style* (the "Chicago Style Manual"), also published by the University of Chicago Press.

SAMPLE RESEARCH PAPER

Here is a sample, a student's complete research paper, to show what the final product can look like. The ongoing national debate about energy led him to the *Encyclopaedia Britannica* for a survey of the subject. The most recent *Reader's Guide* and *Social Sciences Index* soon gave him more than enough articles — a virtual flood to choose from. The card catalog, under "Energy," gave him almost as many books in as short a time. When he talked over his project, I referred him to several articles more. He had already made a working thesis favoring solar power. He found his specific answer in Barry Commoner's article, roughed out a pro-and-con strategy as he sorted his cards (setting about half of them aside not to be used at all), and started his first draft.

To convey an idea of the process, I have shown bibliographical cards with notes corresponding to the footnotes on page 1 of the finished paper. This paper follows the conventional format: title page with outline (unnumbered if one page, numbered with Roman numerals if more than one page); double-spaced text with single-spaced footnotes, each page except the first numbered in Arabic at the top; and the bibliography at the end, on a separate page or pages. Our paper combines title page with outline; perhaps more common is a separate title page. To set up a separate title page, center the title on the width of the page somewhat above the middle and the other elements — name, designation of course, instructor's name, date — below as shown:

Renewable Energy:

The Imperative Choice

Edwin W. Greenspan

[12 to 15 lines of space]

English 123

Mr. Baker

June 10, 1980

Our bibliography is alphabetized by authors' last names or by titles when the author is unknown or anonymous. Keeping this alphabetization for each group, you can divide a longer bibliography into *primary sources* — works of literature, historical documents, scientific tables, letters, and so on — and *secondary sources*, or works *about* your subject.

Edwin W. Greenspan
English 123
Mr. Baker
June 10, 1980

Renewable Energy: The Imperative Choice

<u>Thesis</u>: To solve the energy crisis, America must shift from nu-

clear power to a system based on a renewable source of

natural solar energy--methane gas.

Topic outline
I. Nuclear power
  A. Present dependence
    1. Output
    2. Risks
      a. Accidents
      b. Radioactive wastes
  B. Breeder reactors
    1. Renewability
    2. Risks
      a. Accidents
      b. Radioactive wastes
      c. Theft by terrorists
  C. Nuclear fusion
    1. Prospects
    2. Risks

II. Solar power
  A. Varieties
    1. Direct collectors
    2. Indirect collectors
      a. Wind and water
      b. Trees and plants
      c. Derived gases
        i. hydrogen
        ii. methane
  B. Methane versus central electric power
    1. Cogenerators
    2. Pipelines
      a. Present system
      b. Storage
      c. Economy

ALL ON
ONE SIDE

H-825   _Fortune_ editorial
          "It's Time to End the Holy War
          Over Nuclear Power" (editorial),
          Fortune, 12 Mar. 1979, p. 81.

12.5% electricity from 72 nuclear plants.
126 more are ordered or being built—with
these, by mid or late '80's, 25% electricity
from nuclear.
"Around Chicago, and in parts of New England
and the Southwest, atomic plants provide
about half of the electric power."

FRONT

H-825   Faltermayer, Edmund
          "Nuclear Power After Three Mile
          Island," _Fortune_, 7 May 1979,
          114-18, 120-22.

Three Mile Island on Mar. 28, 1979:
"The system _did_ stick together." (114)

France is speeding up to reach 50% nuclear
electricity by 1985. (114)

U.S. has 500-yr. supply of coal. (117)
Coal may heat up atmosphere (118), and

BACK

nuclear power remains cheaper. (120)

For plants already built—with rising
construction costs—nuclear power
comes out 2% cheaper than coal. (122)

Renewable Energy: The Imperative Choice

Opener   A battered car, its fender dangling, races its motor at

the stoplight. As the light changes, it roars away in a squeal

of rubber and a cloud of blue smoke. The next car accelerates

Narrowing to slowly and quietly to a moderate speed. Someone, at least, is
thesis

trying to save energy, a problem increasingly on the public

conscience through newspapers, magazines, and television. Some

say there is no crisis; others, that nuclear power will save us.

But most people seem to agree that we must eventually rely on

the sun. For a lasting solution to the energy crisis, America

must shift from nuclear power to a system based on renewable

sources of natural solar energy.

Opening   In spite of the nuclear disaster pictured in The China
contra:
nuclear power Syndrome and threatened at Three Mile Island, Pennsylvania, on

March 28, 1979, 72 nuclear generators still supply 12.5 percent

Specific of America's electricity--about 50 percent around Chicago and
evidence

in some parts of New England and the Southwest--and 126 more nu-

clear generators are either under construction or ordered, which

will increase the nuclear output of electricity to 25 percent by

More the middle 1980's.[1] Edmund Faltermayer notes with approval that
specifics:
citing an France is speeding nuclear construction to produce 50 percent of
authority

its electricity by 1985, and he remains positive even after

Three Mile Island: after all, he writes, "the system did stick

together."[2] After more than twenty years of operation, no one

Unsigned   [1]"It's Time to End the Holy War Over Nuclear Power" (edi-
editorial torial), Fortune, 12 Mar. 1979, p. 81.

Author named [2]"Nuclear Power After Three Mile Island," Fortune, 7 May
in text 1979, p. 114.

2

Summarizing
paraphrase

has yet been killed or injured in a nuclear plant. In spite of
soaring prices for construction and safety, says Faltermayer, nuclear power will still be two percent cheaper than coal, which is
not only dirtier but may dangerously heat up the atmosphere.[3]

More nuclear
contra:
historical
background

This positive view of nuclear energy is not new. In 1953,
Palmer C. Putnam worked out for the Atomic Energy Commission a
detailed estimate of the world's conventional sources of energy
for the next 150 years in terms of consumption per capita.[4] The
picture became statistically obvious. Gas and oil will run out
soon in the next century, but coal will outlast them by a great
distance before its end--in about five hundred years, in Faltermayer's later estimate (p. 117). Wind, water, and other means

Citing more
authorities

can carry only a little of the load. In 1958, Hans Thirring sur-
veyed the problem even more closely in Energy for Man: Windmills
to Nuclear Power, seeing atomic power as the only answer to
shrinking agricultural production, shrinking fuel supplies, and
a global population growing from 2.4 billion to as many as 8
billion by A.D. 2050, at the rate of 70,000 a day.[5] He saw huge
atomic reactors generating enough electricity to heat and light
the world and run its trains and cars, with smaller nuclear power
plants for ships and even large airplanes (p. 391). In 1975,

Distinguished
authorities

with the crisis more threatening, Edward Teller was even more
positive: "It is certain that by encouraging international use
of nuclear reactors, a great contribution can be made toward a

Second
citation:
author named
in text

[3]Pp. 118, 112. See also Bernard L. Cohen, "Tale of Two
Wastes," Commentary, Nov. 1978, pp. 63-65.

Author and
book named
in text

[4]Energy in the Future (New York: Van Nostrand, 1953).

[5]Bloomington, Indiana: Indiana University Press,
1958, p. 9.

3

worldwide alleviation of the shortage of energy."[6] By building

reactors, drilling for more domestic oil and gas, economizing,

and using more coal, Teller believed that by 1985 the United

States could export 13 percent of its output of fossil fuels, or

about three million barrels of oil and one million tons of coal

a day (p. 8). Glenn T. Seaborg, the first chairman of the Atomic

Energy Commission, also saw atomic power as the world's salva-

tion: "Nuclear power came just in time," he said in 1971.[7]

Richard Bailey, speaking for Great Britain, summarizes the broad

consensus of opinion today, still with emphasis on atomic energy:

> The answer clearly is to conserve oil reserves and use more
> coal, which is abundant, while developing nuclear power, and
> the as yet unrealized potential of the alternative energy
> sources from wind, solar, and geo-thermal power.[8]

Controversial
authority
adding
interest

Ralph Nader takes the opposite view:

> This is the first time this country has permitted the devel-
> opment of an industry that can wipe this country out. . . .
> The danger of catastrophic nuclear power plant accidents is
> a public safety problem of the utmost urgency in the country
> today.[9]

To be sure, Nader's view is extreme--even uninformed. The esti-

mate of the worst possible nuclear accident made by the Union of

Strong
evidence for
nuclear power
from its
opponents

Concerned Scientists is only 2.4 deaths per reactor-year over the

long run--a figure, as Faltermayer says, "no more than all the

mining, pollution, and other deaths that are believed to result

from generating the same amount of electricity at a coal-burning

[6]Energy: A Plan for Action (New York: Commission on Crit-
ical Choices for Americans, 1975), p. 63.

Quotation in
anonymous
work

[7]Energy Crisis in America, anon. monograph (Washington,
D.C.: Congressional Quarterly, Inc., 1973), p. 57.

[8]Energy: The Rude Awakening (London and New York: McGraw-
Hill, 1977), p. 4.

[9]Quoted in Energy Crisis, p. 57.

Switching to
pro thesis
plant, and it may be as much as ten times less."[10]   Nevertheless,
the problem of public safety is real.

   The biggest problem with nuclear energy derives not from the
possibility of an accident but from radioactive wastes.   Plutoni-

Turning
contra
evidence pro
um is lethal for 250,000 years, even though, according to the
heading of one of Faltermayer's charts, "With Reactor Wastes, the
Worst Is Over in Six Centuries"--only six hundred years of
threatening disaster after each new burial.[11]   Although breathing plutonium dust is lethal, Bernard L. Cohen, a physicist at
the University of Pittsburgh, has offered "to eat as much plutonium 239 as an anti-nuclear critic will eat of caffeine, which he
contends is just as dangerous."[12]   Mr. Cohen no doubt said, or
meant to say, "harmless"--unless one failed to hold his breath
while eating the lethal dust.

Specific
evidence
   Nuclear waste is admittedly lethal, to be handled with extreme care for at least six hundred years.   The United States
already has on hand 600,000 tons of this radioactive waste from
making atomic missiles, and a typical nuclear power plant exudes
30 tons each year.[13]   None of this has yet been permanently disposed.   The Department of Energy is just now beginning a Waste
Isolation Pilot Project to insulate radioactive waste within
ceramic blocks and bury them in salt beds in New Mexico that
have not moved for two hundred million years, a solution Falter-

   [10]"Exorcising the Nightmare of Reactor Meltdowns," Fortune,
12 Mar. 1979, p. 84.

First and
subsequent
citations to
article (see
footnotes 2,
10, and 19 for
other articles
by same
author)
   [11]"Burying Nuclear Trash Where It Will Stay Put," Fortune,
26 Mar. 1979, p. 102.

   [12]Faltermayer, "Burying," p. 102.

   [13]Faltermayer, "Burying," p. 100.

5

Contra set up
for refutation

mayer believes completely satisfactory.[14] Teller concurs, esti-
mating that burying waste in deep salt strata, or cooling it into
almost unbreakable rods to be buried in earthen bunkers, is both
safe and inexpensive. He believes that objections to breeder reactors, which produce more plutonium than they use, "are probably not
justified" (pp. 61-62). Corwin L. Rickard and Richard C. Dahlberg
believe breeders are the final solution to both energy and disposal, since advanced converters built near breeders could use
their excess fuel and increase output still further.[15]

Pro: refuting
contra

But such combinations of breeders and converters require gi-
gantic installations that would wholly remodel our landscape and

Con: detailed
description
for refutation

way of life. A study by the Atomic Energy Commission at Oak
Ridge National Laboratory produced an artist's model of a nuclear-
powered agroindustrial complex, or "nuplex," with an industrial
center of ten square miles and 300,000 adjacent acres of "food
factory," to be irrigated by deep underground wells or electri-
cally desalinated sea water, all pumped by nuclear-produced electricity, and the whole to be connected to similar complexes by
canals.[16]

Back to pro

If this is an acceptable solution for the future, with
breeder reactors converting our vanishing uranium into an inex-
haustible fuel, the consumption or disposal of nuclear waste
nevertheless remains an unknown quantity, or, at best, a specula-

Pro authority

tion. Barry Commoner believes that radioactive waste would pile

[14]"Burying," p. 104.

[15]"Nuclear Power: A Balanced Approach," Science, 10 Nov.
1978, pp. 581-84.

Two authors

[16]Marsha Freeman and John Schoonover, "Nuplex City Building, The Transition to Fusion," Fusion, Nov. 1978, pp. 45-47.

6

higher:

> Thus, to the already formidable difficulties and costs that
> would be involved in a transition to a breeder-based power
> system, we must add the nearly immeasurable problems that
> would be created by the need to cope with huge amounts of
> radioactive material without poisoning the environment and
> the people in it.[17]

Commoner believes that we must turn from the nuclear route as

soon as possible, particularly to avoid the mounting accumulation

of radioactive waste. Many others agree. According to Energy

Crisis in America:

> The number of shipped containers, about 30 per year in 1970,
> could rise to 500 per week by the year 2000, making chances
> of truck or railroad accidents almost a certainty, based on
> Department of Transportation accident rates.[18]

In fact, all of our present sources of energy pose serious

threats:

> Continued reliance on fossil fuels and nuclear fission, in
> particular, could have serious adverse effects on the
> nation's environment through increased strip mining and off-
> shore drilling, thermal pollution or radiation hazards, and
> deteriorating air quality. (p. 54)

Contra:
summarizing
The only replies to these objections are those of Rickard

and Dahlberg, who believe "advanced converters" will improve

enough to consume all of the extra plutonium from breeders, and

of Teller and Faltermayer, who believe that we can bury nuclear

waste safely and continuously in the world's limited space.

Faltermayer convincingly sets aside the threat of theft by ter-

rorists or small governments as too dangerous and difficult,

Pro: keeping
the thesis
visible
adding that radioactive waste can be "spiked" with other iso-

[17]"Reflections: The Solar Transition--II," The New Yorker,
30 Apr. 1979, p. 52.

Title cited in
text; cross-
reference for
additional
support
[18]P. 58. See also L. J. Carter, "Interagency Group Cautious on Nuclear Waste Disposal," Science, 30 Mar. 1979, pp.
1320-21.

topes to make it useless for explosives.[19] Nevertheless, the environmental threat in nuclear fission remains.

Con: another
alternative

Another hope for the future is nuclear fusion, the dynamics of the hydrogen bomb made peaceful--forcing atomic nuclei to merge, rather than splitting them:

> While large amounts of energy will be produced from nuclear fission, the total will be insignificant compared with the potential of nuclear fusion. The attainment of practical power from controlled fusion is perhaps the most formidable technical challenge that man has faced. If the problem can be solved, deuterium (heavy hydrogen) is available from water in quantity sufficient to provide virtually unlimited energy.[20]

Pro: refutation
by authority

But Commoner sets fusion aside as too far in the future for decisions that must be made now. He also thinks it is potentially dangerous and perhaps uneconomical:

> . . . some radioactivity would be produced, most of it in the especially dangerous form of radioactive hydrogen, or tritium; and fusion power plants would necessarily be very large and demanding of capital, and therefore economically inefficient. (p. 46)

Pro: inductive
question with
partial answer

Without the atom, then, where can we turn for energy? One immediate answer is synthetic fuel. In November 1979, the U.S. Senate enacted President Carter's twenty-billion-dollar synthetic-fuel program. Most immediately, this will support operations already underway to turn coal and oil-bearing shale into

Pro: rejecting
the final
contra

oil and gas.[21] But the process is expensive, and its environmental risks are considerable. In addition to moving mountains of coal and rock, it deposits still other mountains of waste and

[19]"Keeping the Peaceful Atom from Raising the Risk of War," Fortune, 9 Apr. 1979, pp. 90-93.

[20]Charles R. Russell, "Energy Sources," Macropaedia, Encyc. Brit., 1979.

Unsigned
article

[21]"Tapping the Riches of Shale," Time, 19 Nov. 1979, pp. 62-63.

8

requires immense quantities of water, to be returned to the land
unpolluted. At best, it merely stretches our supply of exhaust-
ible fossil fuels until we find some renewable source.

The ultimate renewable source, as everyone agrees, is the
sun. Wilson Clark believes that solar power is the only alternative to extinction. He also suspects that nuclear power, in

addition to its danger, may cost more energy in construction,
mining, shipping, handling, disposal, and guarding than it produces.[22] James R. Bolton agrees, proposing as the most promising

solution some system similar to natural photosynthesis that would
electrolyze water to produce hydrogen to drive electric genera-

tors.[23] But most writers go beyond mere sunlight to include, as
"solar energy," all sources that renew themselves from the sun--

trees for fuel, grain for alcohol, winds, rivers, and tides for
milling and generating electricity directly, and the natural
heating and cooling of night and day. People have used most of
these for centuries, and can now return to and increase their
use. All agree that we must do so immediately to conserve fossil
fuels until some other dependable system emerges, one based on
renewable solar energy.

The most feasible system appears to be one that converts
organic matter directly into fuel: methane gas from sewage and
other wastes, and grain alcohol, or ethanol, from grains and

other vegetation. Both of these solar fuels already supply energy in many parts of the country. Several American oil compan-

---

[22]_Energy for Survival: The Alternative to Extinction_ (Garden City, New York: Anchor Books, Doubleday, 1974), pp. 312-13.

[23]"Solar Fuels," _Science_, 17 Nov. 1978, p. 710.

ies now sell "gasohol," which is gasoline improved by ten percent
ethanol to replace high-octane unleaded fuel. Brazil is rapidly
converting to automobiles that run on pure ethanol derived from
sugar cane.[24] On the other hand, the city of Modesto, California,
runs many of its cars and trucks on methane gas from its sewage-
disposal plant at the cost of thirty-five cents for the equivalent of a gallon of gasoline, "and the vehicles using it last
longer because of its clean-burning and low-emission characteristics."[25]

Indeed, methane promises to be the solar fuel of the future,
supplemented by ethanol. John Van Geldern, whose company is
building a series of systems in Arkansas to convert poultry
wastes into methane, terms it "the best and least costly" of alternative fuels. More than half a million cars now on American
roads, he says, can burn either gasoline or methane.[26] Moreover,
producing methane yields further solar energy in the form of feed
and fertilizer to continue the biological cycle, and carbon di-
oxide for cooling and freezing foods.

More important still, methane can mix with, or entirely replace, natural gas, which is itself a form of methane. The People's Gas Company now adds to its piped gas daily a million cubic feet of methane produced from cow manure in feeding lots in
Oklahoma, at a saving of twelve cents per thousand cubic feet:

Thus, every pot of water on a gas-burning stove in Chicago

[24]Barry Commoner, "A Reporter at Large: Once and Future
Fuel," The New Yorker, 29 Oct. 1979, p. 112.

[25]Chuck Nerpel, "Dual Fuel Test," Motor Trend, May 1979,
pp. 90, 92.

[26]"Synthetic Fuels," New York Times, 30 Sept. 1979, Sec. 3,
p. 14.

Margin notes:

Specific
example with
statistical
support

Further
support

The answer
still more
sharply
specified

Specific and
statistical
support

is now heated in part--so far, a very small part--by solar energy.[27]

Effects argued from causes

By extending present pipelines and using methane-powered cogenerators in buildings and homes, America could eliminate the enormous and relatively inefficient central electric generators that must inevitably evolve into breeder reactors as the fossil fuels and uranium run out.[28]

The economic argument saved for last as most persuasive

The savings in both energy and expense are impressive. Transporting gas now costs only 85¢ per million British thermal units as compared to $4.16 for the equivalent in electricity. No gigantic new installations are necessary. Pipelines are already extensive. Methane is already produced in a number of

Specific support

small systems. New York City's sewage-disposal plants, for instance, already emit methane as a by-product. Every cannery,

Specifics for emphasis

slaughter house, feeding lot, vegetable market, and garbage system in the country could build a convenient methane plant to

The final economic persuasion

turn its waste into profit and national benefit. Finally, no massive storage tanks are needed. Methane from abundant years and areas can be pumped right back into natural-gas wells and drawn again at need, as man renews nature's work with natural solar fuel.[29]

Thesis restated: the inverted funnel

Renewable solar power, therefore, is as feasible as it is

[27]Commoner, "Reflections," p. 57.

Explanatory footnote: too much detail for text

[28]"Reflections," pp. 51, 54. A cogenerator is essentially an automobile engine for generating both electricity and heat. By capturing rather than exhausting the heat, it becomes 90 percent efficient as compared to 30 percent for the most efficient conventional engine. Though cogenerators are usually both large and expensive, the Fiat Company now sells a small one, suitable for homes, for $6,000. Mass production and competition can reduce that price, and the eliminated electric bills can make it economical.

[29]Commoner, "Reflections," pp. 57-58.

11

necessary, with methane by far the most promising single source. Both methane and ethanol can extend and eventually replace diminishing supplies of natural gas and petroleum. Both burn without

Con
reintroduced
for unity and
climatic
refutation

pollution. Together, they can eliminate the threat of nuclear radioactivity and the still unsolved problem of ever-increasing nuclear wastes, which even now will plague the world for 250,000 years. We must, immediately and imperatively, turn away from the road leading to enormous nuclear electric plants with their towering and wasteful networks of cables and wires. We must increase our solar energy and efficiency in every way we can, and,

The clincher

especially, extend our underground pipelines and use our thousands of available sources of methane gas now going to waste.

Bibliography

Bailey, Richard. _Energy: The Rude Awakening_. London and New
 York: McGraw-Hill, 1977.

Bolton, James R. "Solar Fuels." _Science_, 17 Nov. 1978, pp.
 705-10.

Carter, L. J. "Interagency Group Cautious on Nuclear Waste Disposal." _Science_, 30 Mar. 1979, pp. 1320-21.

Clark, Wilson. _Energy for Survival: The Alternative to Extinc-
 tion_. Garden City, New York: Anchor Books, Doubleday, 1974.

Cohen, Bernard L. "Tale of Two Wastes." _Commentary_, Nov. 1978,
 pp. 63-65.

Commoner, Barry. "Reflections: The Solar Transition--II." _The
 New Yorker_, 30 Apr. 1979, pp. 46-93.

Article by
same author

 _____. "A Reporter at Large: Once and Future Fuel."
 The New Yorker, 29 Oct. 1979, pp. 106-26.

Energy Crisis in America. Anon. monograph. Washington, D.C.:
 Congressional Quarterly, Inc., 1973.

Faltermayer, Edmund. "Burying Nuclear Trash Where It Will Stay
 Put." _Fortune_, 26 Mar. 1979, pp. 98-104.

 _____. "Exorcising the Nightmare of Reactor Melt-
 downs." _Fortune_, 12 Mar. 1979, pp. 82-87.

 _____. "Keeping the Peaceful Atom from Raising the
 Risk of War." _Fortune_, 9 Apr. 1979, pp. 90-93.

 _____. "Nuclear Power After Three Mile Island."
 Fortune, 7 May 1979, pp. 114-22.

Two authors

Freeman, Marsha, and John Schoonover. "Nuplex City Building: The
 Transition to Fusion." _Fusion_, Nov. 1978, pp. 43-50.

Unsigned
editorial

"It's Time to End the Holy War Over Nuclear Power." Editorial.
 Fortune, 12 Mar. 1979, p. 81.

Nerpel, Chuck. "Dual Fuel Test." _Motor Trend_, May 1979, pp.
 90-93.

Putnam, Palmer C. _Energy in the Future_. New York: Van Nostrand, 1953.

Rickard, Corwin L., and Richard C. Dahlberg. "Nuclear Power: A
 Balanced Approach." _Science_, 10 Nov. 1978, pp. 581-84.

Signed
article in
encyclopedia

Russell, Charles R. "Energy Sources." Encyclopaedia Britannica:
    Macropaedia. 1979 ed.

Unsigned
article

"Tapping the Riches of Shale." Time, 19 Nov. 1979, pp. 62-63.

Teller, Edward. Energy: A Plan for Action. New York: Com-
    mission on Critical Choices for Americans, 1975.

Thirring, Hans. Energy for Man: Windmills to Nuclear Power.
    Bloomington, Indiana: Indiana University Press, 1958.

Signed
newspaper
article

Van Geldern, John. "Synthetic Fuels." New York Times, 30 Sept.
    1979, Sec. 3, p. 14.

EXERCISES

1. *Consult the current* World Almanac and Book of Facts *for the date of some memorable event; the sinking of the* Titanic *or the* Lusitania, *Lindbergh's flight over the Atlantic, the United States' entry into war, the founding of the United Nations, the great stock-market crash, or the like. Now go to another collection, like* Facts on File, *and some of the other almanacs and yearbooks for the year of your event; write an essay entitled, let us say,* "1929" — *a synopsis of the monumental and the quaint for that year, as lively and interesting as you can make it.*

2. *Look up some event of the recent past (after 1913) in the* New York Times Index. *Write a paper on how the event is reported in the* Times *and in the other newspapers available in your library.*

3. *Choose a subject like the origin of man, Watergate (or a similar affair),* apartheid — *anything that interests you — and compile a bibliographical list of the articles given in the* Reader's Guide, *beginning with the most recent issue and going backward in time until you have eight or ten titles. You may have to look under several headings, such as "archeology," "anthropology," and "evolution," for the origin of man; under "U.S. Government" and others in addition to "Watergate" itself for the Watergate affair; and under "South Africa," "racism," and "apartheid" itself for* apartheid. *Then look in the scholarly* Indexes *discussed on p. 100, make another bibliographical listing of your subject for the same period. Which articles appear in the* Humanities *or* Social Sciences Index *(or both) only? Which articles appear in the* Reader's Guide *only? Which appear in both the* Indexes *and the* Guide? *Write a brief commentary about the differences in coverage in these two (or three) indexes. What does comparing them tell you about research?*

4. *In the* Essay and General Literature Index, *look up three essays published in anthologies between 1965 and 1969 on Gerard Manley Hopkins, recording each entry and then following it by full data on the book, with call number, from the card catalog.*

5. *Select some well-known literary work:* Walden, David Copperfield, Huckleberry Finn, Alice in Wonderland, The Wind in the Willows, A Farewell to Arms. *Describe how thoroughly it is cataloged by your library. Check cards for author, title, and subject. How many editions does the library have? Is the work contained within any* Works? *How many cards treat it as a subject? Does your library own a first edition? This last may require that you find the date of the first edition by looking up your author in an encyclopedia, checking available books about him, and perhaps checking in the British Museum's* General Catalogue of Printed Books, *or, for a twentieth-century book,* United States Catalog of Printed Books, *or* Cumulative Book Index *to discover the earliest cataloging.*

A
WRITER'S
HANDBOOK

10

A Writer's Grammar

You have already seen, in preceding chapters, many of the ills of writing—the ailing thesis that weakens the whole system, the *of*-and-*which* disease, the recurring rashes of wordiness. But many a sentence suffers from ailments more deeply genetic. You can probably tell when a sentence feels bad, especially after your instructor has marked it up. You can, in other words, detect the symptoms, but to work an efficient cure you need also to find the causes and to treat them directly. You need some skill in the ancient remedies of grammar.

THE BASIC PARTS OF SPEECH

The parts of speech are the elements of the sentence. A grasp of the basic eight—nouns, pronouns, verbs, adjectives, adverbs, prepositions, conjunctions, and interjections—will give you a sense of the whole.

Nouns.   Nouns name something. A *proper noun* names a particular person, place, or thing. A *common noun* names a general class of things; a common noun naming a group as a single unit is a *collective noun*. A phrase or clause functioning as a noun is a *noun phrase* or a *noun clause*. Here are some examples:

> COMMON: **stone, tree, house, girl, artist, nation, democracy**
> PROPER: **George, Cincinnati, Texas, Europe, Declaration of Independence**
> COLLECTIVE: **committee, family, quartet, herd, navy, clergy, kind**
> NOUN PHRASE: *Riding the surf* **takes stamina.**
> NOUN CLAUSE: *What you say* **may depend on** *how you say it.*

Pronouns.   As their name indicates, pronouns stand "for nouns." The noun a pronoun represents is called its *antecedent*. Pronouns show *case* — nominative (*I, we, he, she, they*), possessive (*my, our, his, her, their*), and objective (*me, us, him, her, them*). Pronouns may be classified as follows:

> PERSONAL *(standing for persons):* **I, you, he, she, we, they; me, him, her, us, them; my, his, our,** and so on
> REFLEXIVE *(turning the action back on the doer):* **I hurt** *myself.* **They enjoy** *themselves.* **(himself, herself, itself)**
> INTENSIVE *(emphasizing the doer):* **He** *himself* **said so.**
> RELATIVE *(linking subordinate clauses):* **who, which, that, whose, whomever, whichever,** and so on
> INTERROGATIVE *(beginning a question):* **who, which, what**
> DEMONSTRATIVE *(pointing to persons or things):* **this, that, these, those, such**
> INDEFINITE *(standing for indefinite numbers of persons or things):* **any, each, few, some, anyone, no one, everyone, somebody,** and so on
> RECIPROCAL *(plural reflexives):* **each other, one another**

Note that pronouns describing nouns function as adjectives:

> PRONOUNS: *Few* **would recognize** *this.*
> PRONOUNS AS ADJECTIVES: *Few* **readers would recognize** *this* **allusion.**

Verbs.   Verbs express actions or states of being. A verb may be *transitive*, requiring an object to complete the thought, or *intransitive*, requiring no object for completeness. Some verbs can function either transitively or intransitively. *Linking verbs* link the subject to a state of being.

> TRANSITIVE: **He** *put* **his feet on the chair. She** *hit* **the ceiling. They** *sang* **a sad old song. She** *lays* **carpets.**
> INTRANSITIVE: **He** *smiled.* **She** *cried.* **They** *sang* **like birds. They** *are* **coming. He** *lies* **down.**
> LINKING: **He** *is* **happy. She** *feels* **angry. This** *looks* **bad. It** *is* **she.**

Adjectives.   Adjectives describe, or modify, nouns or pronouns. An *adjectival phrase* or *adjectival clause* functions in a sentence as a single adjective would.

> ADJECTIVES: The *red* house faces west. He was a *handsome* devil. The *old haunted* house was *empty. These* books belong to *that* student.
> ADJECTIVAL PHRASE: He had reached the end *of the book.*
> ADJECTIVAL CLAUSE: Here is the key *that unlocks the barn.*

Articles, which point out nouns, are classified with adjectives. *The,* the "definite" article, points to specific persons or things; *A* and *an,* the "indefinite" articles, point out persons or things as members of groups.

> ARTICLES: *The* hunter selected *a* rifle from *an* assortment.

Adverbs.   Adverbs describe verbs, adjectives, or other adverbs, completing the ideas of *how, how much, when,* and *where.* An *adverbial phrase* or *adverbial clause* functions as a single adverb would.

> ADVERBS: Though *slightly* fat, he runs *quickly* and plays *extremely well.*
> ADVERBIAL PHRASE: He left *after the others.*
> ADVERBIAL CLAUSE: She lost the gloves *after she left the store.*

Prepositions.   A preposition links a noun or pronoun to another word in the sentence. A preposition and its object form a *prepositional phrase,* which acts as an adjective or adverb:

> The repairman opened the base OF *the telephone.* [adjective, modifies *base*]
> BY *late afternoon,* Williams was exhausted, [adverb, modifies *was*]
> He walked TO *his car* and drove FROM *the field.* [adverbs, modify *walked* and *drove*]

Certain forms of verbs, alone or in phrases, serve as nouns, adjectives, and adverbs. *Participles* act as adjectives. *Present participles* are verbs plus *-ing,* and *past participles* are regular verbs plus *-ed* (see the Glossary of Usage for *irregular verbs*). *Gerunds,* like present participles, are verbs plus *-ing* but work as nouns; past participles occasionally function as nouns, also. *Infinitives, to* plus verbs, serve as nouns, adjectives, or adverbs. Unlike participles and gerunds, infinitives can have subjects, which are always in the objective case.

> PRESENT PARTICIPLES: *Feeling miserable* and *running a fever,* she took to her bed. [adjectives]
> PAST PARTICIPLES: The nurses treated the *wounded* soldier. [adjective]
> The nurses treated the *wounded.* [noun]
> GERUND PHRASE: *His going* ended the friendship. [noun, subject of sentence]

INFINITIVES: *To err* is human; *to forgive*, divine. [nouns, subjects of sentence]
I saw *him* [*to*] go. [phrase serving as noun, object of *saw*; *him* subject of *to go*]
Ford is the man *to watch*. [adjective]
Coiled, the snake waited *to strike*. [adverb]

Conjunctions. Conjunctions join words, phrases, and clauses. *Coordinating* conjunctions —*and, but, or, yet* —join equals:

May *and* I won easily.
Near the shore *but* far from home, the bottle floated.
He was talented, *yet* he failed.
Could you take Karl *and* me water-skiing?

Subordinating conjunctions attach clauses to the basic subject-and-verb:

Since it was late, they left.
He worked hard *because* he needed an A.
They stopped *after* they reached the spring.

Interjections. Interjections interrupt the usual flow of the sentence to emphasize feelings:

But, *oh*, the difference to me.
Mr. Dowd, *alas*, has ignored the evidence.
The consumer will suddenly discover that, *ouch*, his dollar is cut in half.

AGREEMENT: NOUNS AND VERBS

Make Your Verb and Its Subject Agree.

Match singulars with singulars, plurals with plurals. First, find the verb, since that names the action —*sways* in the following sentence: "The poplar tree sways in the wind, dropping yellow leaves on the lawn." Then ask *who* or *what* sways, and you have your simple subject: *tree*, a singular noun. Then make sure that your singular subject matches its singular verb. (A reminder: contrary to nouns, the majority of singular verbs end in *s* —the actor performs; actors perform.) You will have little trouble except when subject and verb are far apart, or when the number of the subject itself is doubtful. (Is *family* singular or plural? What about *none*? What about *neither he nor she*?)

Subject and
verb widely
separated

FAULTY: *Revision* of their views about markets and averages *are* mandatory.

REVISED: *Revision* of their views about markets and averages *is* mandatory.

Sidestep the plural constructions that fall between your singular subject and its verb:

Mistaken
plurals

FAULTY: The *attention* of the students *wander* out the window.
REVISED: The *attention* of the students *wanders* out the window.

FAULTY: The *plaster*, as well as the floors, *need* repair.
REVISED: The *plaster*, as well as the floors, *needs* repair.

Collective nouns (*committee, jury, herd, group, family, kind, quartet*) are single units (plural in British usage); give them singular verbs, or plural members:

Collective
nouns

FAULTY: Her *family were* ready.
REVISED: Her *family was* ready.

FAULTY: The *jury have disagreed* among themselves.
REVISED: The jurors have disagreed among themselves.

FAULTY: These *kind* of muffins *are* delicious.
REVISED: *These muffins are* delicious.
REVISED: *This kind* of muffin *is* delicious.

Watch out for the indefinite pronouns—*each, neither, anyone, everyone, no one, none, everybody, nobody*. Each of these is (not *are*) singular in idea, yet each line flirts with the crowd from which it singles out its idea: each of *these*, either of *them*, none of *them*. Give all of them singular verbs.

Indefinite
pronouns

None of these men *is* a failure.
None of the class, even the best prepared, *wants* the test.
Everybody, including the high-school kids, *goes* to Andy's Drive-In.
Neither the right nor the left *supports* the issue.

None of them are is very common. From Shakespeare's time to ours, it has persisted alongside the more precise *none of them is*, which seems to have the edge in careful prose.

When one side of the *either-or* contrast is plural, you have a problem, conventionally solved by matching the verb to the nearer noun:

"Either-or"

Either the players or the coach *is* bad.

Since *players is* disturbs some feelings for plurality, the best solution is probably to switch your nouns:

Either the coach or the players *are* bad.

When both sides of the contrast are plural, the verb is naturally also plural:

Neither the rights of man nor the needs of the commonwealth *are* relevant to the question.

Don't let a plural noun in the predicate lure you into a plural verb:

FAULTY: His most faithful rooting *section are* his family and his girl.
REVISED: His most faithful rooting *section is* his family and his girl.
REVISED: His family and his girl *are* his best rooting section.

ALIGNING THE VERBS

Verbs have *tense* (past, present, future), *mood* (indicative, imperative, subjunctive), and *voice* (active, passive). These can sometimes slip out of line, as your thought slips, so a review should be useful here:

Use the Tense that Best Expresses Your Idea.

Each tense (from Latin *tempus*, meaning time) has its own virtues for expressing what you want your sentences to say. Use the *present tense*, of course, to express present action: "Now she *knows*. She *is leaving*." Use the present also for habitual action: "He *sees* her every day," and for describing literary events: "Hamlet *finds* the king praying, but he *is* unable to act; he *lets* the opportunity slip." And use the present tense to express timeless facts: "The Greeks knew the world *is* round." The present can also serve for the future: "Classes begin next Monday." Apply the *past tense* to all action before the present:

> One day I *was watching* television when the phone *rang;* it *was* the police.
> In the center of the cracked facade, the door *sagged;* rubble *lay* all around the foundations.

Use the *future tense* for action expected after the present:

> He *will finish* it next year.
> When he *finishes* next year, . . . [The present functioning as future]
> He *is going to finish* it next year. [The "present progressive" *is going* plus an infinitive, like to *finish*, commonly expresses the future.]

Use the *present perfect tense* for action completed ("perfected") but relevant to the present moment:

> I *have gone* there before.
> He *has sung* forty concerts.
> She *has driven* there every day.

Use the *past perfect tense* to express "the past of the past":

> "When we *arrived* [past], they *had finished* [past perfect]."

Similarly, use the *future perfect tense* to express "the past of the future":

> When we *arrive* [future], they *will have finished* [future perfect].
> You *will have worked* thirty hours by Christmas. [future perfect].
> The flare *will signal* [future] that he *has started* [perfect].

Set your tense, then move your reader clearly forward or back from it as your thought requires:

Hamlet *finds* the king praying. He *had sworn* instant revenge the night before, but he *will achieve* it only by accident and about a week later. Here he *is* unable to act; he *loses* his best opportunity.

But avoid mixtures like this: "Hamlet *finds* the king praying, but he *was* unable to act; he *let* the opportunity slip." Here, all the verbs should be in the present, corresponding to *finds*.

Keep Your Moods in Mind.

The *indicative mood,* which indicates matters of fact (our usual verb and way of writing), and the *imperative mood,* which commands ("Do this," "Keep your moods in mind"), will give you no trouble. The *subjunctive mood,* which expresses an action or condition not asserted as actual fact, occasionally will. The conditional, provisional, wishful, suppositional ideas expressed by the subjunctive are usually subjoined (*subjunctus,* "yoked under") in subordinate clauses. The form of the verb is often plural, and often in past tense, even though the subject is singular, and the condition present or future.

He looked as if he *were* confident.
If I *were* you, Miles, I would ask her myself.
If this *be* error, and upon me [*be*] proved. . . .
Had he *been* sure, he would have said so.
I demand that he *make* restitution.
I move that the nominations *be closed,* and that the secretary *cast* a unanimous ballot.

Don't let *would have* (colloquial *would've*) seep into your conditional clause from your main clause:

FAULTY: **If he *would have known,* he never would have said that.**
REVISED: **If he *had known,* he never would have said that.**
REVISED: *Had* **he** *known,* **he never would have said that.**

Be careful not to write *would of* or *should of* for *would have* (*would've*) or *should have* (*should've*).

Don't Mix Active and Passive Voice.

One parting shot at our friend the passive. Avoid misaligning active with passive in the same sentence:

As he *entered* the room, voices *were heard* [he *heard*].
After they *laid out* the pattern, electric shears *were used* [they *used* electric shears].

You can also think of this as an awkward shift of subject, from *he* to *voices,* from *they* to *shears.* Here is a slippery sample, where the subject stays the same:

FAULTY: This plan *reduces* taxes and *has been used* successfully in three other cities.

Past tense; not passive voice

REVISED: This plan *reduces* taxes and *has been* successful in three other cities.

REVISED: This plan *reduces* taxes and *has proved* workable in three other cities.

REFERENCE OF PRONOUNS

Match Your Pronouns to What They Stand For.

Pronouns stand for (*pro*) nouns. They *refer* back to nouns already expressed (*antecedents*), or they stand for conceptions (people, things, ideas) already established or implied, as in *"None of them* is perfect."* Pronouns must agree with the singular and plural ideas they represent, and stand clearly as subjects or objects.

When a relative pronoun (*who, which, that*) is the subject of a clause, it takes a singular verb if its antecedent is singular, a plural verb if its antecedent is plural:

> Phil is the only *one* of our swimmers WHO *has* won three gold medals. [The antecedent is *one*, not *swimmers*.]
> [The antecedent is *one*, not *swimmers*.]
> Phil is one of the best *swimmers* WHO *have* ever been on the team. [The antecedent is *swimmers*, not *one*.]

Pronouns may stand either as subjects or objects of the action, and their form changes accordingly.

Use Nominative Pronouns for Nominative Functions.

Those pronouns in the predicate that refer back to, or complement, the subject are troublesome; keep them nominative:

Subjective complement

He discovered that it was *I*.
It was *they* who signed the treaty.

Another example is that of the pronoun in *apposition* with the subject (that is, *positioned near, applied to,* and meaning the same thing as, the subject):

Apposition with subject

We students would rather talk than sleep.

After *than* and *as,* the pronoun is usually the subject of an implied verb:

Implied verb

She is taller than *I* [am].
You are as bright as *he* [is].
She loves you as much as *I* [do].

But note: "She loves you as much as [she loves] *me*." Match your pronouns to what they stand for, subjects for subjects, objects for objects. (But a caution: Use an objective pronoun as the subject of an infinitive. See pp. 135, 136.)

Use a nominative pronoun as subject of a noun clause. This is the trickiest of pronominal problems, because the subject of the clause also looks like the object of the main verb:

> FAULTY: The sergeant asked *whomever* did it to step forward.
> REVISED: The sergeant asked *whoever* did it to step forward.

Similarly, parenthetical remarks like *I think*, *he says*, and *we believe* often make pronouns seem objects when they are actually subjects:

> FAULTY: Ellen is the girl *whom* I think *will succeed*.
> REVISED: Ellen is the girl *who* I think *will succeed*.

Use Objective Pronouns
for Objective Functions.

Compound objects give most of the trouble. Try the pronoun by itself: "invited *me*," "sent *him*," and so forth. These are all correct:

Compound objects

> The mayor invited my wife and *me* to dinner. [*not* my wife and *I*]
> Between *her* and *me*, an understanding grew.
> They sent it to Stuart and *him*.
> . . . for you and *me*.
> He would not think of letting *us* girls help him.

Again, *see if the pronoun would stand by itself* ("letting we"? No, *letting us*):

> FAULTY: The credit goes to *he* who tries. ["to he"?]
> REVISED: The credit goes to *him* who tries.

Pronouns in apposition with objects must themselves be objective:

Apposition with object

> FAULTY: The mayor complimented us both—Bill and *I*.
> REVISED: The mayor complimented us both—Bill and *me*.
>
> FAULTY: She gave the advice specifically to us—Helen and *I*.
> REVISED: She gave the advice specifically to us—Helen and *me*.
>
> FAULTY: Between us—Elaine and *I*—an understanding grew.
> REVISED: Between us—Elaine and *me*—an understanding grew.
>
> FAULTY: He would not think of letting *we* girls help him.
> REVISED: He would not think of letting *us* girls help him.

Notice this one:

> FAULTY: Will you please help Leonard and *I* find the manager?
> REVISED: Will you please help Leonard and *me* find the manager?

Leonard and me are objective both as objects of the verb *help* and as subjects of the shortened infinitive *to find.* Subjects of infinitives are always in the objective case, as in "She saw *him* go"; "She helped *him* find his keys."

Use a Possessive Pronoun Before a Gerund.

Since gerunds are *-ing* words used as nouns, the pronouns attached to them must say what they mean:

> FAULTY: **She disliked *him* hunting.**
> REVISED: **She disliked *his* hunting.**

The object of her dislike is not *him* but *hunting.*

Keep Your Antecedents Clear.

If an antecedent is missing, ambiguous, vague, or remote, the pronoun will suffer from "faulty reference."

> MISSING: **In Texas *they* produce a lot of oil.**
> REVISED: **Texas produces a lot of oil.**
> AMBIGUOUS: **Paul smashed into a girl's *car who* was visiting his sister.**
> REVISED: **Paul smashed into the car of a *girl* visiting his sister.**
> VAGUE: **Because Ann had never spoken before an audience, she was afraid of *it.***
> REVISED: **Because Ann had never spoken before an audience, she was afraid.**
> REMOTE: **The castle was built in 1537. The rooms and furnishings are carefully kept up, but the entrance is now guarded by a coin-fed turnstile. *It* still belongs to the Earl.**
> REVISED: **The castle, which still belongs to the Earl, was built in 1537. The rooms and furnishings are carefully kept up, but the entrance is now guarded by a coin-fed turnstile.**

This poses a special problem, especially when heading a sentence ("This is a special problem"). Many good stylists insist that every *this* refer back to a specific noun—*report* in the following example:

"This"   **The commission submitted its *report. This* proved windy, evasive, and ineffectual.**

Others occasionally allow (as I do) a more colloquial *this*, referring back more broadly:

> **The commission submitted its report. This ended the matter.**

Give an Indefinite or General Antecedent a Singular Pronoun.

FAULTY: *Each* of the students hoped to follow in *their* teacher's footsteps.

REVISED: *Each* of the students hoped to follow in *his* [or *his or her*] teacher's footsteps.

REVISED: *All* of the students hoped to follow in *their* teacher's footsteps. [Here, we have a single class.]

FAULTY: If the *government* dares to face the new philosophy, *they* should declare *themselves*.

REVISED: If the *government* dares to face the new philosophy, *it* should declare *itself*.

Keep Person and Number Consistent.

Don't slip from person to person (*I* to *they*); don't fall among singulars and plurals — or you will get bad references:

FAULTY: *They* have reached an age when *you* should know better.
REVISED: *They* have reached an age when *they* should know better.

FAULTY: A motion *picture* can improve upon a book, but *they* usually do not.

REVISED: A motion *picture* can improve upon a book, but *it* usually does not.

MODIFIERS MISUSED AND MISPLACED
Keep Your Adjectives and Adverbs Straight.

The adjective sometimes wrongly crowds out the adverb: "He played a *real* conservative game." And the adverb sometimes steals the adjective's place, especially when the linking verb looks transitive but isn't (*feels, looks, tastes, smells*), making the sense wrong: "He feels *badly*" (adverb) means incompetence, not misery. The cure is to modify your nouns with adjectives, and everything else with adverbs:

He played a *really* conservative game. [adverb]
He feels *bad*. [adjective]
This tastes *good*. [adjective]
I feel *good*. [adjective — spirit]
I feel *well*. [adjective — health]
This works *well*. [adverb]

Some words serve both as adjectives and adverbs: *early, late, near, far, hard, only, little, right, wrong, straight, well, better, best, fast,* for example, to be squeezed for their juice.

Think *little* of *little* things.

Near is a hard case, serving as an adjective (*the near future*) and as an adverb of place (*near the barn*), and then also trying to serve for *nearly,* the adverb of degree:

FAULTY: We are nowhere *near* knowledgeable enough.
REVISED: We are not *nearly* knowledgeable enough.

FAULTY: It was a *near* treasonous statement.
REVISED: It was a *nearly* treasonous statement.

FAULTY: With Dodge, he has a tie of *near*-filial rapport.
REVISED: With Dodge, he has an *almost* filial rapport.

Slow has a long history as an adverb, but *slowly* keeps the upper hand in print. Notice that adverbs usually go after, and adjectives before:

The *slow* freight went *slowly*.

Make Your Comparisons Complete.

Ask yourself "Than what?"—when you find your sentences ending with a *greener* (adjective) or a *more smoothly* (adverb):

FAULTY: The western plains are *flatter*.
REVISED: The western plains are *flatter than* those east of the Mississippi.

FAULTY: He plays more *skillfully*.
REVISED: He plays more *skillfully than* most boys his age.

FAULTY: Jane told her more than Ellen.
REVISED: Jane told her more than she told Ellen.

FAULTY: His income is lower than a *busboy*.
REVISED: His income is lower than a *busboy's*.

Don't Let Your Modifiers Squint.

Some modifiers squint in two directions at once. Place them to modify one thing only.

FAULTY: They agreed *when both sides ceased fire* to open negotiations.
REVISED: They agreed to open negotiations *when both sides ceased fire*.

FAULTY: Several delegations *we know* have failed.
REVISED: *We know* that several delegations have failed.

FAULTY: They hoped to try *thoroughly* to understand.
REVISED: They hoped to try to understand *thoroughly*.

FAULTY: He resolved to *dependably* develop plans.
REVISED: He resolved to develop *dependable* plans.

Don't Let Your Modifiers
or References Dangle.

The *-ing* words (the gerunds and participles) tend to slip loose from the sentence and dangle, referring to nothing or the wrong thing.

FAULTY: **Going home, the walk was slippery. [participle]**
REVISED: **Going home, I found the walk slippery.**

FAULTY: **When getting out of bed, his toe hit the dresser. [gerund]**
REVISED: **When getting out of bed, he hit his toe on the dresser.**

Infinitive phrases also can dangle badly:

FAULTY: **To think clearly, some logic is important.**
REVISED: **To think clearly, you should learn some logic.**

Any phrase or clause may dangle:

FAULTY: **When only a freshman [phrase], Jim's history teacher inspired him.**
REVISED: **When Jim was only a freshman, his history teacher inspired him.**

FAULTY: **After he had taught thirty years [clause], the average student still seemed average.**
REVISED: **After he had taught thirty years, he found the average student still average.**

EXERCISES

1. *Straighten out these disagreements and misalignments:*

1. These kinds of questions are sheer absurdities.
2. Conservatism, as well as liberalism, are summonses for change in American life, as we know it.
3. Neither the fringe on his jacket nor the price of his guitar impress us.
4. Her family were bitter about it.
5. The grazing ground of both the antelope and the wild horses are west of this range.
6. The campus, as well as the town, need to wake up.
7. The extinction of several species of whales are threatened.
8. None of the group, even Smith and Jones, want to play.
9. Holden goes to New York. He looked up his old teacher and called his old girl friend. Before he started, he had decided to call his sister, but actually he took almost the whole book to get around to calling her. In the end, she proved to be his best friend.
10. If I would have studied harder, I would have passed.
11. They insisted that he shows up.
12. The sit-in accomplished its purpose and was tested by fire.
13. First he investigated the practical implications, and then the moral implications that were involved were examined.

2. *Revise these faulty pronouns, and their sentences where necessary:*

1. None of us are perfect.
2. Doug is the only one of the boys who always stand straight.
3. We are stronger than them.
4. He took my wife and I to dinner.
5. Jim will vote for whomever they say is a winner.
6. He opened the bird's cage, and it flew away.
7. It was him all right.
8. She disliked him whistling the same old tune.
9. He will give the ticket to whomever wants it: he did it for you and I.
10. My mother insists on me buying my own clothes: the average girl likes their independence.
11. The buffalo is far from extinct. Their numbers are actually increasing.
12. The program was turned into a fiasco by bad planning. This was bad.
13. All things come to he who waits.

3. *Straighten out these adjectives and adverbs:*

1. The demonstration reached near riot proportions.
2. It smells awfully.
3. The dress fitted her perfect.
4. He has a reasonable good chance.
5. His car had a special built engine.

4. *Complete and adjust these partial thoughts.*

1. He swims more smoothly.
2. The pack of a paratrooper is lighter than a soldier.
3. The work of a student is more intense than his parents.
4. This is the best painting.
5. The moon is smaller.

5. *Unsquint these modifiers:*

1. She planned on the next day to call him.
2. They asked after ten days to be notified.
3. The party promised to completely attempt reform.
4. Several expeditions we know have failed.
5. We wanted to win enough to cry.

6. *Mend these danglers:*

1. What we need is a file of engineers broken down by their specialties.
2. Following the games on television, the batting average of every player was at his fingertips.
3. When entering the room, the lamp fell over.
4. To study well, a quiet room helps.
5. After he arrived at the dorm, his father phoned.

7. *Correct the following:*

1. No one likes dancing backward all their lives.
2. His pass hit the wide receiver real good.
3. The ball was laying under the bench.
4. If they would of come earlier, they would of seen everything.
5. Williams hated him leaving early.
6. I feel badly about it.
7. This is the candidate whom I think will win.

8. *Cure the following grammatical ailments:*

1. The professor as well as the students were glad the course was over.
2. We study hard at State, but you do not have to work all the time.
3. Holden goes to New York and learned about life.
4. As he looked up, a light could be seen in the window.
5. A citizen should support the government, but they should also be free to criticize it.
6. It will all come true, for you and I.
7. The students always elect whomever is popular.
8. She hated me leaving so early.
9. This is one of the best essays that has been submitted.
10. While playing the piano, the dog sat by me and howled.
11. The team had a near perfect record.
12. Run-on sentences show a failure deeper than fragments.

Punctuation, Spelling, Capitalization

Punctuation gives the silent page some of the breath of life. It marks the pauses and emphases with which a speaker points his meaning. Loose punctuators forget what every good writer knows: that even silent reading produces an articulate murmur in our heads, that language springs from the breathing human voice, that the beauty and meaning of language depend on what the written word makes us *hear*, on the sentence's tuning of emphasis and pause. Commas, semicolons, colons, periods, and other punctuation transcribe our meaningful pauses to the printed page.

THE PERIOD: MARKING THE SENTENCE

A period marks a sentence, a subject completed in its verb:

She walked.

A phrase—which lacks a verb, though it may contain a verb *form* (see

p. 135)—subordinates this idea, making it *depend* on some other main clause:

> *While walking,* **she thought.**

A subordinate clause does the same, making the whole original sentence subordinate:

> *While she walked,* **she thought.**

Like a period, and a question mark, an exclamation mark marks a sentence, but much more emphatically: *Plan to revise!* Use it sparingly if you want it to count rhetorically.

Take special care not to break off a phrase or clause with a period, making a fragment that looks like a sentence but isn't (unless you intend a rhetorical fragment—see pp. 66–67), and don't use the comma as a period (see p. 156).

> FAULTY: **She dropped the cup. Which had cost twenty dollars.**
> REVISED: **She dropped the cup, which had cost twenty dollars.**
>
> FAULTY: **He swung furiously, the ball sailed into the lake.**
> REVISED: **He swung furiously. The ball sailed into the lake.**

THE COMMA

Here are the four basic commas:

> I.   THE INTRODUCER — after introductory phrases and clauses.
> II. THE COORDINATOR — between "sentences" joined by *and, but, or, nor, yet, so, for.*
> III. THE INSERTER — a PAIR around any inserted word or remark.
> IV. THE LINKER — when adding words, phrases, or clauses.

I. The Introducer. A comma after every introductory word or phrase makes your writing clearer, more alive with the breath and pause of meaning:

> **Indeed, the idea failed.**
> **After the first letter, she wrote again.**
> **In the autumn of the same year, he went to Paris.**

Without the introductory comma, your reader frequently expects something else:

> **After the first letter she wrote, she. . . .**
> **In the autumn of the same year he went to Paris, he. . . .**

But beware! What looks like an introductory phrase or clause may actually be the subject of the sentence *and should take no comma.* A comma can break up a good marriage of subject and verb. The comma in each of these is an interloper, and should be removed:

That handsome man in the ascot tie, is the groom.
The idea that you should report every observation, is wrong.
The realization that we must be slightly dishonest to be truly kind,
   comes to all of us sooner or later.

If your clause-as-subject is unusually long, or confusing, you may
relieve the pressure by inserting some qualifying remark after it, between two commas:

The idea that you should report every observation, *however insignificant,* is wrong.
The realization that we must be slightly dishonest to be truly kind,
obviously the higher motive, comes to all of us sooner or later.

II. **The Coordinator.**   Between "sentences" joined by coordinate
conjunctions. You will often see the comma omitted when your two
clauses are short: "He hunted and she fished." But nothing is wrong
with "He hunted, and she fished." The comma, in fact, shows the
slight pause you make when you say it.

Think of the "comma-and" (**, and**) as a unit equivalent to the
period. The period, the semicolon, and the "comma-and" (**, and**) all
designate independent clauses — independent "sentences" — but give
different emphases:

.   He was tired. He went home.
;   He was tired; he went home.
, and   He was tired, and he went home.

A comma tells your reader that another subject and predicate are
coming:

He hunted the hills and dales.
He hunted the hills, and she fished in the streams.
She was naughty but nice.
She was naughty, but that is not our business.
Wear your jacket or coat.
Wear your jacket, or you will catch cold.
It was strong yet sweet.
It was strong, yet it was not unpleasant.

Of course, you may use a comma in *all* the examples above if
your sense demands it. The contrasts set by *but, or,* and *yet* often urge
a comma, and the even stronger contrasts with *not* and *either-or*
demand a comma, whether or not full predication follows:

It was strong, yet sweet.
It was a battle, not a game.
. . . either a bird in the hand, or two in the bush.

Commas signal where you would pause in speaking.

The meaningful pause also urges an occasional comma in compound predicates, usually not separated by commas:

> He granted the usual permission and walked away.
> He granted the usual permission, and walked away.

Both are correct. In the first sentence, however, the granting and walking are perfectly routine, and the temper unruffled. In the second,
some kind of emotion has forced a pause, and a comma, after *permission*. Similarly, meaning itself may demand a comma between the two
verbs:

> He turned and dropped the vase.
> He turned, and dropped the vase.

In the first sentence, he turned the vase; in the second, himself. Your
, and in compound predicates suggests some touch of drama, some
meaningful distinction, or afterthought.

You need a comma before *for* and *still* even more urgently.
Without the comma, their conjunctive meaning changes; they assume
their ordinary roles, *for* as a preposition, *still* as an adjective or adverb:

> She liked him still. . . . [That is, either *yet* or *quiet!*]
> She liked him, still she could not marry him.
> She liked him for his money.
> She liked him, for a good man is hard to find.

An observation: *for* is the weakest of all the coordinators. Almost a
subordinator, it is perilously close to *because*. *For* can seem moronic if
cause and effect are fairly obvious: "She liked him, for he was kind."
Either make a point of the cause by full subordination—"She liked
him *because* he was kind"—or flatter the reader with a semicolon:
"She liked him; he was kind." *For* is effective only when the cause is
somewhat hard to find: "Blessed are the meek, for they shall inherit
the earth."

To summarize the basic point about the comma as coordinator:
put a comma before the coordinator (*and, but, or, nor, yet, so, still,
for,*) when joining independnent clauses, and add others necessary for
emphasis or clarity.

III. The Inserter. Put a PAIR of commas around every inserted
word, phrase, or clause—those expressions that seem parenthetical
and are called "nonrestrictive." A corporation recently told its stock-
holders, "Abilene, Kansas looks promising," as if the chairman were
telling his wife that things looked good in Kansas. When you cut a sentence in two to insert something necessary, you need to tie off *both*
ends, or your sentence will die on the table:

> When he packs his bag, however he goes. [, however,]
> The car, an ancient Packard is still running. [, an ancient Packard,]
> April 10, 1985 is agreeable as a date for final payment. [, 1985,]
> John Jones, Jr. is wrong. [, Jr.,]
> I wish, Sandra you would do it. [, Sandra,]

You do not mean that 1985 is agreeable, nor are you telling John Jones that Junior is wrong. Such parenthetical insertions need a PAIR of commas:

> The case, *nevertheless*, was closed.
> She will see, *if she has any sense at all*, that he is right.
> Sam, *on the other hand*, may be wrong.
> Note, *for example*, the excellent brushwork.
> John Jones, *M.D.*, and Bill Jones, *Ph.D.*, doctored the punch to per-
> fection.
> He stopped at Kansas City, *Missouri*, for two hours.

The same rule applies to all *nonrestrictive* remarks, phrases, and clauses — all elements simply additive, explanatory, and hence parenthetical:

> John, *my friend*, will do what he can.
> Andy, *his project sunk*, *his hopes shattered*, was speechless.
> The taxes, *which are reasonable*, will be paid.
> That man, *who knows*, is not talking.

Think of *nonrestrictive* as "nonessential" to your meaning, hence set off by commas. Think of *restrictive* as essential and "restricting" your meaning, hence not set off at all (use *which* for nonrestrictives, *that* for restrictives; see p. 75).

> RESTRICTIVES:
> The taxes that are reasonable will be paid.
> Southpaws who are superstitious will not pitch on Friday nights.
> The man who knows is not talking.

> NONRESTRICTIVES:
> The taxes, which are reasonable, will be paid.
> Southpaws, who are superstitious, will not pitch on Friday nights.
> The man, who knows, is not talking.

The difference between restrictives and nonrestrictives is one of meaning, and the comma-pair signals that meaning. How many grandmothers do I have in the first sentence below (restrictive)? How many in the second (nonrestrictive)?

> My grandmother who smokes pot is ninety.
> My grandmother, who smokes pot, is ninety.

In the first sentence, I still have two grandmothers, since I am distin-
guishing one from the other by my restrictive phrase (no commas) as the one with the unconventional habit. In the second sentence, I have but one grandmother, about whom I am adding an interesting though nonessential, nonrestrictive detail within a pair of commas. Read the two aloud, and you will hear the difference in meaning, and how the pauses at the commas signal that difference. Commas are often op-
tional, of course. The difference between a restictive and a nonre-

strictive meaning may sometimes be very slight. For example, you may take our recent bridegroom either way (but not halfway):

> **That handsome man, in the ascot tie, is the groom.** [nonrestrictive]
> **That handsome man in the ascot tie is the groom.** [restrictive]

Your meaning will dictate your choice. But use *pairs* of commas or none at all. Never separate subject and verb, or verb and object, with just one comma.

Some finer points. One comma of a pair enclosing an inserted remark may coincide with, and, in a sense, overlay, a comma "already there":

> **In each box, a bottle was broken.**
> **In each box, however, a bottle was broken.**
>
> **The team lost, and the school was sick.**
> **The team lost, in spite of all, and the school was sick.**
>
> **The program will work, but the cost is high.**
> **The program will work, of course, but the cost is high.**

Between the coordinate clauses, however, a semicolon might have been clearer:

> **The team lost, in spite of all; and the school was sick.**
> **The program will work, of course; but the cost is high.**

Beware: *however*, between commas, cannot substitute for *but*, as in the perfectly good sentence: "He wore a hat, *but* it looked terrible." You would be using a comma where a full stop (period or semicolon) should be:

> WRONG:
> **He wore a hat, however, it looked terrible.**
>
> RIGHT *(notice the two meanings)*:
> **He wore a hat; however, it looked terrible.**
> **He wore a hat, however; it looked terrible.**

But a simple **,** **but** avoids both the ambiguity of the floating *however* and the ponderosity of anchoring it with a semicolon, fore or aft: "He wore a hat, but it looked terrible."

Another point. *But* may absorb the first comma of a pair enclosing an introductory remark (although it need not do so):

> **At any rate, he went.**
> **But, at any rate, he went.**
> **But at any rate, he went.**
> **But [,] if we want another party, we had better clean up.**
> **The party was a success, but [,] if we want another one, we had better clean up.**

But avoid a comma *after* "but" in sentences like this:

> I understand your argument, but [,] I feel your opponent has a stronger case.

Treat the "he said" and "she said" of dialogue as a regular parenthetical insertion, within commas, and without capitalizing, unless a new sentence begins:

> "I'm going," he said, "whenever I get up enough nerve."
> "I'm going," he said. "Whenever I get up enough nerve, I'm really going."

And American usage puts the comma *inside* ALL quotation marks:

> "He is a nut," she said.
> She called him a "nut," and walked away.

Finally, the comma goes after a parenthesis, never before:

> On the day of her graduation (June 4, 1982), the weather turned broiling hot.

IV. The Linker. This is the usual one, linking on additional phrases and afterthoughts:

Additional phrase; afterthought
> They went home, having overstayed their welcome.
> The book is too long, overloaded with examples.

It also links items in series. Again, the meaningful pause demands a comma:

Items in series
> words, phrases, or clauses in a series
> to hunt, to fish, and to hike
> He went home, he went upstairs, and he could remember nothing.
> He liked oysters, soup, roast beef, and song.

Put a linker before the concluding *and*. By carefully separating all elements in a series, you keep alive a final distinction long ago lost in the daily press, the distinction Virginia Woolf makes (see p. 67): "urbane, polished, brilliant, imploring and commanding him. . . ." *Imploring and commanding* is syntactically equal to each one of the other modifiers in the series. If Woolf customarily omitted the last comma, as she does not, she could not have reached for that double apposition. The muscle would have been dead. These other examples of double apposition will give you an idea of its effectiveness:

Double apposition
> They cut out his idea, root and branch.
> He lost all his holdings, houses and lands.
> He loved to tramp the woods, to fish and hunt.

A comma makes a great deal of difference, of sense and distinction.

But adjectives in series, as distinct from nouns in series, change the game a bit. Notice the difference between the following two strings of adjectives:

Adjectives in
series

a good, unexpected, natural rhyme
a good old battered hat

With adjectives in series, only your sense can guide you. If each seems to modify the noun directly, as in the first example above, use commas. If each seems to modify the total accumulation of adjectives and noun, as with *good* and *old* in the second phrase, do not use commas. Say your phrases aloud, and put your commas in the pauses that distinguish your meaning.

Finally, a special case. Dramatic intensity sometimes allows you to join clauses with commas instead of conjunctions:

Special case:
clauses joined
by commas

She sighed, she cried, she almost died.
I couldn't do it, I tried, I let them all get away.
It passed, it triumphed, it was a good bill.
I came, I saw, I conquered.

The rhetorical intensity of this construction—the Greeks called it *asyndeton*—is obvious. The language is breathless, or grandly emphatic. As Aristotle once said, it is a person trying to say many things at once. The subjects repeat themselves, the verbs overlap, the idea accumulates a climax. By some psychological magic, the clauses of this construction usually come in three's. The comma is its sign. But unless you have a stylistic reason for such a flurry of clauses, go back to the normal comma and conjunction, the semicolon, or the period.

THE FRAGMENT, THE COMMA
SPLICE, AND THE RUN-ON

As you have seen (p. 66), the *fragment*—any piece of a sentence, with subject or predicate missing—may have superb rhetorical force: "So what." But when fragments slip in unnoticed, they reveal a failure to grasp the sentence completely. You have lost the fundamental connection between subject and verb:

Fragments

FAULTY: **She dropped the cup. Which had cost twenty dollars.**
REVISED: **She dropped the cup, which had cost twenty dollars.**

FAULTY: **He does not spell everything out. But rather hints that something is wrong, and leaves the rest up to the reader.**
REVISED: **He does not *spell* everything out, but rather *hints* ..., and leaves. ... [subject with compound verb, set off by commas]**

FAULTY: **Yet here is her husband treating their son to all that she considers evil. Plus the fact that the boy is offered beer.**
REVISED: **Yet here is her husband treating their son to all that she considers evil, especially beer.**

FAULTY: **He points out that one never knows what the future will bring. Because it is actually a matter of luck.**
REVISED: **He points out that one never knows what the future will**

> bring, because it is actually a matter of luck. [dependent clause now properly connected]

FAULTY: They are off. Not out of their minds exactly but driven, obsessed. (*Time*, August 21, 1978, p. 30)

REVISED: They are off, not out of their minds exactly, but driven, obsessed.

The *comma splice* is the beginner's most common error, the exact opposite of the fragment—putting a comma where we need a period, splicing two sentences together with a comma:

Comma splice   **The comma splice is a common error, it is the exact opposite of a fragment.**

The *run-on* sentence (fortunately, less common) omits even the splicing comma, running one sentence right on to another without noticing:

Run-on   **The comma splice is a common error it is the exact opposite of a fragment.**

Here the writer is in deeper trouble, having somehow never gotten the feel of a sentence as based on subject and verb, and thus needing special help. But most of us can see both the comma splice and run-on as really being two sentences, to be restored as such:

> **The comma splice is a common error. It is the exact opposite of a fragment.**

Or to be coordinated by adding a conjunction after the comma:

> **The comma splice is a common error, and it is. . . .**

Or to be subordinated by making the second sentence a phrase:

> **The comma splice is a common error, the exact opposite. . . .**

Here are some typical comma splices, usually invited by two thoughts in close sequence, especially if the first is negative:

> **She cut class, it was boring.**
> **The class was not merely dull, it was useless.**
> **Figures do not lie, they mislead.**
> **He was more than satisfied, he was delighted.**

Each of these pulls together a pair of closely sequential sentences. But a comma without its *and* or *but* will not hold the coordination. Though experienced writers occasionally employ comma splices with strong effect, prudence urges that you make them the sentences they are:

> **She cut class. It was boring.**
> **Figures do not lie. They mislead.**

Or coordinate them with a colon or dash (with a semicolon *only* if they contrast sharply):

> The class was not merely dull: it was useless.
> He was more than satisfied—he was delighted.

Or subordinate in some way:

> She cut class because it was boring.
> The class was not merely dull but useless.
> More than satisfied, he was delighted.

You will accidentally splice with a comma most frequently when adding a thought (a complete short sentence) to a longer sentence:

> The book describes human evolution in wholly believable terms, comparing the social habits of gorillas and chimpanzees to human behavior, it is very convincing. [Either ". . . believable terms. Comparing. . . ," or "human behavior. It. . . ."]

Conjunctive adverbs (*however, therefore, nevertheless, moreover, furthermore*, and others) may also cause comma splices and trouble:

> She continued teaching, however her heart was not in it.

Here are three mendings:

> She continued teaching, but her heart was not in it.
> She continued teaching; however, her heart was not in it.
> She continued teaching; her heart, however, was not in it.

Similarly, transitional phrases (*in fact, that is, for example*) may splice your sentences together:

> He disliked discipline, that is, he really was lazy.

You can strengthen the weak joints like this:

> He disliked discipline; that is, he really was lazy.
> He disliked discipline, that is, anything demanding.

SEMICOLON AND COLON

Use the semicolon only where you could also use a period, unless desperate. This dogmatic formula, which I shall loosen up in a moment, has saved many a punctuator from both despair and a reckless fling of semicolons. Confusion comes from the belief that the semicolon is either a weak colon or a strong comma. It is most effective as neither. It is best, as we have seen (p. 58), in pulling together and contrasting two independent clauses that could stand alone as sentences:

> The dress accents the feminine. The pants suit speaks for freedom.
Semicolon > The dress accents the feminine; the pants suit speaks for freedom.

This compression and contrast by semicolon can go even farther, allowing us to drop a repeated verb in the second element (note also how the comma marks the omission):

> Golf demands the best of time and space; tennis demands the best of personal energy.
> Golf demands the best of time and space; tennis, the best of personal energy.
> Tragedy begins with the apple; comedy, with the banana peel.*

Use a semicolon with a transitional word (*moreover, therefore, then, however, nevertheless*) to signal close contrast and connection:

> He was lonely, blue, and solitary; moreover, his jaw ached.

Used sparingly, the semicolon emphasizes your crucial contrasts; used recklessly, it merely clutters your page. *Never* use it as a colon: its effect is exactly opposite. A colon, as in the preceding sentence, signals the meaning to go ahead; a semicolon, as in this sentence, stops it. The colon is a green light; the semicolon is a stop sign.

Consequently, a wrong semicolon frequently makes a fragment. *Use a semicolon only where you could also use a period* — forget the exceptions — or you will make semicolon-fragments like the italicized phrases following the erroneous semicolons circled below:

> The play opens on a dark street in New York City; *one streetlight giving the only illumination.*
> The geese begin their migration in late August or early September; *some groups having started, in small stages, a week or so earlier.*

Each of those semicolons should have been a comma.

Of course, you may occasionally need a semicolon to unscramble a long line of phrases and clauses, especially those in series and containing internal commas:

> Composition is hard because we often must discover our ideas by writing them out, clarifying them on paper; because we must also find a clear and reasonable order for ideas the mind presents simultaneously; and because we must find, by trial and error, exactly the right words to convey our ideas and our feelings about them.

The colon waves the traffic on through the intersection: "Go right ahead," its says, "and you will find what you are looking for." The colon emphatically and precisely introduces a series, the clarifying detail, the illustrative example, and the formal quotation:

Colon
> The following players will start: Corelli, Smith, Jones, Baughman, and Stein.
> Pierpont lived for only one thing: money.
> In the end, it was useless: Adams really was too green.
> We remember Sherman's words: "War is hell."

---

* Adapted from Guy Davenport, *Life*, 27 Mar. 1970, p. 12.

PARENTHESIS AND DASH

The dash says aloud what the parenthesis whispers. Both enclose interruptions too extravagant for a pair of commas to hold. The dash is the more useful—since whispering tends to annoy—and will remain useful only if not overused. It can serve as a conversational colon. It can set off a concluding phrase—for emphasis. It can bring long introductory matters to focus, concluding a series of parallel phrases: "—all these are crucial." It can insert a full sentence—a clause is really an incorporated sentence—directly next to a key word. The dash allows you to insert—with a kind of shout!—an occasional exclamation. You may even insert—and who would blame you?—an occasional question. The dash affords a structural complexity with all the tone and alacrity of talk.

With care, you can get much the same power from a parenthesis:

> **Many philosophers have despaired (somewhat unphilosophically) of discovering any certainties whatsoever.**
> **Thus did Innocent III (we shall return to him shortly) inaugurate an age of horrors.**
> **But in such circumstances (see page 34), be cautious.**
> **Delay had doubled the costs (a stitch in time!), so the plans were shelved.**

But dashes seem more generally useful, and here are some special points. When one of a pair of dashes falls where a comma would be, it absorbs the comma:

> **If one wanted to go, he certainly could.**
> **If one wanted to go—whether invited or not—he certainly could.**

Not so with the semicolon:

> **He wanted to go—whether he was invited or not; she had more sense.**

To indicate the dash, type two hyphens (--) flush against the words they separate—not one hyphen between two spaces, nor a hyphen spaced to look exactly like a hyphen.

Put commas and periods *outside* a parenthetical group of words (like this one), even if the parenthetical group could stand alone as a sentence (see the preceding "Innocent III" example). (But if you make an actual full sentence parenthetical, put the period inside.)

Change has had its way with the parenthesis around numbers. Formal print and most guides to writing, including this one, still hold to the full parenthesis:

Numbered
items
> **The sentence really has only two general varieties: (1) the "loose" or strung-along, in Aristotle's phrase, and (2) the periodic.**
> **He decided (1) that he did not like it, (2) that she would not like it, and (3) that they would be better off without it.**

Popular print now omits the first half of the parenthesis:

> . . . **decided 1) that he did not like it, 2) that she. . . .**

But for your papers — keep the full parenthesis.

BRACKETS

Brackets indicate your own words inserted or substituted within a quotation from someone else: "Byron had already suggested that [they] had killed John Keats." You have substituted "they" for "the gentlemen of the *Quarterly Review*" to suit your own context; you do the same when you interpolate a word of explanation: "Byron had already suggested that the gentlemen of the *Quarterly Review* [especially Croker] had killed John Keats." *Do not use parenetheses:* they mark the enclosed words as part of the original quotation. Don't claim innocence because your typewriter lacks brackets. Just leave spaces and draw them in later, or type slant lines and tip them with pencil or with the underscore key: ⌐. .⌐

In the example below, you are pointing out with a *sic* (Latin for "so" or "thus"), which you should not italicize, that you are reproducing an error exactly as it appears in the text you are quoting:

> **"On no occassion [sic] could we trust them."**

Similarly you may give a correction after reproducing the error:

> **"On the twenty-fourth [twenty-third], we broke camp."**
> **"In not one instance [actually, Baldwin reports several instances] did our men run under fire."**

Use brackets when you need a parenthesis within a parenthesis:

> **(see Donald Allenberg, *The Future of Television* [New York, 1973], pp. 15–16)**

Your instructor will probably put brackets around the wordy parts of your sentences, indicating what you should cut:

> **In fact, [the reason] he liked it [was] because it was different.**

QUOTATION MARKS AND ITALICS

Put quotation marks around quotations that "run directly into your text" (like this), but *not* around quotations set off from the text and indented. You normally inset poetry, as it stands, without quotation marks:

> **An aged man is but a paltry thing,**
> **A tattered coat upon a stick, unless**
> **Soul clap its hands and sing. . . .**

But if you run it into your text, use quotation marks, with virgules (slants) showing the line-ends: "An aged man is but a paltry thing,/A tattered coat. . . ." Put periods and commas *inside* quotation marks; put semicolons and colons *outside:*

Quotation marks

Now we understand the full meaning of "give me liberty, or give me death."

"This strange disease of modern life," in Arnold's words, remains uncured.

In Greece, it was "know thyself"; in America, it is "know thy neighbor."

He left after "Hail to the Chief": he could do nothing more.

Although logic often seems to demand the period or comma outside the quotation marks, convention has put them inside for the sake of appearance, even when the sentence ends in a single quoted word or letter:

Clara Bow was said to have "It."
Mark it with "T."

If you have seen the periods and commas outside, you were reading a British book or some of America's little magazines.

When you have dialogue, signal each change of speaker with a paragraph's indentation:

"What magazines in the natural sciences should I read regularly?" inquired the student.

"Though moderately difficult, *Scientific American* and *Science* are always worth your time, but you'll want to explore afield from these," responded his advisor.

If in a dialogue a single speaker carries on for several paragraphs, place quotation marks before *each* paragraph, but after only the *last* paragraph.

Omit quotation marks entirely in *indirect* quotations:

She asked me if I would help her.

The insurance agent told Mr. Jones that his company would pay all valid claims within thirty days.

In his review of the play, J. K. Beaumont praised the plot as strong and incisive, but faulted the dialogue as listless and contrived in a few scenes. [Here, you are summarizing the reviewer's comments.]

If you are quoting a phrase that already contains quotation marks, reduce the original double marks (") to single ones ('):

Original	**Your Quotation**
Hamlet's "are you honest?" is easily explained.	He writes that "Hamlet's 'are you honest?' is easily explained."

Single quotation marks (on the right)

Notice what happens when the quotation within your quotation falls at the end:

Original	Your Quotation
A majority of the informants thought *infer* meant "imply."	Kirk reports that "a majority of the informants thought *infer* meant 'imply.' "

And notice that a question mark or exclamation point falls between the single and the double quotation marks at the end of a quotation containing a quotation:

> "Why do they call it 'the Hippocratic oath'?" she asked.
> "Everything can't be 'cool'!" he said.

But heed the following exception:

> "I heard someone say, 'Is anyone home?' " she declared.

Do not use *single* quotation marks for your own stylistic flourishes; use *double* quotation marks or, preferably, none:

> It was indeed an "affair," but the passion was hardly "grand."
> It was indeed an affair, but the passion was hardly grand.
>
> Some "cool" pianists use the twelve-tone scale.

Once you have thus established this slang meaning of *cool*, you may repeat the word without quotation marks. In general, of course, you should favor that slang your style can absorb without quotation marks.

Do not use quotation marks for calling attention to words as words. Use italics (an underscore when typing) for the word, quotation marks for their meanings.

Italics
> This is taking *tergiversation* too literally.
> The word *struthious* means "like an ostrich."

Similarly, use italics for numbers as numbers and letters as letters:

> He writes a 5 like an *s*.
> Dot your *i*'s and cross your *t*'s.

But common sayings like "Watch your p's and q's" and "from A to Z" require no italics.

Use quotation marks for titles *within* books and magazines: titles of chapters, articles, short stories, songs, and poems, and for unpublished works, lectures, courses, TV episodes within a series. But use italics for titles or names of books, newspapers, magazines, plays, films, long poems, sculptures, paintings, ships, trains, and airplanes.

Titles and names
> Poe's description of how he wrote "The Raven" was attacked in the *Atlantic Monthly* [or: the *Atlantic*.]
> We saw Michelangelo's *Pietà*, a remarkable statue in white marble.
> We took the Sante Fe *Chief* from Chicago to Los Angeles.
> He read all of Frazer's *The Golden Bough*.
> His great-grandfather went down with the *Titanic*.

> She read it in the *New York Times.*
> They loved *Saturday Night Fever* [film].

Handle titles within titles as follows:

> *"Tintern Alley" and Nature in Wordsworth* [book]
> " 'Tintern Abbey' and Natural Imagery" [article]
> "The Art of *Tom Jones*" [article]
> *The Art of* Tom Jones [book]

In the last example, notice that what is ordinarily italicized, like the "book" part (Tom Jones) of a larger book title here, is set in roman when the larger setting is in italics.

Italicize foreign words and phrases, unless they have been assimilated into English through usage (your dictionary should have a method for noting the distinction; if not, consult one that has):

> The statement contained two clichés and one *non sequitur.*
> The author of this naïve exposé suffers from an *idée fixe.*

Other foreign expressions *not* italicized are: etc., e.g., et al., genre, hubris, laissez faire, leitmotif, roman à clef, raison d'être, tête-à-tête.

Use neither quotation marks nor italics for the Bible, for its books or parts (Genesis, Old Testament), for other sacred books (Koran, Talmud, Upanishad), nor for famous documents like the Magna Carta, the Declaration of Independence, the Communist Manifesto, and the Gettysburg Address, nor for instrumental music known by its form, number, and key:

> Beethoven's C-minor Quartet
> Brahms's Symphony No. 4, Opus 98

When a reference in parentheses falls at the end of a quotation, the quotation marks *precede* the parentheses:

> As Ecclesiastes tells us, "there is no new thing under the sun" (i.9).

ELLIPSIS

1. Use three spaced periods . . . (the ellipsis mark) when you omit something from a quotation. Do *not* use them in your own text in place of a dash, or in mere insouciance.

2. If you omit the end of a sentence, put in a period (no space) and add the three spaced dots. . . .

3. If your omission falls after a completed sentence, just add the three spaced dots to the period already there. . . . The spacing is the same as for case 2.

Here is an uncut passage, followed by a shortened version illustrating the three kinds of ellipsis:

To learn a language, learn as thoroughly as possible a few everyday sentences. This will educate your ear for all future pronunciations. It will give you a fundamental grasp of structure. And start soon.

(1)

To learn a language, learn . . . a few everyday sentences. This
(2)
will educate your ear. . . . It will give you a fundamental grasp
(3)
of structure. . . .

You can omit beginning and ending ellipses when you use a quotation within a sentence:

Lincoln was determined that the Union, "cemented with the blood of . . . the purest patriots," would not fail.

APOSTROPHE

It's may be overwhelmingly our most frequent misspelling as in "The dog scratched *it's* ear." No, no! *It's* means *it is. Who's* means *who is. They're* means *they are.* NO pronoun spells *its* possessive with an apostrophe: *hers, its, ours, theirs, yours, whose, oneself.*

For nouns, add apostrophe -*s* to form the singular possessive: *dog's life, hour's work, Marx's ideas.* Add apostrophe -*s* even to singular words already ending in *s: Yeats's poems, Charles's crown. Sis' plans* and *the boss' daughter* are not what we say. We say *Sissuz* and *bossuz and keatsuz,* and should say the same in our writing: *sis's boss's, Keats's.* Plurals *not* ending in *s* also form the possessive by adding '*s: children's hour, women's rights.* But most plurals take the apostrophe after the *s* already there: *witches' sabbath, ten cents' worth, three days' time, the Joneses' possessions.*

I repeat, the rule for making singulars possessive is to add '*s* regardless of length and previous ending. French names ending in silent *s*-sounds also add '*s: Camus's works, Marivaux's life, Berlioz's Requiem.* If your page grows too thick with double *s*'s, substitute a few pronouns for the proper names, or rephrase: *the death of Themistocles, the Dickens character Pip.*

The apostrophe can help to clarify clusters of nouns. These I have actually seen: *Alistair Jones Renown Combo, the church barbecue chicken sale, the uniform policeman training program, the members charter plane.* And of course, *teachers meeting* and *veterans insurance* are so common as to seem almost normal. But an apostrophe chips one more noun out of the block. It makes your meaning one word clearer, marking *teachers'* as a modifier, and distinguishing *teacher* from *teachers.* Inflections are helpful, and the written word needs all the help it can get: *Jones's Renowned, church's barbecued, uniformed policeman's, members' chartered.* Distinguish your modifiers, and keep your possessions.

Compound words take the *'s* on the last word only: *mother-in-law's hat, the brothers-in-law's attitude* (all the brothers-in-law have the same attitude), *somebody else's problem.* Joint ownerships may similarly take the *'s* only on the last word (*Bill and Mary's house*), but *Bill's and Mary's* house is more precise, and preferable.

Again, possessive pronouns have no apostrophe: *hers, its, theirs, yours, whose, oneself.* Remember that *it's* means *it is,* and that *who's* means *who is;* for possession, use *its* and *whose.*

The double possessive uses both an *of* and an *'s: a friend of my mother's, a book of the teacher's, a son of the Jones's, an old hat of Mary's.* Note that the double possessive indicates one possession among several of the same kind: mother has several friends; the teacher, several books.

Use the apostrophe to indicate omissions: *the Spirit of '76, the Class of '02, can't, won't, don't.* Finally, use the apostrophe when adding a grammatical ending to a number, letter, sign, or abbreviation: *1920's;* his *3's* look like *8's; p's* and *q's;* he got four *A's;* too many *of's* and *and's;* she *X'd* each box; *K.O.'d* in the first round. (Some of these are also italics, or underlined when typed. See p. 162.)

HYPHEN

For clarity, hyphenate groups of words acting as one adjective or one adverb: *eighteenth-century attitude, early-blooming southern crocus, of-and-which disease.* Distinguish between a *high school,* and a *high-school teacher.* Similarly, hyphenate compound nouns when you need to distinguish, for example, *five sentence-exercises* from *five-sentence exercises.*

Hyphenate prefixes to proper names: *ex-Catholic, pro-Napoleon,* and all relatively new combinations like *anti-marriage.* Consult your dictionary.

Hyphenate after prefixes that demand emphasis or clarity: *ex-husband, re-collect* ("to collect again," as against *recollect,* "to remember"), *re-emphasize, pre-existent.*

When you must break a word at the end of a line, hyphenate where your dictionary marks the syllables with a dot; *syl·lables, syl-lables.* If you must break a hyphenated word, break it after the hyphen: *self-/sufficient.* Don't hyphenate an already hyphenated word: *self-suf-/ficient.* It's hard on the eyes and the printer. When you write for print, underline those line-end hyphens you mean to keep as hyphens, making a little equals sign: self=/sufficient.

Hyphenate suffixes to single capital letters (*T-shirt, I-beam, X-ray*). Hyphenate *ex-champions* and *self-reliances.* Hyphenate to avoid double *i*'s and triple consonants: *anti-intellectual, bell-like.*

Hyphenate two-word numbers: *twenty-one, three-fourths.* Use the "suspensive" hyphen for hyphenated words in series: "We have ten-, twenty-five-, and fifty-pound sizes."

VIRGULE (SLANT, SLASH)

Spare this "little rod" (/), and don't spoil your work with the legalistic *and/or.* Don't write "bacon and/or eggs"; write "bacon or eggs, or both." Likewise, don't use it for a hyphen: not "male/female conflict" but "male-female conflict." Use the virgule when quoting poetry in your running text: "That time of year thou mayst in me behold / When yellow leaves, . . ."

SPELLING

The dictionary is your best friend as you face the inevitable anxieties of spelling, but three underlying principles and some tricks of the trade can help immeasurably:

Principle I. Letters represent sounds: proNUNciation can help you spell. No one proNOUNcing his words correctly would make the familiar errors of "similiar" and "enviorment." Simply sound out the letters: *envIRONment* and *goverNment* and *FebRUary* and *intRAmural.* Of course, you will need to be wary of some words *not* pronounced as spelled: *Wednesday* pronounced "Wenzday," for instance. But sounding the letters can help your spellings. You can even say "conver*t*ible" and "indel*i*ble" and "plaus*i*ble" without sounding like a fool, and you can silently stress the *able* in words like "proba*ble*" and "immov*able*" to remember the difficult distinction between words ending in *-ible,* and *-able.*

Consonants reliably represent their sounds. Remember that *c* and often *g* go soft before *i* and *e.* Consequently, you must add a *k* when extending words like *picnic* and *mimic—picnicKing, mimicKing—*to keep them from rhyming with *slicing* or *dicing.* Conversely, you just keep the *e* (where you would normally drop it) when making *peace* into *peacEable* and *change* into *changEable,* to keep the *c* and *g* soft.

Single *s* is pronounced *zh* in words like *vision, occasion, pleasure.* Knowing that *ss* hushes ("sh-h-h") will keep you from errors like *occassion,* which would sound like *passion.*

Vowels sound short and light before single consonants: *hat, pet, kit, hop, cup.* When you add any vowel (including *y*), the first vowel will say its name: *hate, Pete, kite, hoping, cupid.* Notice how the *a* in *-able* keeps the main vowel saying its names in words like *unmistakable, likable,* and *notable.* Therefore, to keep a vowel short protect it with double consonant: *petting, hopping.* This explains the troublesome *rr* in *occuRRence:* a single *r* would make it say *cure* in the middle. *Putting* a golf ball and *putting* something on paper must both use *tt* to keep from being pronounced *pewting*. Compare *stony* with *sonny* and *bony* with *bonny*. The *y* is replacing the *e* in *stone* and *bone*, and the rule is working perfectly. It works in any syllable that is accented: compare *forgeTTable* as against *markeTing*, *begiNNing* as against *buttoNing*, and *compeLLing* as against *traveLing*.

Likewise, when *full* combines and loses its stress, it also loses an *l*. Note the single and double *l* in *fulFILLment*. Similarly, *SOULful*, *GRATEful*, *AWful* — even *SPOONful*.

Principle II. This is the old rule of *i* before *e*, and its famous exceptions:

> *I* before *e*
> **Except after** *c*,
> **Or when sounded like** *a*
> **As in** *neighbor* **and** *weigh*.

It works like a charm: *achieve, believe. receive, conceive*. Note that *c* needs an *e* to make it sound like *s*. Remember also that *leisure* was once pronounced "lay-sure," and *foreign*, "forayn," and *heifer*, "hayfer." Memorize these important exceptions: *seize, weird, either, sheik, forfeit, counterfeit, protein*. Note that all are pronounced "ee" (with a little crowding) and that the *e* comes first. Then note that another small group goes the opposite way, having a long *i* sound as in German "Heil": *height, sleight, seismograph, kaleidoscope. Financier*, another exception, follows its French origin and its original sound. *Deity* sounds both vowels as spelled.

Principle III. Most big words, following the Latin or French from which they came, spell their sounds letter for letter. Look up the derivations of the words you misspell (note that double *s*, and explain it). You will never again have trouble with *desperate* and *separate* once you discover that the first comes from *de-spero*, "without hope," and that SePARate devides equals, the PAR values in stocks or golf. Nor with *definite* or *definitive*, once you see the kinship of both with *finite* and *finish*. Derivations can also help you a little with the devilment of *-able* and *-ible*, since, except for a few ringers, the *i* remains from Latin, and the *-ables* are either French (*ami-able*) or Anglo-Saxon copies (*workable*). Knowing origins can help at crucial points: *resemblAnce* comes from Latin *simulAre*," "to copy"; *existEnce* comes from Latin *existEre;* "to stand forth."

The biggest help comes from learning the common Latin prefixes, which, by a process of assimilation (*ad-similis*, "like to like"), account for the double consonants at the first syLLabic joint of so many of our words:

AD- (**toward, to**): *abbreviate* (**shorten down**), *accept* (**grasp to**).
CON- (**with**): *collapse* (**fall with**), *commit* (**send with**).
DIS- (**apart**): *dissect* (**cut apart**), *dissolve* (**loosen apart**).
IN- (**into**): *illuminate* (**shine into**), *illusion* (**playing into**).
IN- (**not**): *illegal* (**not lawful**), *immature* (**not ripe**).
INTER- (**between**): *interrupt* (**break between**), *interrogate* (**ask between**).
OB- (**toward, to**): *occupy* (**take in**), *oppose* (**put to**), *offer* (**carry to**).
SUB- (**under**): *suffer* (**bear under**), *suppose* (**put down**).
SYN- (**"together"**—this one is Greek): *symmetry* (**measuring together**), *syllogism* (**logic together**).

Spelling takes a will, an eye, and an ear. And a dictionary. Keep a list of your favorite enemies. Memorize one or two a day. Write them in the air in longhand. Visualize them. Imagine a blinking neon sign, with the wicked letters red and tall—definIte—definIte. Then print them once, write them twice, and blink them a few times more as you go to sleep. But best of all, make up whatever devices you can— the crazier the better—to remember their tricky parts:

DANCE attenDANCE.
EXISTENCE is TENSE.
There's IRON in this envIRONment.
The resISTANCE took its STANCE.
There's an ANT on the defendANT.
LOOSE as a goose.

LOSE loses an o.
ALLOT isn't A LOT.
Already isn't ALL RIGHT.
I for gaIety.
The LL in paraLLel gives me el.
PURr in PURsuit.

When an unaccented syllable leads to misspelling, you can also get some help by trying to remember a version of the word that accents the troublesome syllable: acad*e*my—acaDEMic; defin*i*tely —defiNItion; irrit*a*ble—irriTATE; prep*a*ration—prePARE.
Many foreign words, though established in English, retain their native diacritical marks, which aid in pronunciation; *naïveté, résumé, séance, tête-à-tête, façade, Fräulein, mañana, vicuña.* Many names are similarly treated: *Müller, Gödel, Göttingen, Poincaré, Brontë, Noël Coward, García Lorca, Havlíček.* As always, your dictionary is your best guide, as it is, indeed, to all words transliterated to English from different alphabets and systems of writing (Russian, Arabic, Chinese, Japanese, and so on).
Here are more of the perpetual headaches:

accept—except
accommodate
acknowledgment—judgment
advice—advise
affect—effect°
all right°—a lot°
allusion—illusion—disillusion°
analysis—analyzing

argue—argument
arrangement
businessman
capital (city)—capitol (building)°
censor—censure°
committee
complement—compliment°
continual—continuous°

° In the Glossary of Usage.

controversy
council — counsel — consul*
criticize — criticism
curriculum* — career —
   occurrence
decide — divide — devices
desert — dessert
dilemma — condemn
disastrous
discreet — discrete*
embarrassment — harassment
eminent — imminent —
   immanent*
exaggerate
explain — explanation
familiar — similar
forward — foreword
genius — ingenious* —
   ingenuous*
height — eighth
hypocrisy — democracy
irritable

its — it's*
lonely — loneliness
marriage — marital — martial
misspell — misspelling
Negroes — heroes — tomatoes
obstacle
possession
primitive
principal — principle*
proceed — precede — procedure
rhythm
questionnaire
stationary — stationery
succeed — successful
suppressed
their — they're
truly
until — till
unnoticed
weather — whether
who's — whose*

CAPITALIZATION

You know about sentences and names, certainly; but the following points are troublesome. Capitalize:

1.   Names of races, languages, and religions — Negro, Caucasian, Mongolian, Protestant, Jewish, Christian, Roman Catholic, Indian, French, English, Black (as in Black English). But "blacks and whites in this neighborhood," "black entrepreneurs," "white storekeepers," — especially in phrases that contrast blacks and whites, since *white* is never capitalized.

2.   North, south, east, and west *only when they are regions* — the mysterious East, the new Southwest — or parts of proper nouns: the West Side, East Lansing.

3.   The *complete* names of churches, rivers, hotels, and the like — the First Baptist Church, the Mark Hopkins Hotel, the Suwannee River (not First Baptist church, Mark Hopkins hotel, Suwannee river).

4.   All words in titles, except prepositions, articles, conjunctions,

° In the Glossary of Usage.

and the "to" of infinitives. But capitalize even these if they come first or last, or if they are longer than four letters—I'm Through with Love," *Gone with the Wind*, "I'll Stand By," *In Darkest Africa*, *How to Gain Friends and Influence People*, *To Catch a Thief*. Capitalize nouns, adjectives, and prefixes in hyphenated compounds—*The Eighteenth-Century Background*, *The Anti-Idealist* (but *The Antislavery Movement*). But hyphenated single words, the names of numbered streets, and the written-out numbers on your checks are *not* capitalized after the hyphen: *Self-fulfillment, Re-examination. Forty-second Street, Fifty-four . . . Dollars.*

When referring to magazines, newspapers, and reference works in sentences, footnotes, and bibliographies, you may drop the *The* as part of the title; the *Atlantic Monthly*, the *Kansas City Star*, the *Encyclopaedia Britannica*. (Euphony and sense preserve *The* for a few: *The New Yorker, The Spectator.*)

5.   References to a specific section of a work—the Index, his Preface, Chapter 1, Volume IV, Act II, but "scene iii" is usually not capitalized because its numerals are also in lower case.

6.   Abstract nouns, when you want emphasis, serious or humorous—". . . the truths contradict, so what is Truth?"; Very Important Person; the Ideal.

Do not capitalize the seasons—spring, winter, midsummer.

Do not capitalize after a colon, unless what follows is normally capitalized:

> **Again we may say with Churchill: "Never have so many owed so much to so few."**
>
> *Culture, People, Nature: An Introduction to General Anthropology* [title of book]
>
> **Many lost everything in the earthquake: their homes had vanished along with their supplies, their crops, their livestock.**

Do not capitalize proper nouns serving as common nouns: *china, cognac, napoleon* (a pastry), *chauvinist, watt* (electricity). Usage divides on some proper adjectives: *French [french] pastry, Cheddar [cheddar] cheese, German [german] measles, Venetian [venetian] blinds.* Also somewhat uncertain are names with lower-case articles or prepositions like [Charles] de Gaulle, [John] von Neumann; your best bet when omitting first names is to capitalize in full: *De Gaulle, Von Neumann.* But if you, instead, follow the lower-case form within sentences—*de Gaulle, von Neumann*—always capitalize in full at the beginning of a sentence. Breeds of animals, as in *Welsh terrier*, and products of a definite origin, as in *Scotch whiskey*, are less uncertain. When in doubt, your best guide, as in spelling, is your dictionary.

EXERCISES

1. *Correct these omissions of the comma, and, in your margin, label the ones you insert as* INTRODUCER, COORDINATOR, INSERTER, *or* LINKER:

1. We find however that the greatest expense in renovation will be for labor not for materials.
2. They took chemistry fine arts history and English.
3. We met June 1 1982 to discuss the problem which continued to plague us.
4. A faithful sincere friend he remained loyal to his roommate even after the unexpected turn of events.
5. Though she was a junior-college instructor teaching advanced calculus given at night during the winter did not intimidate her.
6. C. Wright Mills's *The Power Elite* which even after two decades is still one of the finest examples of sociological analysis available ought to be required reading in any elementary sociology course.
7. My father, who is a good gardener keeps things well trimmed.

2. *Correct these fragments, comma splices, and run-ons, adding commas and other marks as necessary:*

1. His lectures are not only hard to follow they are boring.
2. Stephano and Trinculo are the comics of the play never presented as complete characters they are not taken seriously.
3. The book deals with the folly of war its stupidity, its cruelty however in doing this the author brings in too many characters repeats episodes over and over and spoils his comedy by pressing too hard.
4. He left his second novel unfinished. Perhaps because of his basic uncertainty, which he never overcame.
5. She seems to play a careless game. But actually knows exactly what she is doing, and intends to put her opponent off guard.
6. His idea of democracy was incomplete, he himself had slaves.
7. She knows her cards that is she never overbids.
8. The problem facing modern architects is tremendous, it involves saving energy on a grand scale with untested devices and still achieving beautiful buildings.
9. The solution was elegant, besides being inexpensive, it was a wholly new approach.
10. Don't underestimate the future, it is always there.

3. *Add or subtract commas and semicolons as necessary in these sentences:*

1. Their travels are tireless, their budget however needs a rest.
2. They abhor economizing, that is, they are really spendthrifts.
3. Muller wants efficiency, Smithers beauty.
4. Abramson won the first set with a consistent backhand; some beautiful forehand volleys also helping at crucial moments.
5. The downtown parking problem remains unsolved; the new structures, the new meters, and the new traffic patterns having come into play about three years too late.

4. *Adjust the following sentences concerning the colon:*

1. Many things seem unimportant, even distasteful, money, clothes, popularity, even security and friends.
2. People faced with inflation, of which we have growing reminders daily, seem to take one of two courses; either economizing severely in hopes of receding prices, or buying far beyond their immediate needs in fear of still higher prices.
3. Depressed, refusing to face the reality of his situation, he killed himself, it was as simple as that.
4. To let him go was unthinkable: to punish him was unbearable.

5. *Add quotation marks and italics to these:*

1. Like the farmer in Frost's Mending Wall, some people believe that Good fences make good neighbors.
2. Here see means understand, and audience stands for all current readers.
3. For him, the most important letter between A and Z is I.
4. Why does the raven keep crying Nevermore: he asked.
5. In America, said the Chinese lecturer, people sing Home, Sweet Home; in China, they stay there.
6. The boys' favorite books were Huckleberry Finn, the Bible, especially Ecclesiastes, and Walden.
7. Germaine Greer's The Female Eunuch is memorable for phrases like I'm sick of peering at the world through false eyelashes and I'm a woman, not a castrate.

6. *Make a list of your ten most frequent misspellings. Then keep it handy and active, removing your conquests and adding your new troubles.*

7. *Capitalize the following, where necessary:*

go west, young man.	the missouri river
the south left the union.	my christian name begins with
the east side of town	c.
the introduction to *re-establishing toryism*	the new york public library *the neo-positivistic approach* [book]
east side, west side	the st. louis post-dispatch [add italics]
the tall black spoke french.	twenty-five dollars [on a check]
she loved the spring.	33 thirty-third street
health within seconds [book]	the tundra occupies a large portion of northern canada.
clear through life in time [book]	
a doberman pinscher	
the methodist episcopal church	

12

A
Glossary
of Usage

Speech keeps a daily pressure on writing, and writing returns the compliment, exacting sense from new twists in the spoken language and keeping old senses straight. Usage, generally, is "the way they say it." Usage is the current in the living stream of language; it keeps us afloat, it keeps us fresh—as it sweeps us along. But to distinguish yourself as a writer, you must always swim upstream. You may say, *hoojaeatwith?*; but you will write: *With whom did they compare themselves? With the best, with whoever seemed admirable.* Usage is, primarily, talk; and talk year by years gives words differing social approval, and differing meanings. Words move from the gutter to the penthouse, and back down the elevator shaft. *Bull*, a four-letter Anglo-Saxon word, was unmentionable in Victorian circles. One had to use *he-cow*, if at all. Phrases and syntactical patterns also have their fashions, mostly bad. *Like unto me* changes to *like me* to *like I do; this type of thing* becomes *this type thing; -wise*, after centuries of dormancy in only a few words (*likewise, clockwise, otherwise*), suddenly sprouts out the end of everything: *budgetwise, personalitywise, beautywise, prestigewise. Persuade them to vote* becomes *convince them to vote.* Suddenly, everyone is saying *hopefully.* As usual, the marketplace changes more than your money.

But the written language has always refined the language of the marketplace. The Attic Greek of Plato and Aristotle (as Aristotle's remarks about local usages show) was distilled from commercial exchange. Cicero and Catullus and Horace polished their currency against the archaic and the Greek. Mallarmé claimed that Poe had given *un sens plus pur aux mots de la tribu*—which Eliot rephrases for himself: "to purify the dialect of the tribe." It is the very nature of writing so to do; it is the writer's illusion that he has done so:

> I have laboured to refine our language to grammatical purity, and to clear it from colloquial barbarisms, licentious idioms, and irregular combinations. Something, perhaps, I have added to the elegance of its construction, and something to the harmony of its cadence.

—wrote Samuel Johnson in 1752 as he closed his *Rambler* papers. And he had almost done what he hoped. He was to shape English writing and speech for the next hundred and fifty years, until it was ready for another dip in the stream and another purification. His work, moreover, lasts. We would not imitate it now; but we can read it with pleasure, and imitate its enduring drive for excellence and meaning— making words mean what they say.

Johnson goes on to say that he has "rarely admitted any word not authorized by former writers." Writers provide the second level of usage, the paper money. But even this usage requires principle. If we accept "what the best writers use," we still cannot tell whether it is valid: we may be aping their bad habits. Usage is only a court of first appeal, where we can say little more than "He said it." Beyond that helpless litigation, we can test our writing by asking what the words mean, and by simple principles: clarity is good, economy is good, ease is good, gracefulness is good, fullness is good, forcefulness is good. As with all predicaments on earth, we judge by appeal to meanings and principles, and we often find both in conflict. Do *near* and *nearly* mean the same thing? Do *convince* and *persuade? Lie* and *lay?* Is our writing economical but unclear? Is it full but cumbersome? Is it clear but too colloquial for grace? Careful judgment will give the ruling.

THE GLOSSARY

A, an. *A* goes before consonants and *an* before vowels. But use *a* before *h* sounded in a first syllable: *a hospital, a hamburger.* Use *an* before a silent h: *an honor, an heir, an hour.* Use *a* before vowels pronounced as consonants: *a use, a euphemism.*

Abbreviations. Use only those conventional abbreviations your reader can easily recognize: *Dr., Mr., Mrs., Ms., Messrs.* (for two or more men, pronounced "messers," as in *Messrs. Adams, Pruitt, and Williams*), *Jr., St., Esq.* (Esquire, following a British gentleman's name, between commas and with *Mr.* omitted), *S.J.* (Society of Jesus, also following a name). All take periods. College degrees are usually recognizable: *A.B., M.A., Ph.D., D.Litt., M.D., LL.D.* Similarly, dates and times: B.C., A.D., A.M., P.M. Though these are conventionally printed as small capitals, regular capitals in your classroom papers are perfectly acceptable as are "lowercase" letters for a.m. and p.m. Write them without commas: *2000 B.C. was Smith's estimate.* A number of familiar abbreviations go without periods: *TV, FBI, USSR, USA, YMCA,* though periods are perfectly OK or O.K. Certain scientific phrases also go without periods, especially when combined with figures: *55 mph, 300 rpm, 4000 kwh.* But *U.N.* and *U.S. delegation* are customary. Note that in formal usage *U.S.* serves only as an adjective; write out *the United States* serving as a noun.

Abbreviations, conventional in running prose, unitalicized, are "e.g." (*exempli gratia,* "for example"), "i.e." (*id est,* "that is"), "etc." (*et cetera,* better written out "and so forth"), and "viz." (*videlicet,* pronounced "vi-DEL-uh-sit," meaning "that is," "namely"). These are followed by either commas or colons after the period:

> **The commission discovered three frequent errors in management, i.e., failure to take appropriate inventories, erroneous accounting, and inattention to costs.**
> **The semester included some outstanding extracurricular programs, e.g.: a series of lectures on civil rights, three concerts, and a superb performance of** *Oedipus Rex.*

The abbreviation *vs.,* usually italicized, is best spelled out, unitalicized, in your text: "The antagonism of Capulet versus Montague runs throughout the play." The abbreviation *c.* or *ca.,* standing for *circa* ("around") and used with approximate dates in parentheses, is italicized: "Higden wrote *Polychronicon* (*c.* 1350)." For further abbreviations in footnoting, see Chapter 9, "Research," pp. 109–11.

Above. For naturalness and effectiveness, avoid such references as "The above statistics are . . . ," and "The above speaks for itself." Simply use "These" or "This."

Action. A horribly overused catchall. Be specific: *invasion, rape, murder, intransigence, boycott.*

Adapt, adopt. To *adapt* is to modify something to fit a new purpose. To *adopt* is to take it over as it is.

Advice, advise. Frequently confused. *Advice* is what you get when advisers *advise* you.

Affect, effect. *Affect* means "to produce an *effect.*" Avoid *affect* as a noun; just say *feeling* or *emotion. Affective* is a technical term for *emotional* or *emotive*, which are clearer.

Aggravate. Means to add gravity to something already bad enough. Avoid using it to mean "irritate."

Wrong	Right
He aggravated his mother.	The rum aggravated his mother's fever.

All, all of. Use *all* without the *of* wherever you can to economize: *all this, all that, all those, all the people, all her lunch.* But some constructions need *of: all of them, all of Faulkner.*

All ready, already. Two different meanings. *All ready* means that everything is ready; *already* means "by this time."

All right, alright. *Alright* is not *all right;* you are confusing it with the spelling of *already.*

Allusion, illusion, disillusion. The first two are frequently confused, and *disillusion* is frequently misspelled *disallusion.* An *allusion* is a reference to something; an *illusion* is a mistakem conception. You disillusion someone by bringing him back to hard reality from his illusions.

Alot. You mean *a lot*, not *allot.*

Among. See *Between.*

Amount of, number of. Use *amount* with general heaps of things; use *number* with amounts that might be counted: *a small amount of interest, a large number of votes.*

And/or. an ungainly thought stopper. See p. 166.

Anxious. Use to indicate *Angst*, agony, and anxiety. Does not mean cheerful expectation: "He was *anxious* to get started." Use *eager* instead.

Any. Do not overuse as a modifier.

Poor	Good
She was the best of any senior in the class.	She was the best senior in the class.
If any people know the answer, they aren't talking.	If anyone knows the answer, he's not talking.

Add *other* when comparing likes: "She was better than *any other* senior in the class." But "This junior was better than any senior."

Any more. Written as two words, except when an adverb in negatives and questions:

She never wins *anymore.*
Does she play *anymore?*

Anyplace, someplace. Use *anywhere* and *somewhere* (adverbs), unless you mean "any *place*" and "some *place.*"

Appear. Badly overworked for *seem.*

Appreciate. Means "recognize the worth of." Do not use to mean simply "understand."

Loose	Careful
I *appreciate* your position.	I *understand* your position.
I *appreciate* that your position is grotesque.	I *realize* your position is grotesque.

Area. Drop it. *In the area of finance* means *in finance,* and *conclusive in all areas* means simply *conclusive,* or *conclusive in all departments (subjects, topics).* Be specific.

Around. Do not use for *about:* it will seem to mean "surrounding."

Poor	Good
Around thirty people came.	*About* thirty people came.
He sang at *around* ten o'clock.	He sang at *about* ten o'clock.

As. Use where the cigarette people have *like:* "It tastes good, *as* a goody should," or "it tastes good the way a goody should." (See also *Like.*)

Do not use for *such as:* "Many things, *as* nails, hats, toothpicks. . . ." Write "Many things, *such as* nails. . . ."

Do not use *as* for *because* or *since;* it is ambiguous:

Ambiguous	Precise
As I was walking, I had time to think.	Because I was walking, I had time to think.

As if. Takes the subjunctive: ". . . as if he *were* cold."

As of, as of now. Avoid, except for humor. Use *at,* or *now,* or delete entirely.

Poor	Improved
He left, as of ten o'clock.	He left at ten o'clock.
As of now, I've sworn off.	I've just sworn off.

As to. Use only at the beginning of a sentence: "As to his first allegation, I can only say. . . ." Change it to *about,* or omit it, within a sentence: "He knows nothing *about* the details"; "He is not sure [whether] they are right."

As well as. You may mean only *and.* Check it out. Avoid such ambiguities as *The Commons voted as well as the Lords.*

Aspect. Overused. Try *side, part, portion.* See *Jargon.*

At. Do not use after *where.* "Where is it *at?*" means "Where is it?"

Awhile, a while. You usually want the adverb: *linger awhile, the custom endured awhile longer.* If you want the noun, emphasizing a period of time, make it clear: *the custom lasted for a while.*

Bad, badly. *Bad* is an adjective: *a bad trip. Badly* is an adverb: *he wrote badly.* Linking verbs take *bad: he smells bad; I feel bad; it looks bad.*

Balance, bulk. Make them mean business, as in "He deposited the balance of his allowance" and "The bulk of the crop was ruined." Do not use them for people:

Poor	Improved
The *balance* of the class went home.	The *rest* of the class went home.
The *bulk* of the crowd was indifferent.	*Most* of the crowd was indifferent.

Basis. Drop it: *on a daily basis* means *daily.*

Be sure and. Write *be sure to.*

Because of, due to. See *Due to.*

Besides. Means "in addition to," not "other than."

Poor	Improved
Something *besides* smog was the cause [unless smog was also a cause].	Something *other than* smog was the cause.

Better than. Unless you really mean *better than,* use *more than.*

Poor	Improved
The lake was *better than* two miles across.	The lake was *more than* two miles across.

Between, among. *Between* ("by twain") has *two* in mind; *among* has more than two. *Between,* a preposition, takes an object; *between us, between you and me.* ("Between you and I" is sheer embarassment; see *Me,* below.) *Between* also indicates geographical placing: "It is midway between Chicago, Detroit, and Toledo." "The grenade fell between Jones and me and the gatepost"; but "The grenade fell among the fruit stands." "Between every building was a plot of petunias" conveys the idea, however nonsensical "between a building" is. "Between all the buildings were plots of petunias" would be better, though still a compromise.

Bimonthly, biweekly. Careless usage has damaged these almost beyond recognition, confusing them with *semimonthly* and *semiweekly.* For clarity, better say "every two months" and "every two weeks."

But, cannot but. "He can but fail" is old but usable. After a negative, however, the natural turn in *but* causes confusion:

Poor	Improved
He cannot but fail.	He can only fail.
He could not doubt but that it. . . .	He could not doubt that it. . . .
He could not help but take. . . .	He could not help taking. . . .

When *but* means "except," it is a preposition. "Everybody laughed but me."

But that, but what. Colloquial redundancies.

Poor	Improved
There is no doubt but that John's is the best steer.	There is no doubt that John's is the best steer.
	John's is clearly the best steer.
There is no one but what would enjoy it.	Anyone would enjoy it.

Can, may (could, might). *Can* means ability; *may* asks permission, and expresses possibility. *Can I go?* means, strictly, "Have I the physical capability to go?" In speech, *can* usually serves for both ability and permission, though the clerk will probably say, properly, "May I help you?" In assertions, the distinction is clear: "He can do it." "He may do it." "If he can, he may." Keep these distinctions clear in your writing.

Could and *might* are the past tenses, but when used in the present time they are subjunctive, with shades of possibility, and hence politeness: "*Could* you come next Tuesday?" *Might* I inquire about your plans?" *Could* may mean ability almost as strongly as *can:* "I'm sure he could do it." But *could* and *might* are usually subjunctives, expressing doubt:

> Perhaps he could make it, if he tries.
> I might be able to go, but I doubt it.

Cannot, can not. Use either, depending on the rhythm and emphasis you want. *Can not* emphasizes the *not* slightly.

Can't hardly, couldn't hardly. Use *can hardly, could hardly,* since *hardly* carries the negative sense.

Can't help but. A marginal mixture in speech of two clearer and more formal ideas, *I can but regret* and *I can't help regretting.* Avoid it in writing.

Capital, capitol. Frequently confused. You mean *capital,* the head thing, unless describing the Capitol Building and Hill in Washington, D.C., the *capital* of the United States.

Case. Chop out this deadwood:

Poor	Improved
In many cases, ants survive. . . .	Ants often. . . .
In such a case, surgery is recommended.	Then surgery is recommended.
In case he goes. . . .	If he goes. . . .
Everyone enjoyed himself, except in a few scattered cases.	Almost everyone enjoyed himself.

Cause, result. Since *all* events are both causes and results, suspect yourself of wordiness if you write either word.

Wordy	Economical
The invasions caused depopulation of the country.	The invasions depopulated the country.
He lost as a result of poor campaigning.	He lost because his campaign was poor.

Cause-and-effect relationship. Verbal adhesive tape. Recast the sentence, with some verb other than the wordy *cause:*

Poor	Improved
Othello's jealousy rises in a cause-and-effect relationship when he sees the handkerchief.	Seeing the handkerchief arouses Othello's jealousy.

Censor, censure. Frequently confused. A *censor* cuts out objectionable passages. *To censor* is to cut or prohibit. *To censure* is to condemn: "The *censor censored* some parts of the play, and *censured* the author as an irresponsible drunkard."

Center around. A physical impossibility. Make it *centers on,* or *revolves around,* or *concerns,* or *is about.*

Clichés. Don't use unwittingly. But they can be effective. There are two kinds: (1) the rhetorical—*tried and true, the not too distant future, sadder but wiser, in the style to which she had become accustomed;* (2) the proverbial—*apple of his eye, skin of your teeth, sharp as a tack, quick as a flash, twinkling of an eye.* The rhetorical ones are clinched by sound alone; the proverbial are metaphors caught in the popular fancy. Proverbial clichés can lighten a dull passage. You may even revitalize them, since they are frequently dead metaphors (see pp. 87–88). Avoid the rhetorical clichés unless you turn them to your advantage; *tried and untrue, gladder and wiser, a future not too distant.*

Compare to, compare with. To compare *to* is to show similarities (and differences) between different kinds; to compare *with* is to show differences (and similarities) between like kinds.

> Composition has been compared *to* architecture.
> He compares favorably *with* Mickey Spillane.
> Compare Shakespeare *with* Ben Jonson.

Complement, compliment. Frequently confused. *Complement* is a completion; *compliment* is a flattery: "When the regiment reached its full *complement* of recruits, the general gave it a flowery *compliment.*"

Concept. Often jargonish and wordy.

Poor	Improved
The concept of multiprogramming allows. . . .	Multiprogramming allows. . . .

Connotation, denotation. Words denote things, acts, moods, whatever: *tree, house, running, anger.* They usually also *connote* an attitude toward these things. *Tree* is a purely neutral denotation, but *oak* connotes sturdiness and *willow* sadness in addition to denoting different trees. *A House Is Not a Home,* wrote a certain lady, playing on connotations and a specific denotation: a house of prostitution. *Woman* and *lady,* both denote the human female, but carry connotations awakened in differing contexts:

> A *woman* usually outlives a man. (Denotation)
> She is a very able *woman*. (Connotation positive)
> She is his *woman*. (Connotation negative)
> She acts more like a *lady* than a *lady* of pleasure. (Connotations plus
> and minus)

Usage changes denotations: *a gay party* changes from a festive to a homosexual gathering. Usage also changes connotations. *Negro*, once polite, is now taboo for the once impolite *black*. *Chairman*, once a neutral denoter, now has acquired enough negative connotations to change a number of letterheads and signatures.

Beware of unwanted, or exaggerated, or offensive connotations: your reader may find you prejudiced.

Contact. Don't *contact* anyone: call, write, find, tell him.

Continual, continuous. You can improve your writing by *continual* practice, but the effort cannot be *continuous*. The first means "frequently repeated"; the second, "without interruption."

> It requires *continual* practice.
> There was a *continuous* line of clouds.

Contractions. We use them constantly in conversation: *don't, won't, can't, shouldn't, isn't*. Avoid them in writing, or your prose will seem too chummy. But use one now and then when you want some colloquial emphasis: *You can't go home again.*

Convince, persuade. *Convince* THAT and *persuade* TO are the standard idioms. *Convince* OF is also standard. *Convince* is wrongly creeping in before infinitives with *to*.

Wrong	**Right**
They *convinced* him to run.	They *persuaded* him *to* run.
	They *convinced* him *that* he should run.
	They *convinced* him *of* their support.

Could, might. See *Can, may.*

Could care less. You mean *couldn't care less*. Speech has worn off the *n't*, making the words say the opposite of what you mean. A person who cares a great deal could care a great deal less; one who does not care "*couldn't* care less": He's already at rock bottom.

Could of, would of. Phonetic misspellings of *could've* ("could have"), and *would've* ("would have"). In writing, spell them all the way out: *could have* and *would have*.

Couldn't hardly. Use *could hardly*.

Council, counsel, consul. *Council* is probably the noun you mean: a group of deliberators. *Counsel* is usually the verb "to advise." But *counsel* is also a noun: an adviser, an attorney, and their advice. Check your dictionary to see that you are writing what you mean. A *counselor* gives you his *counsel* about your courses, which may be submitted to an academic *council*. A *consul* is an official representing your government in a foreign country.

Curriculum. The plural is *curricula*, though *curriculums* will get by in informal prose. The adjective is *curricular*.

Definitely. A high-school favorite, badly overused.

Denotation, Connotation. See *Connotation*.

Different from, different than. Avoid *different than*, which confuses the idea of differing. Things differ *from* each other. Only in comparing several differences does *than* make clear sense: "All three of his copies differ from the original, but his last one is *more* different *than* the others." But here *than* is controlled by *more*, not by *different*.

Wrong	Right
It is different *than* I expected.	It is different *from* what I expected.
	It is not what I expected.
He is different *than* the others.	He is different *from* the others.

Discreet, discrete. Frequently confused. *Discreet* means someone tactful and judicious; *discrete* means something separate and distinct: "He was *discreet* in examining each *discrete* part of the evidence."

Disinterested. Does not mean "uninterested" nor "indifferent." *Disinterested* means impartial, without private interests in the issue.

Wrong	Right
You seem disinterested in the case.	You seem uninterested in the case.
	The judge was disinterested and perfectly fair.
He was disinterested in it.	He was indifferent to it.

Double negative. A negation that cancels another negation, making it accidentally positive: "He couldn't hardly" indicates that "He could easily," the opposite of its intended meaning. "They can't win nothing" really says that they *must* win something.

But some doubled negations carry an indirect emphasis—a mild irony, really—in such tentative assertions as "One cannot be certain that she will not prove to be the century's greatest poet," or "a not unattractive offer."

Due to. Never begin a sentence with "*Due* to circumstances beyond his control, he. . . ." *Due* is an adjective and must always relate to a noun or pronoun: "The catastrophe *due* to circumstances beyond his control was unavoidable," or "The catastrophe was *due* to circumstances beyond his control" (predicate adjective). But you are still better off with *because of, through, by,* or *owing to*. *Due to* is usually a symptom of wordiness, especially when it leads to *due to the fact that,* a venerable piece of plumbing meaning *because.*

Wrong	Right
He resigned *due to* sickness.	He resigned *because of* sickness.
He succeeded *due to* hard work.	He succeeded *through* hard work.
He lost his shirt *due to* leaving it in the locker room.	He lost his shirt *by* leaving it in the locker room.
The Far East will continue to worry the West, *due to* a general social upheaval.	The Far East will continue to worry the West, *owing to* a general social upheaval.
The program failed *due to the fact that* a recession had set in.	The program failed *because* a recession had set in.

Either, neither. One of two, taking a singular verb: *Either is a good candidate, but neither speaks well. Either ... or (neither ... nor)* are paralleling conjunctions. See pp. 64–65.

Eminent, imminent, immanent. Often confused. *Eminent* is something that stands out; *imminent* is something about to happen. *Immanent,* much less common, is a philosophical term for something spiritual "remaining within, indwelling." You usually mean *eminent.*

Enormity. Means "atrociousness"; does not mean "enormousness."

the *enormity* of the crime
the *enormousness* of the mountain

Enthuse. Don't use it; it coos and gushes.

Wrong	Right
She *enthused* over her new dress.	She gushed on and on about her new dress.
He was *enthused.*	He was *enthusiastic.*

Environment. Frequently misspelled *enviorment* or *envirnment.* It is business jargon, unless you mean the world around us.

Wordy	Improved
in an MVT environment	in MVT; with MVT; under MVT
He works in an environment of cost analysis.	He analyzes cost.

Equally as good. A redundant mixture of two choices, *as good as* and *equally good.* Use only one of these at a time.

Everyday, every day. You wear your *everyday* clothes *every day.*

Everyone, everybody. Avoid the common mismatching *their:*

"Everyone does *his* [or *her* but not *their*] own thing."

Exists. Another symptom of wordiness.

Poor	Improved
a system like that which exists at the university	a system like that at the university

The fact that. Deadly with *due to*, and usually wordy by itself.

Poor	Improved
The fact that Rome fell *due to* moral decay is clear.	*That* Rome fell *through* moral decay is clear.
This disparity is in part *a result of the fact that* some of the best indicators make their best showings in an expanding market.	This disparity arises in part *because* some of the best indictors. . . .
In view of the fact that more core is installed. . . .	Because more cores. . . .

Factor. Avoid it. We've used it to death. Try *element* when you mean "element." Look for an accurate verb when you mean "cause."

Poor	Improved
The increase in female employment is a factor in juvenile delinquency.	The increase in female employment has contributed to juvenile delinquency.
Puritan self-sufficiency was an important factor in the rise of capitalism.	Puritan self-sufficiency favored the rise of capitalism.

Farther, further. The first means distance; the second means time or figurative distance. You look *farther* and consider *further*.

Feasible. See *Viable*.

Fewer, less. See *Less, few*.

The field of. Try to omit it—you usually can—or bring the metaphor to life. It is trite and wordy.

Poor	Improved
He is studying in the field of geology.	He is studying geology.

Firstly. Archaic. Trim all such terms to *first, second, third*, and so on.

Flaunt, flout. *Flaunt* means to parade, to wave impudently; *flout* means to scoff at. The first is metaphorical; the second, not: "She *flaunted* her wickedness and *flouted* the police."

For. See p. 151.

Former, latter. Passable, but they often make the reader look back. Repeating the antecedents is clearer:

Poor	Improved
The Athenians and Spartans were always in conflict. *The former* had a better civilization; *the latter* had a better army.	The Athenians and Spartans were always in conflict. Athens had the better culture; Sparta, the better army.

Further. See *Farther*.

Good, well. *Good* is the adjective: *good time*. *Well* is the adverb: *well done*. In verbs of feeling, we are caught in the ambiguities of health. *I feel good* is more accurate than *I feel well*, because *well* may mean that your feelers are in working order. But *I feel well* is also an honest statement: "I feel that I am well." Ask yourself what your readers might misunderstand from your statements, and you will use these two confused terms clearly.

Got, gotten. Both acceptable. Your rhythm and emphasis will decide. America prefers the older *gotten* in many phrases; Britain goes mainly for *got*.

Hanged, hung. *Hanged* is the past of *hang* only for the death penalty.

> **They hung the rope and hanged the man.**

Hardly. Watch the negative here. "I can't *hardly*" means "I *can* easily." Write: "One can hardly conceive the vastness."

Healthy, healthful. Swimming is *healthful;* swimmers are *healthy*.

His/her, his (her). Shift to the neutral plural, or otherwise rephrase to avoid this awkwardness. *His* stands for both sexes, if you can stand it.

Historically. A favorite windy throat-clearer. Badly overused.

History. The *narrative*, written or oral, of events, not the events themselves. Therefore, avoid the redundancy "*recorded* history," likewise "*annals* of history," "*chronicles* of history." *History* alone will suffice: "Archaeologists have uncovered evidence of events previously unknown to history"; "World War II was the most devastating conflict in history."

Hopefully. An inaccurate dangler, a cliché. "Hopefull, they are at work" does not mean that they are working hopefully. Simply use "I hope" or "one hopes" (but *not* "it is hoped"): not "They are a symbol of idealism, and, hopefully, are representative," but "They are a symbol of idealism and are, one hopes, representative."

However. Initial *however* should be an adverb: "However long the task takes, it will be done." For the "floating" *however*, and however versus *but*, see p. 153.

Hung. See *Hanged*.

The idea that. Like *the fact that*—and the cure is the same. Cut it.

I (we, you, one). See *Point of View*.

If, whether. *If* is for uncertainties; *whether*, for alternatives. Usually the distinction is unimportant: *I don't know if it will rain; I don't know whether it will rain* [*or not*].

Imminent, immanent. See *Eminent*.

Imply, infer. The author *implies;* you *infer* ("carry in") what you think he means.

> **He *implied* that all women are hypocrites.**
> **From the ending, we *infer* that tragedy ennobles as it kills.**

Importantly. Often an inaccurate (and popular) adverb, like *hopefully.*

Inaccurate	Improved
More importantly, he walked home.	*More important,* he walked home.

In connection with. Always wordy. Say *about.*

Poor	Improved
They liked everything *in connection with* the university.	They liked everything *about* the university.

Includes. Jargonish, as a general verb for specific actions.

Poor	Improved
The report includes rural and urban marketing.	The report analyzes rural and urban marketing.

Individual. Write *person* unless you really mean someone separate and unique.

Infer. See *Imply, infer.*

Ingenious, ingenuous. Sometimes confused. *Ingenious* means clever; *ingenuous,* naïve. *Ingenius* is a common misspelling for both.

Instances. Redundant. *In many instances* means *often, frequently.*

Interesting. Make what you say interesting, but never tell the reader *it is interesting:* he may not believe you. *It is interesting* is merely a lazy preamble.

Poor	Improved
It is interesting to note that nicotine is named for Jean Nicot, who introduced tobacco into France in 1560.	Nicotine is named for Jean Nicot, who introduced tobacco into France in 1560.

Irregardless. A faulty word. The *ir-* (meaning *not*) is doing what the *-less* already does. You are thinking of *irrespective,* and trying to say *regardless.*

Irregular verbs. Here are some to watch; learn to control their past and past-participial forms. (See, also, *Hanged, hung; Lay; Rise, raise; Set, sit.*) Alternate forms are in parentheses.

arise, arose, arisen
awake, awoke, awaked (*but* was awakened)
bear, bore, borne
beat, beat, beaten
begin, began, begun
bid ("order"), bade, bidden
bid ("offer"), bid, bid
burst, burst, burst

drag, dragged (not drug), dragged
fit, fitted (fit, *especially intransitively*), fitted (*but* a fit person)
fling, flung, flung
get, got, got (gotten)
light, lit (lighted), lit (lighted)
prove, proved, proven (proved)
ride, rode, ridden
sew, sewed, sewn (sewed)

shine ("glow"), shone, shone
shine ("polish"), shined, shined
show, showed, shown (showed)
shrink, shrank (shrunk), shrunk (shrunken)

sow, sowed, sown (sowed)
spring, sprang, sprung
swim, swam, swum
swing, swung, swung
wake, woke (waked), waked

Is when, is where. Avoid these loose attempts:

Loose	Specific
Combustion is when [where] oxidation bursts into flame.	Combustion is oxidation bursting into flame.

It. Give it a specific reference, as a pronoun. See pp. 74, 142, 143.

Its, it's. Don't confuse *its*, the possessive pronoun, with *it's*, the contraction of *it is*.

-ize. A handy way to make verbs from nouns and adjectives (*patronize, civil-ize*). But handle with care. Manufacture new *-izes* only with a sense of humor and daring ("they Harvardized the party"). Business overdoes the trick: *finalize*, a relative newcomer, has provoked strong disapproval from writers who are not commercially familiarized.

Jargon. A technical, wordy phraseology that becomes characteristic of any particular trade, or branch of learning, frequently with nouns modifying nouns, and in the passive voice. Break out of it by making words mean what they say.

Jargon	Clear Meaning
The plot structure of the play provides no objective correlative.	The play fails to act out and exhibit the hero's inner conflicts.
	The plot is incoherent.
	The structure is lopsided.
The character development of the heroine is excellent.	The author sketches and deepens the heroine's personality skillfully.
	The heroine matures convincingly.
Three motivation profile studies were developed in the area of production management.	The company studied its production managers, and discovered three kinds of motivation.
He structured the meeting.	He organized (planned, arranged) the meeting.

Kind of, sort of. Colloquialisms for *somewhat, rather, something*, and the like. Usable, but don't overuse.

Lay. Don't use *lay* to mean *lie*. *To lay* means "to put" and needs an object; *to lie* means "to recline." Memorize both their present and past tenses, frequently confused:

> I *lie* down when I can; I *lay* down yesterday; I have *lain* down often. [Intransitive, no object.]
> The hen *lays* an egg; she *laid* one yesterday; she has *laid* four this week. [Transitive, *lays* an object.]
> Now I *lay* the book on the table; I *laid* it there yesterday; I have *laid* it there many times.

Lend, loan. Don't use *loan* for *lend*. *Lend* is the verb; *loan*, the noun: "Please *lend* me a five; I need a *loan* badly." Remember the line: "I'll *send* you to a *friend* who'll be willing to *lend*."

Less, few. Don't use one for the other. *Less* answers "How much?" *Few* answers "How many?"

Wrong	Right
We had *less* people than last time.	We had *fewer* people this time than last.

Level. Usually redundant jargon. *High level management* is *top management* and *college level courses* are *college courses*. What is a *level management,* or a *level course* anyway?

Lie, lay. See *Lay.*

Lighted, lit. Equally good past tenses for *light* (both "to ignite" and "to descend upon"), with *lit* perhaps more frequent. Rhythm usually determines the choice. *Lighted* seems preferred for adverbs and combinations: *a clean well-lighted place; it could have been lighted better.*

Like, as, as if. Usage blurs them, but the writer should distinguish them before he decides to go colloquial. Otherwise, he may throw his readers off.

> He looks *like* me.
> He dresses *as* [the way] I do.
> He acts *as if* he were high.

Note that *like* takes the objective case, and that *as*, being a conjunction, is followed by the nominative:

> She looks like *her.*
> He is as tall as *I* [am].
> He is tall, like *me.*

Like sometimes replaces *as* where no verb follows in phrases other than comparisons (*as . . . as):*

> It works *like* a charm. (. . . *as* a charm *works.*)
> It went over *like* a lead balloon. (. . . *as* a lead balloon *does.*)
> They worked *like* beavers. (. . . *as* beavers *do.*)

Literally. Often misused, and overused, as a general emphasizer: "We *literally* wiped them off the field."

Loan. See *Lend.*

Loose, lose. You will *lose* the game if your defense is *loose.*

Lots, lots of, a lot of. Conversational for *many, much, great, consider-able.* Try something else. See *Alot.*

Majority. Misused for *most:* "*The majority* of the play is comic" [wrong].

Maximum (minimum) amount. Drop *amount.* The minimum and the maximum *are* amounts. Don't write *a minimum of* and *as a minimum:* write *at least.*

May. See *Can, may.*

Maybe. Conversational for *perhaps.* Sometimes misused for *may be.* Unless you want an unmistakable colloquial touch, avoid it altogether.

Me. Use *me* boldly. It is the proper object of verbs and prepositions. Nothing is sadder than faulty propriety: "between you and *I*," or "They gave it to John and *I*," or "They invited my wife and *I*." Test yourself by dropping the first member "between *I*" (*no*), "gave it to *I*" (*no*), "invited *I*" (*no*). And do NOT substitute *myself.*

Medium, media. The singular and the plural. Avoid *medias,* unless you choose to begin *In medias res.*

Might. See *Can, may.*

Most. Does not mean *almost.*

Wrong	Right
Most everyone knows.	*Almost* everyone knows.

Must, a must. A *must* is popular jargon. Try something else:

Jargon	Improved
Beatup is really a *must* for every viewer.	Everyone interested in film should see *Beatup.*
This is a *must* course.	Everyone should take this course.

Myself. Use it only reflexively ("I hurt *myself*"), or intensively ("I *myself* often have trouble"). Fear of *me* leads to the incorrect "They gave it to John and *myself.*" Do not use *myself, himself, herself, themselves* for *me, him, her, them.*

Nature. Avoid this padding. Do not write *moderate in nature, moderate by nature, of a moderate nature;* simply write *moderate.*

Near. Avoid using it for degree.

Poor	Improved
a *near* perfect orbit	a *nearly* perfect orbit
	an *almost* perfect orbit
It was *a near* disaster.	It was *nearly a* disaster [or nearly disastrous].

Neither. See *Either.*

No one. Two words in America, not *noone,* or no-one (British).

None. This pronoun means "no one" and takes a singular verb, as do *each, every, everyone, nobody,* and other distributives. See p. 137.

Nowhere near. Use *not nearly,* or *far from,* unless you really mean *near:* "He was nowhere, near the end." See *Near.*

Number of. Usually correct. See *Amount of.*

Numbers. Spell out those that take no more than two words (*twelve, twelfth, twenty-four, two hundred*); use numerals for the rest (*101, 203, 4,510*). Spell out *all* numbers beginning a sentence. But use numerals to make contrasts and statistics clearer: *20 as compared to 49; only 1 of out of 40; 200 or 300 times as great.* Change a two-word number to numerals when it matches a numeral: *with 400* [not *four hundred*] *students and 527 parents.* Numbers are customary with streets: *42nd Street, 5th Avenue,* which may also be spelled out for aesthetic reasons: *Fifth Avenue.* Use numbers also with dates, times, measurements, and money: *April 1, 1984; 6:30* A.M. (but *half-past six*); *3 x 5 cards; 240 by 100 feet; 6'3"* (but *six feet tall*); *$4.99; $2 a ticket* (but *16 cents a bunch*).

Use Roman numerals (see your dictionary) together with Arabic to designate Act, scene, and line in plays, and Book, chapter, and page in the novels that use them:

> Romeo lies on the floor and cries like a child (III.iii.69–90).
> When Tom Jones finds the banknote (XII.iv.483), . . .

You would have already identified, in a footnote, the edition you are using. For further details see pp. 108, 111. Also see *Per cent, percent, percentage.*

Off of. Write *from:* "He jumped *from* his horse."

On the part of. Wordy.

Poor	Improved
There was a great deal of discontent *on the part of* those students who could not enroll.	The students who could not enroll were deeply discontented.

One. As a pronoun—"*One* usually flunks the first time"—see *Point of view.* Avoid the redundant numeral:

Poor	Improved
One of the most effective ways of writing is rewriting.	The best writing is rewriting.
The Ambassadors is one of the most interesting of James's books.	*The Ambassadors* is James at his best.
The meeting was obviously a poor one.	The meeting was obviously poor.

In constructions such as "one of the best that . . ." and "one of the worst who . . . ," the relative pronouns often are mistakenly considered singular. The plural noun of the prepositional phrase (*the best, worst*), not *the one,* is the antecedent, and the verb must be plural too:

Wrong	Right
one of the best [*players*] who *has* ever swung a bat	one of the best [*players*] who *have* ever swung a bat

Only. Don't put it in too soon; you will say what you do not mean.

Wrong	Right
He *only liked* mystery stories.	He liked *only* mystery stories.

Overall. Jargonish. Use *general,* or rephrase.

Dull	Improved
The overall quality was good.	The lectures were generally good.

Parent. Though only recently "promoted" to a verb, as such overworked and exhausted. Refresh your reader with *rear, bring up, supervise, raise, love.*

Per. Use *a:* "He worked ten hours *a* day." *Per* is jargonish, except in conventional Latin phrases: *per diem, per capita* (not italicized in your running prose).

Poor	Improved
This will cost us a manhour *per* machine *per* month a year from now.	A year from now, this will cost us a manhour a machine a month.
As *per* your instructions.	According to your instructions.

Per cent, percent, percentage. *Percent* (one word) seems preferred, though *percentage,* without numbers, still carries polish: "A large *percentage of* nonvoters attended"; "a significant *percentage* of the students." Use the % sign and numerals only in tables and in technical reports. Use numerals and *percent* when comparing several percentages. Otherwise spell out "percent" with the numbers: *ten percent, a hundred percent* (in business reports, a number usually goes with "percent"; *10 percent; 85 percent*). See *Numbers.*

Perfect. Not "more perfect," but "more nearly perfect."

Personally. Almost always superfluous.

Poor	Improved
I want to welcome them *personally.*	I want to welcome them [*myself*].
Personally, I like it.	I like it.

Phase. Do not use when *part* is wanted; "*a phase* of the organization" is better put as "a *part* of the organization." A phase is a stage in a cycle, as of the moon, of business, of the financial markets.

Phenomena. Frequently misused for the singular *phenomenon:* "This is a striking *phenomenon*" (not *phenomena*).

Phenomenal. Misused for a general intensive: "His popularity was *phenomenal*." A phenomenon is a fact of nature, in the ordinary nature of things. Find another word for the extraordinary: "His success was *extraordinary*" (*unusual, astounding, stupendous*).

Plan on. Use *plan to.* "He planned on going" should be "He planned to go."

Point of view. Pronouns establish your point of view: *I, one, we, you.* The essay normally proceeds in the third person with assertions and facts: *Jogging is good for heart and soul. It improves circulation.* Casting that in the first person, with *I*, limits both evidence and authority to just the singular view, the merely personal. But *I* is effective for an illustration from personal experience or for easing an assertion: "Clifton, I think, misses the point." Moving from *I* to *one* generalizes in the right direction, expanding the viewpoint from the singular first person to the collective third, from *I am sure* to *One is sure.* But *one* can seem too formal and get too thick:

> FAULTY: *One* finds *one's* opinion changing as *one* grows older.
> REVISED: Opinions change with age.
> REVISED: *Our* opinions change as *we* grow older.

That *we* is sometimes a useful generalizer, a convenient haven between the isolating *I* and the impersonal *one. We* can seem pompous, but not if it honestly handles those experiences we know we share, or can share.

> As *we* watch program after program, *we* are progressively bored, and *we* begin to wonder what values, if any, they represent.

The indefinite *you*, like the indefinite *they*, is usually too vague, too adolescent.

> FAULTY: You have your own opinion.
> FAULTY: They have their own opinion.
> REVISED: Everyone has his own opinion.
> REVISED: We all have our own opinions.

You as direct address to the reader poses a different problem. I have consistently addressed this book to *you*, the reader. But this is a special case, the relationship of tutor to student projected onto the page. None of my essays, I think, contains any *you* at all. Our stance in an essay is a little more formal, a little more public. We are better holding our pronouns to *one* or *we*, an occasional *I*, or none at all.

Prejudice. When you write "He was *prejudice*," your readers may be *puzzle.* Give it a *d:* "He was *prejudiced*"; then they won't be *puzzled.*

Presently. Drop it. Or use *now.* Many readers will take it to mean *soon:* "He will go *presently.*" It is characteristic of official jargon:

Poor	Improved
The committee is meeting *presently.*	The committee is meeting. The committee is meeting *soon.*
He is *presently* studying Greek.	He is studying Greek.

Principle, principal. Often confused. *Principle* is a noun only, meaning an essential truth, or rule: "It works on the *principle* that hot air rises." Princi*pal* is the *a*djective: The high-school *principal* acts as a noun because usage has dropped the *person* the adjective once modified. Likewise, *principal* is the principal amount of your money, which draws interest.

Process. Often verbal fat. For example, the following can reduce more often than not: *production process,* to *production; legislative* (or *legislation*) *process,* to *legislation; educational* (or *education*) *process,* to *education; societal process* to *social forces.*

Proof, evidence. *Proof* results from enough *evidence* to establish a point beyond doubt. Be modest about claiming proof:

Poor	Improved
This *proves* that Fielding was in Bath at the time.	Evidently, Fielding was in Bath at the time.

Provide. If you *absolutely cannot* use the meaningful verb directly, you may say *provide,* provided you absolutely cannot *give, furnish, allow, supply, enable, authorize, permit, facilitate, force, do, make, effect, help, be, direct, encourage.* . . .

Providing that. Use *provided,* and drop the *that. Providing,* with or without *that,* tends to make a misleading modification.

Poor	Improved
I will drop, *providing that* I get an incomplete.	I will drop, *provided* I get an incomplete.

In "I will drop, *providing that* I get an incomplete," *you* seem to be providing, contrary to what you mean.

Put across. Try something else: *convinced, persuaded, explained, made clear. Put across* is badly overused.

Quality. Keep it as a noun. Too many *professional quality writers* are already producing *poor quality prose,* and *poor in quality* means *poor.*

Quite. An acceptable but overused emphatic: *quite good, quite expressive, quite a while, quite a person.* Try rephrasing it now and then: *good, very good, for some time, an able person.*

Quote, quotation. Quote your quotations, and put them in quotation marks. Distinguish the verb from the noun. The best solution is to use *quote* only as a verb and to find synonyms for the noun: *passage, remark, assertion.*

Wrong	Right
As the following *quote* from Milton shows: . . .	As the following *passage* [or quotation] from Milton shows: . . .

Raise. See *Rise, raise.*

Rarely ever. Drop the *ever:* "Shakespeare *rarely* misses a chance for comedy."

Real. Do not use for *very. Real* is an adjective meaning "actual":

Wrong	Right
It was *real* good.	It was *very* good.
	It was *really* good.

Reason . . . is because. Knock out *the reason . . . is,* and *the reason why . . . is,* and you will have a good sentence.

> [The reason] they have difficulty with languages [is] because they have no interest in them.

Regarding, in regard to. Redundant or inaccurate.

Poor	Improved
Regarding the banknote, Jones was perplexed. [Was he *looking* at it?]	Jones was perplexed by the banknote.
He knew nothing *regarding* money.	He knew nothing about money.
She was careful *in regard to* the facts.	She respected the facts.

Regardless. This is correct. See *Irregardless* for the confusion.

Respective, respectively. Usually redundant.

Poor	Improved
The armies retreated to their *respective* trenches.	The armies retreated to their trenches.
Smith and Jones won the first and second prize *respectively.*	Smith won the first prize; Jones, the second.

Reverend, Honorable. Titles of clergymen and congressmen. The fully proper forms, as in the heading of a letter (*the* would not be capitalized in your running prose), are *The Reverend Mr. Claude C. Smith; The Honorable Adam A. Jones.* In running prose, *Rev. Claude Smith* and *Hon. Adam Jones* will get by, but the best procedure is to give the title and name its full form for first mention, then continue with *Mr. Smith* and *Mr. Jones.* Do not use "Reverend" or "Honorable" with the last name alone.

Rise, raise. Frequently confused. *Rise, rose, risen* means to get up. *Raise, raised, raised* means to lift up. "He *rose* early and *raised* a commotion."

Sanction. Beatifically ambiguous, now meaning both "to approve" and "to penalize." Stick to the root; use it only "to bless," "to sanctify," "to approve," "to permit." Use *penalize* or *prohibit* when you mean just that. Instead of "They exacted *sanctions*," say "They exacted *penalties*" or "enacted *restrictions*."

Seldom ever. Redundant. Cut the *ever*. (But *seldom if ever* has its uses.)

Set, sit. Frequently confused. You *set* something down; you yourself *sit* down. Confine sitting mostly to people (*sit, sat, sat*), and keep it intransitive, taking no object. *Set* is the same in all tenses (*set, set, set*).

Confused	Clarified
The house *sets* too near the street.	The house *stands* [*sits*] too near the street.
The package *set* where he left it.	The package *lay* [*sat*] where he left it.
He *has set* there all day.	He *has sat* there all day.

Shall, will; should, would. The older distinctions—*shall* and *should* reserved for *I* and *we*—have faded; *will* and *would* are usual: "I will go"; "I would if I could"; "he will try"; "they all would." *Shall* in the third person expresses determination: "They shall not pass." *Should,* in formal usage, is actually ambiguous: *We should be happy to comply,* intended to mean "would be happy," seems to say "ought to be happy."

Should of. See *Could of, would of.*

Similar to. Use *like:*

Poor	Improved
This is *similar* to that.	This is *like* that.

Sit. See *Set, sit.*

Situate. Usually wordy and inaccurate. Avoid it unless you mean, literally or figuratively, the act of determining a site, or placing a building: "Do not *situate* heavy buildings on loose soil."

Faulty	Improved
He is well *situated.*	He is rich.
Ann Arbor is a town *situated* on the Huron River.	Ann Arbor is a town on the Huron River.
The control panel is *situated* on the right.	The control panel is on the right.
The company is well *situated* to meet the competition.	The company is well prepared to meet the competition.

Situation. Usually jargon. Avoid it. Say what you mean: *state, market, mess, quandary, conflict, predicament.*

Size. Often redundant. *A small-sized country* is *a small country. Large in size* is *large.*

Slow. GO SLOW is what the street signs and the people on the street all say, but write "Go slowly."

So. Should be followed by *that* in describing extent: "It was *so* foggy *that* traffic almost stopped." Avoid its incomplete form, the teenager's intensive—*so nice, so wonderful, so pretty*—though occasionally this is effective.

Someplace, somewhere. See *Anyplace.*

Sort of. See *Kind of, sort of.*

Split infinitives. Improve them. They are cliché traps: *to really know, to really like, to better understand.* They are one of the signs of a wordy writer, and usually produce redundancies: *to really understand* is *to understand.* The quickest cure for split infinitives is to drop the adverb.

For a gain in grace, and often for a saving of words, you can sometimes change the adverb to an adjective.

Poor	Improved
to adequately *think* out solutions	*to think* out adequate solutions
to enable us *to* effectively *plan* our advertising	to enable us *to plan* effective advertising

Structure. See *Jargon.*

Sure. Too colloquial for writing: "It is *sure* a good plan." Use *surely* or *certainly,* or rephrase.

Tautology. Several words serving where fewer—usually one—are needed, or wanted: useless repetition. Some examples:

attach [together]	mix [together]
[basic] essentials	[pair of] twins
consecutive days [in a row]	(but, two *sets* of twins)
[early] beginnings	[past] history
[final] completion	refer [back]
[final] upshot	repeat [again]
[first] beginnings	sufficient [enough]
[just] merely	whether [or not]

That, which, who. *That* defines and restricts; *which* is explanatory and nonrestrictive; *who* stands for people, and may be restrictive or nonrestrictive. See pp. 59, 74–75, 141.

There is, there are, it is. However natural and convenient—it is WORDY. Notice that *it* here refers to something specific, differing distinctly from the *it* in "It is easy to write badly." (Better: "Writing badly is easy.") This indefinite subject, like *there is* and *there are,* gives the trouble. Of course, you will occasionally need an *it* or a *there* to assert existences:

There are ants in the cupboard.	There are craters on the moon.
There is only one Kenneth.	It is too bad.

They. Often a loose indefinite pronoun; tighten it. See pp. 142, 143.

Till, until. Both are respectable. Note the spelling. Do not use *'til.*

Tool. Overused for "means." Try *instrument, means.*

Toward, towards. *Toward* is the better (towards in Britain), though both are acceptable.

Trite. From Latin *tritus:* "worn out." Many words get temporarily worn out and unusable: *emasculated, viable, situation,* to name a few. And many phrases are permanently frayed; see *Clichés.*

Type. Banish it, abolish it. If you must use it, insert *of:* not *that type person* but *that type OF person,* though even this is really jargon for *that kind of person, a person like that.* See p. 77.

Unique. Something *unique* has nothing in the world like it.

Wrong	Right
The *more unique* the organiza-tion. . . .	The *more nearly unique.* . . .
the *most unique* man I know	the *most unusual* man I know
a *very unique* personality	a *unique* personality

Use, use of. A dangerously wordy word. See p. 76.

Use to. A mistake for *used to.*

Utilize, utilization. Like *use,* wordy. See p. 76.

Poor	Improved
He *utilizes* frequent dialogue to enliven his stories.	Frequent dialogue enlivens his stories.
The *utilization* of a scapegoat eases their guilt.	A scapegoat eases their guilt.

Very. Spare the *very* and the *quite, rather, pretty,* and *little.* I would hate to admit (and don't care to know) how many of these qualifiers I have cut from this text. You can do without them entirely, but they do ease a phrase now and then.

Viable. With *feasible,* overworked. Try *practicable, workable, possible.*

Ways. Avoid it for distance. Means *way:* "He went a short *way* into the woods."

We (I, one, you). See *Point of view.*

Well. See *Good.*

Whether. See *If.*

Which. See *Who, which, that.*

While. Reserve for time only, as in "*While* I was talking, she smoked constantly." Do not use for *although.*

Wrong	Right
While I like her, I don't admire her.	*Although* I like her, I don't admire her.

Who, which, that. *Who* may be either restrictive or nonrestrictive: "The ones *who win* are lucky"; "The players, *who are all outstanding,* win often." *Who* refers only to persons. Use *that* for all other restrictives; *which* for all other nonrestrictives. Cut every *who, that,* and *which* not needed. See pp. 72, 74, "the *of-and-which* disease" (pp. 74–75), and, on restrictives, and nonrestrictives, p. 75.

Avoid *which* in loose references to the whole idea preceding, rather than to a specific word, since you may be unclear:

Faulty	Improved
He never wore the hat, which his wife hated.	His wife hated his going bare-headed.
	He never wore the hat his wife hated.

Whom, whomever. The objective forms, after verbs and prepositions; but each is often wrongly put as the subject of a clause (p. 141).

Wrong	Right
Give the ticket to *whomever* wants it.	Give the ticket to *whoever* wants it. [The whole clause is the object of *to; whoever* is the subject of *wants.*]
The president, *whom* he said would be late. . . .	The president, *who* he said would be late. . . . [Commas around *he said* would clear the confusion.]
Whom shall I say called?	*Who* shall I say called?

BUT:

They did not know *whom* to elect. [The infinitive takes the objective case.]

Who's, whose. Sometimes confused in writing. *Who's* means "who is?" in conversational questions: "*Who's* going?" Never use it in writing (except in dialogue), and you can't miss. *Whose* is the regular possessive of *who:* "The committee, *whose* work was finished, adjourned."

Will. See *Shall.*

-wise. Avoid all confections like *marketwise, customerwise, price-wise, gradewise, confectionwise* — except for humor.

Would. For habitual acts, the simple past is more economical:

Poor	Improved
The parliament *would meet* only when called by the king.	The parliament *met* only when called by the king.
Every hour, the watchman *would make* his round.	Every hour, the watchman *made* his round.

Would sometimes seeps into the premise of a supposition. Rule: Don't use *would* in an *if* clause.

Wrong	Right
If he *would have* gone, he would have succeeded.	If he *had* gone, he would have succeeded.
	Had he gone, he would have succeeded [more economical].

Would of. See *Could of, would of.*

You (I, we, one). See *Point of view.*

Index